7/24

MAINE COMMUNITY COOKBOOK

VOLUME 2

E-(& family) Hoping you find some fun-interesting... even delicious recipes here Love, Mimi

12/22

200 MORE RECIPES

Celebrating Home Cooking
in the Pine Tree State

Introduction by Don Lindgren

Compiled and Edited by Margaret Hathaway & Karl Schatz

Islandport Press, Inc.
P.O. Box 10
Yarmouth, Maine 04096
www.islandportpress.com

Specific permissions and acknowledgments listed on page 274.

For more recipes, stories, and photos visit maine200cookbook.com

First Edition, June 2022

Cover and interior design by Ashley Halsey

ISBN: 978-1-952143-60-1
Library of Congress Catalog Number: 2022932246

Islandport Press

Maine Community Cookbook Volume Two is distributed to the trade by Islandport Press, Inc. and its partners, please contact 207-846-3344 or email info@islandportpress.com for more information.

For you, and your family.

We invite you to personalize this community cookbook with your own family recipe, so that every family in Maine can be included in this celebration of Maine cooking.

RECIPE ____________________

From the Kitchen of: ____________________

Our Family Story: ____________________

INGREDIENTS:

DIRECTIONS:

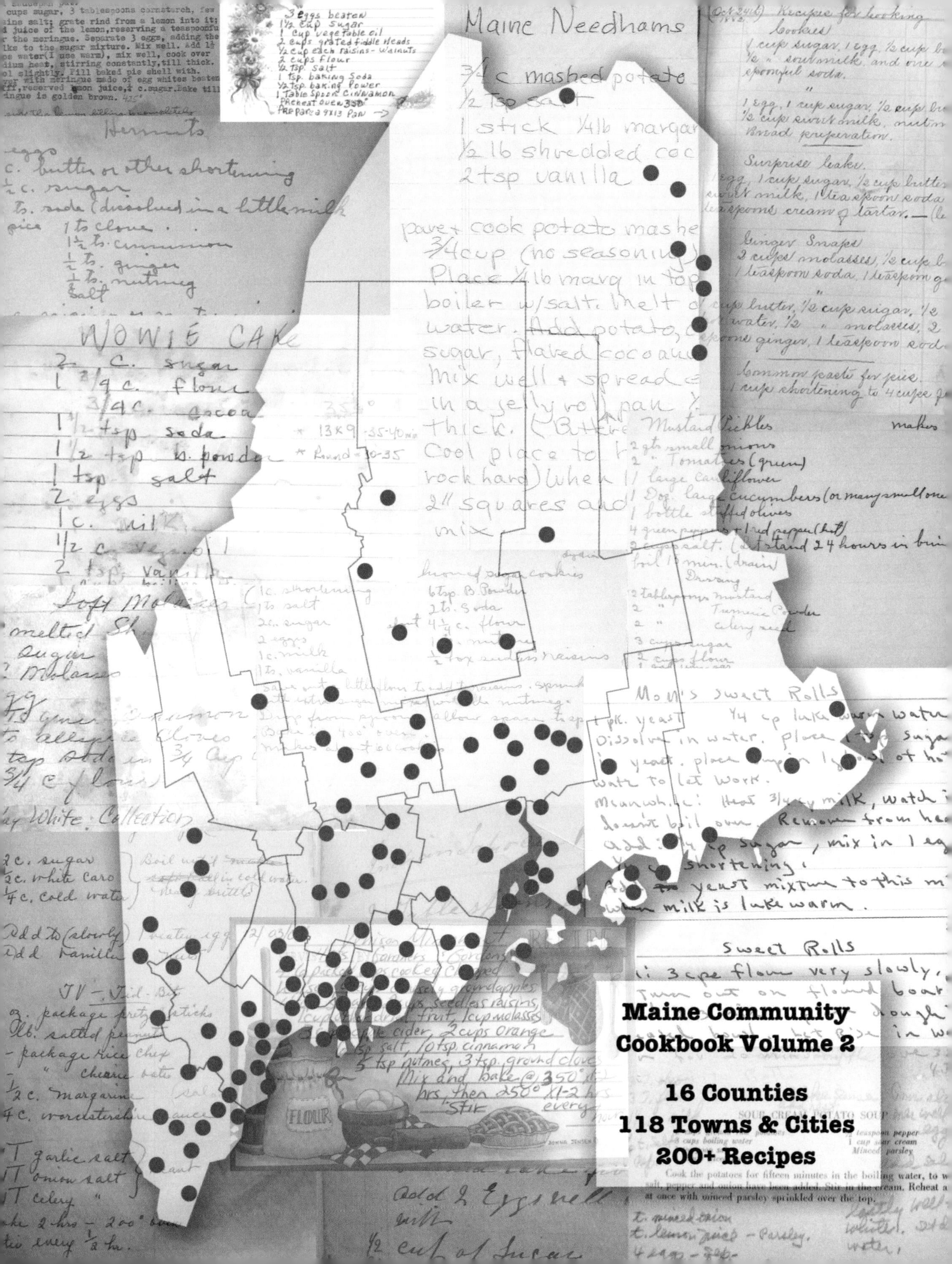

Maine Community Cookbook Volume 2

16 Counties
118 Towns & Cities
200+ Recipes

CONTENTS

About This Project

By Margaret Hathaway & Karl Schatz

This book is the second volume of a project, begun several years ago, that has steadily grown in scope and purpose. What we started in the fall of 2019 was intended to be one book, the *Maine Bicentennial Community Cookbook*, a collection of 200 recipes celebrating home cooking around the state. Here in Maine, we were anticipating that 2020 would be a festive year marking the bicentennial of statehood, and our community cookbook was to be one small piece of that celebration.

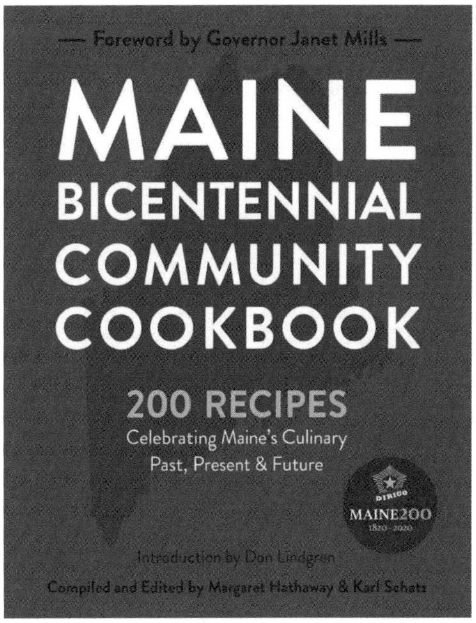

The project was modest, and so was our ambition. We envisioned a book that would highlight Maine's resources and rich food traditions, sharing dishes found in the kitchens of all 16 counties. We hoped to sell the cookbook from a little booth at fairs and festivals across the state, and we worked with a local publisher to distribute it to Maine's bookstores and gift shops. We saw the book as a chance to be inclusive and instructive, and in the manner of all community cookbooks, we planned to give a portion of the proceeds to organizations doing good in the community—in this case fighting hunger in Maine. Soliciting input and essays from food writers across the state, we crowdsourced recipes and reminiscences from Mainers old and new and crowdfunded the production costs through ad placements, a Kickstarter campaign, and presales. We sent our book off to the printer in early March 2020.

It goes without saying that the world, just a few years ago, was a very different place. When we started the book, we looked forward to a summer packed with people and gatherings. By the time finished copies arrived in the warehouse, we were three months into a global pandemic. Schools and businesses were shut down, and bicentennial celebrations had been scaled down, postponed, and then gradually cancelled or moved online. Our community cookbook emerged into a landscape where the whole idea of community was being redefined.

In his essay in the following pages, Don Lindgren explores how community can be formed around any number of things: shared religion, politics, and social causes are just a few of the bonds that can create a sense of togetherness. Our project began in a community bound by geography, but as the *Maine*

Bicentennial Community Cookbook was released into the world, it began to create community of its own.

As the writer Laurie Colwin once noted, "No one who cooks cooks alone." Each dish we make is informed by written recipes, family histories, and legions of home cooks who've come before us. By the summer of 2020, at a time when many of us felt isolated and distant from each other, the invitation into the family kitchens of so many people around Maine was a bright spot of connection. One thing that the whole world had in common was that we were all spending more time at the stoves in our home kitchens. Though we couldn't share meals, we could still share recipes.

From our own home kitchens, Don, Karl and I made many of the recipes that appeared in the book. We simmered New Year's Eve Cioppini, formed Empanadas Colombianas by hand, and baked Luce's Maple Cheesecake and President George H. W. Bush's Lemon Bars. We cooked Thai Fiddlehead Stir Fry in May, brought Whoopie Pies up to camp through the summer, and ate vegan Pumpkin Seed Croquettes with Shiitake Mushroom Gravy at Thanksgiving. Propping our computers on stacks of cookbooks, the three of us Zoomed in to discussions of community cookbooks, and led cook-alongs through libraries and organizations around the state. We were amazed and gratified to see that others shared our curiosity. In fact, the Reverend Elizabeth Bailey-Mitchell, whose recipe for Custard Pie can be found on page 219 of this volume, cooked her way through the entire first book, and kept us up to date on her menus through a blog.

The overwhelmingly positive reception of the *Maine Bicentennial Community Cookbook* inspired us to continue our project, and to expand it. In 2021, the three of us began to solicit recipes for this second volume. We also started a podcast, "Cooking Is Community," which looks in depth at specific community cookbooks, the context in which they were created, and the recipes they contain.

At a time when our country's divisions are increasingly on display, we choose to focus on what connects us. We have no doubt that the people featured in the following pages have a variety of views on the issues of our day. If my own beloved grandmother and mother-in-law were seated at the same table, safe topics of conversation might be limited to their cookie recipes (pages 206 and 205, respectively). But the book's contributors are all united by one thing: they are generous enough to invite us into their kitchens and share their family's food traditions with us. We are so grateful.

As we were putting this book together, we followed many of the same methods as in the first volume. We put out a call in the summer of 2021 for recipes, and have interspersed crowd-sourced submissions with recipes from Don's extensive collection of historic community cookbooks. With virus variants surging through the fall and winter, we were deprived of the opportunity to get together with our crew of fellow food writers, who were so instrumental to the shape of the first book. This time, decisions about which recipes to include fell entirely to us, and we tried to include them all. Readers who have both volumes will notice that the spine of this book is slightly wider because we've added pages to accommodate more recipes.

In the first volume, we received so many recipes for certain dishes that we created several chapters comprised entirely of variations on a single theme, such as donuts and beans. This time, in concert with our lead sponsor the Department of Agriculture, Conservation and Forestry, we've focused a few chapters on some of Maine's most iconic ingredients. You'll find recipes showcasing apples, rhubarb, potatoes, lobster, and wild blueberries grouped in the chapters bearing their names.

As we did in the first volume, we've included essays from Maine scholars, politicians, community leaders, and humorists to help provide context for the state's food history and contemporary challenges. You'll find these tucked between the chapters on pages with a yellow border. In these essays, independent scholar Pamela Snow Sweetser chronicles the career of Avis "Ma" Dudley, a farmer's wife turned early 20th century entrepreneur and renowned chef. Professor Myron Beasley of Bates College honors the memory and culinary traditions of those tragically displaced from Malaga Island more than a century ago. Journalist Avery Yale Kamila traces the deep historical roots of vegetarianism in the state, from spiritual leaders to abolitionists to contemporary food bloggers. Senator Craig Hickman shares the imperatives for the nation's first Right To Food Amendment, passed here in Maine in 2021, which he successfully spearheaded. Author Abdi Nor Iftin, whose bestselling memoir *Call Me American* traces his inspiring journey from Somalia to Maine, suggests ways to welcome new Americans at the table. Finally, Kristen Miale, President of Good Shepherd Food Bank, speaks to the challenge of food insecurity in Maine, and discusses statewide strategies to address hunger. Within the chapters, generally marked by red titles, you'll find shorter essays about particular foods: Author Nancy Harmon Jenkins meditates on apples, memory, and her mother's chowder. Humorist and summer resident John Hodgman creates the perfect burger, food historian Sandy Oliver addresses the importance of molasses to Maine's food, and writer Amy Wight Chapman walks us through her mother's blueberry cake instructions, from the best place to pick berries to which chipped measuring cup to use. We are greatly indebted to these generous writers for making the cookbook that much richer.

The recipes themselves are left as much as possible in the format in which they were submitted. We've tried to edit them as little as necessary, and only for the sake of clarity. In most cases, there is a distinct ingredient list, standardized measurements, and enough instructions to guide the most novice of cooks. We've left spellings as they came in, so you will see the same foodstuff variously referred to as "doughnut" and "donut," and "borscht," "borsht," and "borsch." Similarly, the region of the state known as "Downeast" Maine is spelled and capitalized in a variety of ways. The notes at the top of each recipe are in the words of the person who submitted it, often the cook, but in a few cases, a friend or family member. Recipes from historic community cookbooks are introduced by Don Lindgren, and appear exactly as they do in their primary printing.

As in the first volume, we did not test any of the recipes, but instead trusted that the people who submitted them were sharing their best. Everyone's taste is their own, and you may prefer some dishes with a little more salt, a little less butter, or a slightly longer cooking time. Our hope is that you will take the recipes in this book and make them your own. Adapt them to your tastes, make notes in the margins, and above all, share them with the people you love.

The *Maine Community Cookbook* is illustrated entirely with family photographs, artifacts, and ephemera. Some pictures may be faded or slightly out of focus, but they capture the hearts and memories of the families who submitted them. Keen observers may note that one photo is used twice within these pages.

In this second volume, we revisit several families and home cooks who were featured in the first book. Readers of the *Maine Bicentennial Community Cookbook* will recognize the return of the Foss Sisters of Harmony. This time, a recipe from each sister is featured, along with another reflection on their childhood. We are also delighted to include more reminiscence from the memoir of Professor Thomas W. Easton of Bridgton. Throughout the book, we see generations of families at work and at rest, enjoying each other and sharing moments in the kitchen and at the table. It is a privilege to spend time in their company.

To date, since the publication of the first book, we have distributed more than $20,000 to organizations fighting hunger throughout our state. The need has never been more acute, and we are honored that these books can be part of the solution. Thank you for being part of our community.

Despite our state's wealth of natural resources, Maine ranks 19th in the nation, and 2nd in New England for household food insecurity. According to the USDA's September 2021 Household Food Security report, 11.4% of Maine households are considered food insecure, and 1 in 5 Maine children are unsure of where their next meal will be coming from. $2 from every copy sold of the *Maine Community Cookbook, Volume 2* will go to organizations fighting hunger in Maine. To learn more, and to find updated information about the organizations we support, visit maine200cookbook.com/fighting-hunger-in-maine.

Photo: Faces of the *Maine Bicentennial Community Cookbook*: Some of the many people who enriched our community by sharing their family recipes and stories.

of recipes compiled
-seven years by
rownie" Schrumpf
COOKING
WITH
A MAINE ACCENT
1892
1992
CASTINE
FROM THE MINUTES OF THE CASTINE, MAINE, WOMAN'S CLUB
MIRIAM ANNE BOURNE
MMC
COOK BOOK
mployees' Activity Committee
MAINE MEDICAL CENTER
Portland, Maine
Merrymeeting Merry Eating
A collection of recipes gathered in Maine
HOCKEY
MOTHERS'
COOK
BOOK
— BANGOR BOOSTER CLUB —
AINE
KERY
ND NOW
FISHERMAN'S FARE
a Seafood Cook Book
CASCO BAY CUISINE
Cruising Favorites from the Portland Yacht Club

The Changing Community Cookbook

By Don Lindgren

When Margaret and Karl invited me to join them in the *Maine Bicentennial Community Cookbook* project, I said yes without hesitation. The project appealed to me immediately. Not only was it a chance to work with two good friends, but also an opportunity to spend some time with the hundreds of historical Maine cookbooks I've been collecting for more than a decade.

Tasked with writing the historical introduction to what is now Volume One, I revisited a talk I'd given many times before, a talk that traces the 1877 dawn of the community cookbook in Portland[1] through the rapid explosion of cookbook titles produced in every town and city throughout our state. The books were compiled by members (mostly women) in community organizations of every type. Those organizations included church auxiliaries, grange halls, hospital supporters, civic organizations and much more. I made sure to define the community cookbook with its three elements: published by a recognizable community or organization; compiled with recipes contributed by members of the community; and used to raise funds for a charitable or civic cause. My introduction to Volume One would come from my existing knowledge of the genre, and would be a familiar and comfortable task.

Margaret and Karl also asked me to search books in my collection for historical recipes for inclusion in the *Maine Bicentennial Community Cookbook*, recipes to appear alongside those gathered from the homes of contributors around the state. Spending time with my collection, I sought historical recipes from cookbooks from various decades, and from communities geographically dispersed, aiming to represent every county. From within the books, I sought recipes representing categories commonly found in community cookbooks: bread, soups, salads, candy, drinks, and so on. I hoped that the recipes selected would offer little glimpses into the complexities of recipe writing, with changing recipe formats, shifts in ingredients, or varying levels of specificity. How precise are measurements or timings? Do we encounter specific ingredient names or just general ones?

The historical recipes weren't gathered in a vacuum; we also considered how they might compliment or contrast with the contemporary recipes that would appear alongside them. All of these types of complexities—and these just scratch the surface—were familiar to me, learned by living with, reading, and occasionally cooking from my own collection, and refined through research to produce lectures, essays, and other published works on the subject.

Another important consideration while selecting recipes from the historical books was the wide variety of community organizations that produced the cookbooks. With just twenty historical recipes in the bicentennial cookbook, and with those recipes leaning towards representing the oldest

1

books, it wasn't possible to even suggest how many different kinds of groups chose to use community cookbooks as a fundraising project over the decades. This is an important story. Much has been written in the last few decades about the loss of communal social life in America.[2] It has been said that many of the community organizations that helped create the social fabric of America are gone; the bowling league, the PTA, the rural grange hall, have faded, disappeared, leaving contemporary Americans without opportunities for face-to-face interactions, without the glue that binds us to other community members who might otherwise be strangers. Many types of community organization are a shadow of what they were in the past; some are gone altogether.

But the community cookbooks of Maine (along with those of the rest of the nation), tell a somewhat different story, a story of some groups fading, but also of others emerging as times change, as types of activities change, and as political, cultural, and social desires change. For example, cookbooks compiled as efforts by political groups supporting Woman's Suffrage or Temperance largely disappeared as their goals were achieved or failed; new groups, advocating for civil rights and against discriminatory legislation, offered their books for these newer causes. As a percentage of output, cookbooks by Protestant church groups fell, now joined by those from Italian- or Greek-Americans, or Jewish congregations, and later, books featuring recipes by Maine's immigrant populations from all over the world. Community cookbooks were issued by employees of companies like L.L. Bean. Members of statewide progressive farming organizations like Maine Organic Farmers and Gardeners Association (MOFGA) published community cookbooks to raise funds for their activities or charitable causes. New and diverse social activities, representing harness racing drivers, public librarians, school food service workers, foster grandparents, bikers, legal secretaries, and even caged bird fanciers, compiled, published, and sold community cookbooks in Maine just like the earlier church, grange, and women's clubs had done. The community groups issuing the books changed, and this change helps us see just how much the rich social life of Maine has changed in the nearly one hundred fifty years since the first one appeared. They act as a repository of that social life for us to touch, read, and cook from.

One thing I hadn't anticipated when I joined this project was how participating in the process of producing the *Maine Bicentennial Community Cookbook* allowed me to step out of my role as a collector and food historian and into the practical shoes of a member of "the committee" (we never called ourselves that, but we knew that's what it was). It was in this role that I learned entirely new things about the cookbooks I thought I knew so well. I helped Margaret and Karl acquire the recipes from the public, structure the sections of the book, and put together a meeting of cookbook authors and others to review and select the recipes. We were faced with what must have been many of the common questions and challenges for the committees who met in church basements, living rooms, school offices, and grange halls before us. What does a committee do with four recipes for the same dish from four different contributors? What are the personal or local political considerations of including a recipe or of leaving a recipe out? To what extent should compilers standardize the recipes, which had arrived in many formats and with greatly varying levels of detail? To what degree does the committee seek to project a single “voice” in the edited book. This process, happening in the present, helped me to imagine and better understand how the process may have unfolded for some or many of the compilers of community cookbooks of the past. The books themselves, along with other relevant written and printed materials, tell us a great deal about how groups of women came together to create the books, but they don’t tell us everything. Participating in the process revives something akin to embodied knowledge, offering new angles of inquiry to pursue.

As we’ve worked on this second volume, many questions remain about the history of Maine’s food and about the communities that grew or caught, cooked, served, and ate that food. Some of the questions are about the food itself, about the ingredients, the recipes, and the techniques of cooking, and about how they evolved over time. Are the recipes representative of daily life, of special occasions, or are the recipes aspirational? How does one speak of “local” foodways, when the books so often reveal a national network of recipe swapping and compilation? Other questions are about the social history of those Maine communities: why was a certain book made at a specific moment? Issues are raised of communication between communities, across towns, and across the state and the nation. Perhaps the most important questions arise from the silences. Why was “this” recorded but not “that”? Whose books are missing? What foods and food traditions are not spoken of? Which communities are less represented or not represented at all?

The many questions raised are not a problem but rather a challenge to the reader, the cook, or the historian. By engaging with the seemingly infinite stories told by the community cookbooks of Maine, and by reaching into our own memories and the lives of our neighbors to find a dish to put on our table, we’re continuing a culinary conversation begun almost 150 years ago.

---

1 Ladies of State Street Parish. Fish, Flesh & Fowl (Portland, Me.: 1877).

2 Putnam, Robert D. Bowling Alone (NY: 2000).

Recipes
Houlton Country Club
Houlton, Maine
Ladies' Handbook
and
Household Assistant
DORCA
DISHE
A LITTLE BOOK
COUNTRY COOK
INTRODUCTION BY
KATE DOUGLAS WI
Secrets in Cooking
Disclosed by
sworth Circle, No, 1
Department of Maine
the Grand Army of the Republic
Portland, Maine
The Orono Cook Book
TO MAKE THE BUTTERFLY
A Collection of Practical Recipes
Furnished By
The Ladies of
Norway Grange
NO. 45
Patrons of Husbandry
FARM BUREAU
COOK BOOK
CUMBERLAND COUNTY
Woolwich Grange Cook Book
P. of H.
No. 68
REBEKAH
COOK

THE HOUSEKEEPERS FRIEND
A MERRY CHRISTMAS AND HAPPY NEW YEAR
Published By
JOHN GARNER,
Choice Teas, Coffees, Spices, Fancy Groceries, Flour,
Butter, Cheese, Meats of all kinds, &c.
LEWISTON, ME.
Copyrighted PRICE 25 CENTS 1879
SUNSHINE CLUB
Cook Book
Brewer Library Reading Room
Brewer
Library Cook Bo
1913
Machias
Cookery
1909
THE APPLEDORE COOK BOOK
THE HOUSEKEEPER'S FRIEND.
MERRY CHRISTMAS & HAPPY NEW YEAR
PUBLISHED BY
JOHN GARNER,
PASSENGER & EXCHANGE AGENT,
LEWISTON, MAINE
Fish, flesh and fowl
FOWL, FLESH AND FISH
Each served up
IN A SEPARATE DISH.
A COLLECTION OF
COOKING RECIPES

Land and Food Acknowledgment

The people of the Wabanaki Confederacy have been stewards of the land we now call Maine for thousands of years. They fished, foraged, hunted, and farmed these lands, woods, and shores long before the arrival of European colonists. Indigenous communities here in Maine and across the Americas continually demonstrate resilience and resistance in the face of efforts to separate them from land, culture, community, and food traditions. They continue to be on the front lines of environmental, racial, and food justice. We honor the pasts, presents, and futures of the Maliseet, Mi'kmaq, Passamaquoddy, and Penobscot peoples and support work ongoing to ensure Native land and food sovereignty for the Wabanaki Confederacy and all indigenous people.

Live Laugh Love Live Laugh Love Live Laugh Love

APPLES

Photo: Kathleen Webster and her granddaughter, Morgan, get ready to make apple dumplings together in Kathleen's kitchen in Auburn. The recipe can be found on page 12.

Apple Crisp

Heidi Inman • Bryant Pond, Oxford County

"This is a recipe passed down from our family friend Ada (Hobbs) Cox of Norway. She was born in 1889 and she lived to be 98. Ada was a great cook and seamstress and came from tough Maine stock. This recipe of hers has been passed along down the line and is a beloved family favorite. Thank you Ada!"

6-8 Macintosh apples
½ teaspoon cinnamon
1 tablespoon lemon juice
¼ cup sugar

Topping:
⅓ cup butter
½ cup brown sugar
⅓ cup flour
1 cup quick cook rolled oats

Note: We like lots of topping so we usually double the topping amounts!

Preheat oven to 375 degrees and prepare an 8x8-inch pan with nonstick spray. Peel, core, and slice thin enough apples to fill the pan ¾ full. Mix the cinnamon, lemon juice, and sugar together, pour over the apples. Toss to coat.

To make the topping: Melt the butter, then stir in the brown sugar. Stir in the flour, then mix in the oats. Place this crumble mixture on top of the apples. Bake for 30 minutes. Serve warm with vanilla ice cream.

Gramma's Apple Pandowdy

Betsy Daus • Penobscot, Hancock County

"When I was growing up in the '60s, Gramma used to make this apple pandowdy for us from a handful of simple ingredients. We'd help her peel the apples and butter the bread and we'd bake it in her trusty ancient Wagner cast-iron skillet. Foggy autumn days in Penobscot always make me think of her and this simple kid-friendly dessert."

Good white bread, or cinnamon raisin, or any kind you like
1½ sticks unsalted butter, melted
4 large green cooking apples, peeled, cored, and sliced thin
½ cup dark brown sugar
2-4 teaspoons cinnamon or apple pie spice
½ cup water, buttermilk, or milk
½ stick unsalted butter, softened
More brown sugar for sprinkling on top

Preheat oven to 350 degrees. Line the bottom and sides of a buttered 10-inch cast-iron skillet with fingers of bread (crusts removed) which have been dipped in the melted butter. Arrange the apple slices on top of the bread. Sprinkle the apples with a mixture of the brown sugar and cinnamon. Thickly butter the remaining slices of bread. Pour the ½ cup of water (or buttermilk or milk) over the apple slices and cover the top with a layer of well-buttered fingers of bread. Sprinkle top with additional sugar. Cover with foil and bake 45-50 minutes, then remove foil and bake another 5-8 minutes until top is browned the way you like. Keep an eye on it, as the sugar can burn. Serve hot with whipped cream or vanilla ice cream.

Apple Pie

Nancy Burnette • Brunswick, Cumberland County

"This recipe was altered slightly to please the judges at the Cumberland Fair. I have won first prize with this recipe. One year, my 13 year old son decided to make a pie using this recipe. He won, while I finished third! It is always a crowd favorite. You can use a mix of Cortland and Macintosh apples if you can't find Gravensteins (though Sweetsers in Cumberland has them for a short period of time.) Now my granddaughter, Sadie, helps make the pie."

Crust:
2 cups flour
1 teaspoon salt
1 cup shortening
1 tablespoon vinegar
1 egg
¼ cup water

Filling:
7 cups Red Gravenstein apples, peeled, cored, sliced
1 cup sugar
1 teaspoon cinnamon
⅛ teaspoon mace
⅛ teaspoon salt
¼ cup flour
2 tablespoons butter, cut into small cubes

To make the crust: Mix together flour and salt, and cut shortening into the mixture until it is about the size of peas. In a separate bowl, mix together vinegar, egg, and water, slightly beating the egg. Mix into flour with your hands until crust holds together. Let it rest while you prepare the filling.

When ready to assemble pie, divide dough in two balls, and roll each out between sheets of floured wax paper. This will allow you to move dough easily to the pie tin. Press one crust into the bottom of the pie tin.

To make the filling: Mix everything together in a large bowl, tossing gently. Dump apple mixture into prepared bottom crust. Cover with top crust and flute the edges. Cut three slits in the top crust to allow steam to vent. Bake at 350 degrees for 1 hour.

Apple Cheesecake

Sherry Pike • Winthrop, Kennebec County

"Apple desserts have always been a favorite in our family and this is a well-loved recipe that has traveled to many family events. One year, it was requested by my nephew Ryan in lieu of gifts! It has been known to make a yummy breakfast if you happen to have any leftovers!"

Crust:
¾ cup butter, softened
⅔ cup sugar
½ teaspoon vanilla
1 ½ cups flour

Cream:
16 ounces cream cheese (two 8-ounce packages), softened
½ cup sugar
2 eggs
1 teaspoon vanilla

Topping:
⅓ cup sugar
½ teaspoon cinnamon
4-5 cups peeled, cored, and sliced apples
½ cup sliced almonds

To make the crust: Cream together the butter, sugar, and vanilla. Blend in flour. Spread mixture on the bottom and 1½ inches up sides of a 9-inch springform pan.

To make the cream: Blend together the cream cheese and the sugar. Add eggs one at a time, and mix to thoroughly incorporate. Stir in the vanilla. Pour mixture into crust.

To make the topping: Combine sugar, cinnamon, and apples. Spoon over cream cheese layer. Sprinkle with almonds.

Bake at 450 degrees for 10 minutes. Reduce heat to 400 degrees, and bake for an additional 25 minutes. Cool cheesecake in the pan for 15 minutes, then loosen the rim and run a knife around the outer edge. Tighten the ring back up and let cheesecake cool completely. Serve with whipped cream.

Baked Apple Pudding

Karen Conroy • Caribou, Aroostook County

"Living in a small town and growing up with numerous friends (and cousins) made for many adventures! Whether it was playing in the barn, jumping in hay or throwing apples at each other under the apple trees, we made good memories. We also helped by picking apples so Aunt Irma would make us our favorite BAKED APPLE PUDDING! It always warmed up the kitchen and sent marvelous aroma all through the home."

- 3 cups thin sliced apples
- Juice of 1 lemon
- ½ teaspoon of cinnamon
- 1¾ cups sugar, separated
- 3 tablespoons butter
- 1 cup flour
- 1 teaspoon baking powder
- Dash of salt
- ½ cup milk
- 1 tablespoon cornstarch
- 1 cup boiling water

Preheat oven to 375 degrees. Place sliced apples in an 8x8-inch baking dish. Drizzle with lemon juice and cinnamon.

In a medium-size bowl, mix together ¾ cup sugar, butter, flour, baking powder, and a dash of salt. Add milk, stir to form a batter, and pour mixture over the apples. In a separate bowl, mix together remaining cup of sugar and cornstarch, and sprinkle over the batter. Pour 1 cup boiling water over the whole dish. Bake for 45-60 minutes. Serve warm with whipped cream or ice cream.

My Grandmother's Apple Upside-Down Cake in a Cast-Iron Frying Pan

Judith Couture • Oakland, Kennebec County

"This recipe dates from the 1940s or possibly '30s, and it has always been popular in our family. My grandmother probably made the recipe by what she had available. We could look for it especially after our noon meal on Sundays, but I think that it could also be served at a weekend breakfast."

- 4 tablespoons butter, divided
- 1 cup sugar, divided
- 1 tablespoon molasses
- 4 medium apples, peeled and sliced
- 1 egg
- ½ cup milk
- 1 cup flour
- 1 teaspoon baking powder
- ½ teaspoon salt
- 1 teaspoon vanilla

Preheat oven to 350 degrees.

Melt 3 tablespoons of butter in an 8- or 9-inch frying pan. Add ½ cup sugar and molasses, and stir until well mixed. Arrange apple slices over the sugar mixture, and cook over low heat until apples are soft.

Using a separate small pan (or microwave), melt remaining tablespoon of butter.

In a large bowl, beat together egg, remaining ½ cup of sugar, and milk. Add to this mixture the flour, baking powder, salt, and vanilla, and beat well. Stir in melted butter. Pour batter over the cooked apples. Bake 30 minutes, or until cake tests done and a toothpick in the center comes out clean. Cool slightly, then flip onto a serving plate. Serve warm with whipped cream or vanilla ice cream. Makes 6-8 servings.

Matzoh Apple Pudding

1960 • Cook Book: Kosher Recipes, for the Jewish Housewife or Newlywed
Jewish Home for Aged Ladies' Auxiliary • Portland, Cumberland County

The recipes in this kosher cookbook are not credited, but members of the "Cooking School Committee," Sadye Schatz, Bessie Mack, Bessie Edison, and Mrs. Swonkin, compiled this cookbook, in part to celebrate reaching two hundred members of the Ladies' Auxiliary of the Jewish Home for the Aged. Founded in 1929, the home changed its name to The Cedars in 1991, and serves people of all faiths and backgrounds. —DL

- 2 matzohs
- 2 medium apples
- ¼ lb. raisins
- ½ cup granulated sugar
- 2 tablespoons fat
- 3 eggs
- ¼ lemon rind
- Dash of cinnamon

Soak the matzohs and squeeze water out well. Add the apples cut into small pieces, raisins, a dash of cinnamon, the grated lemon rind, sugar, melted fat. Mix together with well beaten eggs. Pour into a greased dish and bake in a moderate oven for twenty to thirty minutes.

Autumn Delight (a salad)

1937• The North Anson Woman's Club

Woman's Club • North Anson, Somerset County

Composed salads were all the rage for the first half of the 20th century, and the ladies of North Anson have included more than 25 salads in this book, plus a guide for combining salad ingredients. Their Autumn Delight is somewhat similar to the famous Waldorf Salad created for the grand hotel by Chef Oscar Tschirky in 1896. —DL

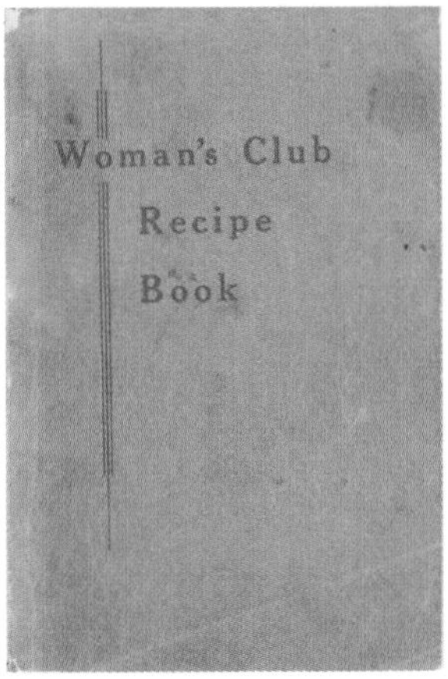

Red apples, thin slices of carrot, raw, minced dates and nuts. Cut the apples into thin slices crosswise, removing core and seeds. Arrange round thin slices of carrots on top of apple. Heap minced dates and nuts in center. Serve in lettuce with French dressing or mayonnaise.

— Elizabeth R. Cummings

Mincemeat and Grinders

Thomas W. Easton • Bridgton, Cumberland County

"Now and then, we would find an abandoned orchard which was still putting out good fruit from a tree or two. We might bring in a bushel or so of apples already out of fashion, varieties which no one grew anymore, and which my grandmother remembered from her childhood, but no one else could identify. These went into pies, of course, and applesauce, and because we didn't care for dried apples, the winter portion was put into mincemeat. Jars and jars of mincemeat lined a whole shelf in the cellar. We made it up with venison, when we had some, or beef, when we had no venison.

To do such things as make mincemeat, we had to grind a lot of different things. Suet puddings required grinding, and so did other foods. The grinder was a cast-iron contrivance, which one can still buy, but which is more likely to appear in modern kitchens as an attachment for the electric mixer. Ours clamped to the edge of a table, was fed large pieces through the top, and produced small pieces out one side. The power for making little ones out of big ones was provided by hand, quite often mine. That's a pale statement of the situation; it took muscles of back as well as arm, and sometimes of leg, too. Turning the crank of that machine was hard, and it was tiring, and because the table had a tendency to walk away from the job, it was aggravating, as well. One tried to wedge the table into the wall and hold it there by bracing one hip on it. Sometimes it worked."

Nana (Nellie) Bonney's Mincemeat Recipe

Pamela Fesq Bonney • Buxton, York County

"This is my husband's grandmother's treasured family recipe. Until the end of her days Nana baked wonderful pies in her Mechanic Falls kitchen, in a wood cook stove with a thermometer that hadn't worked for many, many years. She gauged the temperature just by putting her hand in the oven. Her recipe calls for ground venison, and she always used meat from the deer's neck. Over the years I have eliminated the meat and always use cider rather than vinegar, but the suet is essential–it just doesn't taste right without it. Nana's mincemeat pie is a holiday tradition at our house."

- 2½ pounds ground venison
- ¼ pound (or less) suet
- 3 pounds currants
- 1 pound seedless raisins
- 2 cups molasses
- 2 cups brown sugar
- 7½ pounds apples, peeled, cored, and chopped before weighing
- 2 cups apple cider
- 1 teaspoon cloves
- 1 teaspoon allspice
- 1 teaspoon cinnamon
- 1 tablespoon salt

Combine all ingredients in a large pot and cook over low heat about one hour, stirring occasionally to make sure it doesn't scorch. Makes about 8 quarts. Mincemeat may be frozen in quart containers and thawed before use.

Apple Dumplings

Kathleen Webster • Auburn, Androscoggin County

"My granddaughter Morgan and I enjoyed making these apple dumplings together. She now makes them herself. A family favorite!"

Sauce:

2 cups water
1½ cups sugar
1 teaspoon cinnamon
½ teaspoon nutmeg (or less, to taste)
¼ cup margarine

Dumplings:

2 cups flour
1 teaspoon baking powder
½ teaspoon salt
¾ cup shortening
½ cup milk
3-4 apples, peeled, cored, and cut into thick slices

To make the sauce: Combine water, sugar, spices, and margarine in a saucepan and bring to a boil.

To make the dumplings: In a large bowl, mix together flour, baking powder, and salt, and cut in the shortening. Sprinkle milk over the top, and toss lightly with a fork to make a dough. You may need to knead a little with your hands to bring the dough together. On a floured surface, roll out the dough and cut into squares. Place a slice of apple in the center of each square and shape each dumpling into a ball. Place the dumplings in a greased 9x13-inch baking dish and pour sauce over them. Bake at 350 degrees for 40 minutes. Makes 12 dumplings..

Apfel Kuchen

Cindy Rogers • Union, Knox County

"My mother emigrated to Maine from Germany in 1948 and brought this recipe with her, passed down from her mother. She remembered it from her childhood in Czechoslovakia, made with apples or plums. It takes time, but is so worth the effort! For me, this is the best thing to make with fall apples at least once a year. Great for breakfast or a not-too-sweet snack."

½ cup warm water (110-115°F)
1 packet (2¼ teaspoons) active dry yeast
¾ cup warm milk (110-115°F)
½ cup vegetable shortening or softened butter
½ cup granulated sugar
1 teaspoon kosher salt
1 egg
½ teaspoon ground nutmeg
3-4 cups all-purpose flour
2-3 large or 6-8 small apples
2 teaspoons cinnamon

Streusel topping:
¼ cup butter, softened
½ cup granulated sugar
½ cup all-purpose flour

In a small bowl, whisk water and yeast; let proof for 5 minutes, then add milk and whisk to combine.

In the large bowl of a stand mixer or by hand, cream shortening (or butter) and ½ cup sugar. Add salt, egg, nutmeg, and yeast mixture, beating to combine; it won't be smooth. Add 1 cup of flour, beating well. Continue to add flour ½ cup at a time until a soft, slightly sticky dough is formed, and dough just starts to pull away from the sides of the bowl. Cover the dough in the bowl with a cloth or plastic wrap and let rise in a warm, draft-free place for 1-2 hours. The dough should double in volume.

While dough is rising, make the streusel topping. In a small bowl, using your hands, rub the butter, sugar, and flour together to form ½-inch crumbles. Set aside.

When dough has risen, punch down the dough and turn it out on a well-floured surface. Knead just for a minute or two, and form into a ball. Sprinkle flour over the work surface, rolling pin, and dough, and roll dough to roughly fit a lightly greased 11x14x1-inch sheet pan, pulling and tucking the dough in the pan as needed.

Peel, core, and slice apples into thin wedges. Arrange apples on top of the dough in slightly overlapping rows, right to the edges. Sprinkle with cinnamon. Sprinkle streusel topping evenly over the apples. Cover with a clean cloth and let rise for about ½ hour, just to puff a bit. While dough is rising, preheat oven to 375 degrees.

Bake kuchen for 35-45 minutes, or until streusel and dough edges are golden brown and crisp. Cut into 12 squares (or more smaller ones), and serve warm or cool.

Nana's Apple Squares

Cynthia DiBiase • Standish, Cumberland County

"These apple squares were a traditional treat when visiting my Nana. I remember arriving at Nana's house and watching her pull out a neat, tinfoil-wrapped, shiny portion of her apple squares to enjoy over a chat at her kitchen table. Nana had stacks of these treats in her freezer, ready for when visitors arrived. She loved when family visited unexpectedly. She would say, 'this is an unexpected pleasure,' and happily welcome you into her home. It was a good day when she pulled out some apple squares. I always thought this was Nana's special recipe, but it was actually a recipe my mom brought home from her junior high school home economics class back in 1974. My mom made them for her parents and her brother after learning how to make them in school. My Nana loved them and saved the recipe. She continued to make them as years went by for all special occasions, especially in the fall months with fresh Maine apples."

2 eggs
¾ cup plus 2 tablespoons sugar
1 cup flour
1 teaspoon baking powder
½ teaspoon cinnamon
¼ teaspoon salt
½ cup cooking oil
¼ teaspoon vanilla
½ cup walnuts (optional)
1 cup thinly sliced apples

Preheat oven to 350 degrees. In a large bowl, beat eggs. Add sugar gradually and beat until light and fluffy. Add sifted dry ingredients. Stir in oil and vanilla. Fold in chopped nuts, if you used them. Fold in the apple slices with a rubber scraper. Turn mixture into a greased 8-inch square pan. Bake for 40-45 minutes. Place pan on a rack to cool. Cut into squares. These freeze well.

Apple Fritters

1983 • A Taste of Apple

People's United Methodist Church • Greenville Junction, Piscataquis County

A homemade book, printed by electronic printer on computer paper and with a handwritten title and felt apple collaged onto the stapled wrappers. The forty-three apple-based dishes are not credited, but we know the book was produced for the October Apple Festival, with recipes solicited from the community on the shores of Moosehead Lake. —DL

Beat -- 2 eggs; Stir in -- ½ cup milk; Sift together & beat in -- 1 cup sifted flour, 1 tsp baking powder, 1 tsp salt. Beat in -- 1 tsp melted margarine; Stir in -- 1 ½ - 2 cups peeled, sliced apples. Drop in hot fat, brown, drain; serve with syrup.

Apples I Have Known

Nancy Harmon Jenkins • Rockland, Knox County

I grew up in Camden, in a house overlooking the Megunticook River at a point where the river was no longer a rushing stream but a somnolent pool formed by the mill dam below it. Between the house and the river, sloping ground embraced my father's prized vegetable gardens and a small apple orchard, not more than a couple dozen trees. I never knew if my parents bought the house because of the apples or if they planted the trees after purchasing the land. Maybe a bit of both? There were many varieties and they kept us well supplied with fresh apples, apple sauce, apple jelly, cider, and a bounty of high limbs on which to rest and read a book or contemplate the universe or simply to escape from household chores.

Just beyond the kitchen windows a tall old crabapple, as high as the house and then some, burst into blossom in May. Year in and year out, the tree was covered with white flowers, veined with red and deeply fragrant, that grew into apples no bigger than ping pong balls. Most of those little apples were added to the cider bin but some were turned into crabapple jelly, the most beautiful jelly in the world, a deep ruby orange glow that radiated from jars on the kitchen countertop as the jelly cooled and the lids clicked into a seal. Stored on shelves in the cellarway, the jars were opened on chilly winter mornings to spill a burst of autumn sunlight onto buttered biscuits or hot breakfast cornbread.

There were several Macintosh and Cortland trees in the orchard, of course, the staple apples of Maine farms, then as now. There was a single Northern Spy, one Baldwin and a Wolf River, and there may have been a Wealthy too (memories fade). All of these are cooking apples as well as for fresh eating—but Wolf Rivers are huge, mealy-textured and really only good for baking. Maine cooks say that Wolf Rivers and Wealthies make the finest kind of apple pie. Then there were odd apples—Winter Bananas with slick, oily skins and a curious ripe-banana flavor. And Yellow Transparents, the very first apples, often ripening in late July and only good to eat right off the tree. Brought into the kitchen and piled in a bowl on the counter, they softened within days—and an apple, to be truly a good apple, must be crisp textured. But they were crispy when eaten right off the tree and, my, that first fresh apple crunch was invigorating after months of storage fruit.

And then there was a Gravenstein, my all-time apple favorite. Gravenstein fruits are pale yellow liberally streaked with blood red. Sweet and tart and crisp, they are the epitome of what an apple should be. I see that California now claims Gravensteins as its own heritage fruit but I will point out, diplomatically, that Gravensteins were probably growing in Maine when California was still part of Mexico. Mexico or Maine, however, to my mind there is no better apple, for eating, for cooking, for storing in the cold cellar. Even though Reine des Reinettes is touted as *the* apple for a classic tarte tatin, I make mine with Gravensteins—when I can find them.

But where have all the Gravensteins gone? They are darned difficult to locate. At the one farmstand where I had bought them in the past, I asked about Gravensteins in mid-September. "Too late," said the assistant. "They've all gone by." Which is patently absurd since it's truly a mid-season apple and should last well into October. And that Gravenstein in the orchard where I grew up? About 30 years ago I went back to see if I could take a graft off that tree and recreate it in a meadow I'd acquired on the banks of the Wessaweskeag River in South Thomaston. But the house on the Megunticook had been sold many times over and the old Gravenstein, distressingly, was no more, long since chopped down and turned into—what? Firewood, I hope. It seems like the noblest end for a fine old tree.

And meanwhile, I'll make my tarte tatin with something else. Even with Cortlands it is still a noble dish.

Photo: 2009 poster for The Maine Organic Farmers and Gardeners Association's Common Ground Fair, illustrated by John Bunker.

COMMON GROUND COUNTRY FAIR

CELEBRATE RURAL LIVING WITH MOFGA

Ma Dudley's

By Pamela Snow Sweetser

The future "Ma Dudley," Avis Elzadie Tilley, was born in Castle Hill, and raised in a household where she said, "I learned how to work, and learned to like to work." It was an ethic she followed her whole life. Cooking held a particular fascination for her, and she viewed it as an art form where imagination and curiosity, along with trial and error, helped her find her own magic. Her attitude was a valuable assets for what lay ahead when she married potato grower Forrest Dudley in 1918.

Avis and Forrest worked shoulder to shoulder to make their farm prosper. By 1923, the couple had four children, and Avis was responsible for producing, preserving, cooking and serving food for three meals every day for eight or more hungry mouths. A natural leader, she stepped up to improve local women's and children's health and nutrition through the Extension Service and the first School Lunch programs of the 1930s and '40s. Life as a farmer's wife, mother, and community activist was her universe. Its nucleus was her kitchen table.

On October 26, 1954, however, tragedy struck. Forrest Dudley died unexpectedly. Determined to stay in the big house that was her home, Avis continued the only life she had known—housekeeping, family, and community involvement. Soon public demand soared for the home-cooked food served in her kitchen. Requests for meals at the Dudley Homestead started coming from clubs, professional organizations and family groups. By 1963, she had opened her home to the public. She resisted calling her business venture a restaurant, and it became simply "Ma Dudley's."

Eating at The Dudley Homestead became a must for locals, tourists and seasonal sports enthusiasts. It was enormously popular among the personnel stationed at Loring Air Force Base in Limestone. She recounted that many of them had "eaten around the world and [ranked hers] the best food they've ever had."

Ma Dudley's fare was varied and plentiful, and before long she expanded her kitchen and dining spaces in the farmhouse. Guests might be a group or single individuals. After they were seated, the wait staff began lading the tables, first with Ma Dudley's unique layered—never tossed—green salad accompanied by heaping plates of her signature hot caramel rolls. Then out came platters and bowls brimming with meats, seafood, and vegetables, to be passed around just as you would at home, except the person next to you might be a stranger.

Whole pies appeared for dessert. Each table was like its own family at a holiday feast, where you leisurely shared the food and met new folks.

In 1977, she published her cookbook, *Secrets of the Dudley Homestead*, but she never kept her recipes or methods a secret. That year, Yankee Magazine launched the first in a twenty-year series entitled "Great New England Cooks." Avis Dudley had the honor of being the first of the Great New England Cooks. She was 81 years old, and by then, world famous. She told Yankee Magazine, "A lot of people ask me how at my age I ever do this work every day. And sometimes . . . I don't know myself how I ever do it. But I'm enthused over it and I don't think of it as work. To tell you the truth, I wouldn't know how to live if I retired. I'd be bored to death."

Ma Dudley's recipe for Caramel Rolls can be found on page 38.

Pamela Snow Sweetser is a retired educator, an independent scholar historian, and a time-and-a-half farmer and small business owner. She is a member of the The Rural Women's Studies Association and a contributor to Backstories: The Kitchen Table Talk Cookbook.

CHEF
CHEERIODLE
CHEERIOOO

BREAKFAST & BREADS

Photo: Maine Community Cookbook author Margaret Hathaway, age 4, with her dad, Steve, wearing the chef's hat and oven mitt she got with boxtops from Cheerios. Margaret's recipe for Heath Bar Cookies can be found on page 206.

Tumahsis (Frybread)

Tom Doyle • Sipayik (Pleasant Point Reservation)

"Tumahsis is a traditional Passamaquoddy frybread common across many Native American communities. Among the Passamaquoddy, Tumahsis is often topped with local maple syrup and wild blueberries. The Passamaquoddy people have lived and flourished for fourteen thousand years primarily in Eastern Maine and Western New Brunswick, Canada. Our way of life was to hunt, fish, trap, and gather food and medicine, and employ the environment's natural resources to sustain their communities. Over the past 400 years, the encroachment and degradation of the resources in our homeland forced us to adapt, precipitating a shift away from our traditional indigenous economy. We had to find alternative ways to survive and feed our families. The Passamaquoddy were among the first to harvest wild blueberries and have been doing so for more than one thousand years, making these fruits an essential part of their diet, economy, and culture. Passamaquoddy Wild Blueberry Company has been managing and harvesting wild blueberries on 2,000 acres of barrens since the 1980s. Headquartered in Columbia Falls, Maine, the company is owned, managed, and staffed by Passamaquoddy Tribe members. Passamaquoddy Wild Blueberry Company embodies the long tradition and ongoing commitment to wild blueberry farming and its cultural significance, which has helped sustain the Passamaquoddy People." —Passamaquoddy Wild Blueberry Company

2 cups flour
2 cups water
2 teaspoons baking powder
2 pinches salt

Optional seasonings:
2 pinches garlic salt or cinnamon
Crisco, for frying
Wild blueberries and maple syrup (warmed), for topping

Mix flour, water, baking powder, and salt together in a large bowl. Add optional seasonings if desired. Heat 1 inch of Crisco in a skillet to 350 degrees. Carefully spoon a scoop of the mixture into hot oil, and fry on one side until browned. Using tongs, carefully turn and brown the other side. When browned, transfer breads to a towel-lined plate to cool. Top plain or cinnamon frybread with wild blueberries or maple syrup, as desired.

Aunt Weeza's Homemade Donuts

Victory Glenar • Garland, Penobscot County

"Louise Ernest of Garland was the oldest of the five Foss sisters (Louise, Barbara, Myrtie, Ada and Norma), raised by their widowed father, Roy, in Harmony. My Great Aunt 'Weeza,' as my family fondly called her, never missed Christmas and our birthdays. My brother, sister and I could not wait to receive the metal Maxwell House Coffee can which was always lined with wax paper and filled with our chosen favorite treat. My brother's favorite was molasses cookies, my sister's tollhouse cookies and my favorite was homemade donuts. Aunt Weeza made me 'special' shaped donuts from the scrap pieces of dough. They were 2 to 3 inches long and somehow, they tasted different to me. She would put several in each can of donuts and I was always excited to find them mixed in with the regular shaped donuts. On Christmas morning we would hurry to the Christmas tree and locate our can filled with the homemade treat. This was always the first gift we would open and we would snack on our treat while opening the other presents. We could taste and feel the love!"

- 1½ cups sugar
- 4 tablespoons oil (vegetable or canola)
- 2 eggs
- 5 cups all-purpose flour, plus more if needed
- 1 rounded teaspoon baking soda
- 1 teaspoon nutmeg
- 1½ cups buttermilk
- Fat or oil for frying

In a large bowl, mix together sugar, oil and eggs. In separate bowl sift together dry ingredients. Add the dry ingredients to the egg mixture, alternating with the buttermilk. Mix until combined. Place cover over bowl and refrigerate overnight.

When ready to fry, heat oil over medium heat until 370 degrees. Liberally flour a work space and roll dough out to ½-inch thickness. Cut donuts with a floured donut cutter.

Place donuts gently into hot oil (only a few at a time, as the oil will cool too quickly and make donuts heavy and greasy). The donuts will drop to the bottom, then rise to the top as they cook. Fry until golden brown on one side, then turn each one over to brown the other side. When done cooking, place on paper towels to remove excess grease. While still warm, shake in paper bag with sugar, sugar and cinnamon, or powdered sugar, or eat plain.

Muufo Corn Bread

Habiba Salat • Wales, Androscoggin County

"Habiba Salat is a farmer at Little Jubba Central Maine Agrarian Commons in Wales. Habiba was born in Somalia, and in 1991 fled to a Kenyan refugee camp during the Somali Civil war. She moved to Maine in 2005. She now goes to two farmers markets, in Yarmouth and Norway, and often cooks Somali traditional foods like Muufo Corn Bread. Little Jubba Central Maine Agrarian Commons is the latest step in securing farmland tenure for future generations of Somali Bantu agrarians. We chose the name Little Jubba Central Maine to describe our relationship to land, the Jubba River Valley being our ancestral farmland and Central Maine being our home now. Today in Central Maine, more than 200 Somali Bantu farmers can grow their own, culturally preferred foods, such as the flint corn this recipe is made from." —Muhadin Libah

- 2 cups Maine Grains Liberation Farms Corn Meal, or other corn flour
- 1 cup all-purpose flour
- 1½ teaspoons yeast
- 2 eggs
- 1 cup water
- 1½ teaspoons salt
- 1½ teaspoons sugar

Mix together the corn flour, all-purpose flour, and yeast. Add the eggs, and mix for 10 minutes. Stir in the water, and mix for another 10 minutes. Continue mixing as you add the salt and sugar. Place the dough in a large bowl, and leave it in a cool, dry place to rise for 3 hours.

When the dough has risen, form the dough into balls. Shape them into round, flat breads. Place on a hot griddle, and cook for 10 minutes, flipping the bread when it starts to color. Muufo is done when it's cooked through and reddish brown in color.

Kate Doyle Hanson's Irish Bread

Kathleen Sturtevant • York, York County

"My grandmother Kate Doyle Hanson was an immigrant in 1905 from County Cork Ireland. She joined several brothers and sisters who were already here working in the houses of wealthy people in Boston. She brought this Irish bread recipe with her. She came to York, where there were large summer houses owned by rusticators who needed their houses cleaned, walls painted and wallpapered, and fires lit on cold mornings. She married my grandfather Augustine Charles Hanson, whom she met through these summer connections. He was a carpenter, wallpaperer, and gentle man. They married and settled in York, where they built a house which I live in now. Kate was feisty, funny and not afraid to speak her mind. When there was a KKK organizational meeting advertised in York, this Irish Catholic woman went to the meeting and sat among her friends and neighbors to let them know that she saw them and what they were thinking of doing. The meeting dissolved quickly. She stood for something. Also, a party didn't start until Kate arrived, and if she was running late she'd bustle in saying "me 'ead is here, me arse is coming." I like to think that that's where all of her 8 grandchildren got their senses of humor and the strength to stand for what's right."

3 cups flour
½ cup softened butter
¾-1 cup sugar
4 teaspoons baking powder
1 teaspoon salt
2 eggs
¾ cup milk
Currants, as desired
2 teaspoons caraway seeds

Mix first 5 ingredients together. Then add the eggs, milk, currants (a handful), and caraway seeds. Mix with a spoon or your hands. Dough will be stiff like biscuit dough. Pat out on a floured board. Press dough into a good sized frying-pan (I use a 9-inch greased cake pan). Bake at 350 degrees for 45 minutes.

Anadama Bread

Martha Speed • Edgecomb, Lincoln County

"This is our Thanksgiving treat. The first loaf disappears before it has cooled off."

- ½ cup yellow cornmeal
- 2 cups water
- 2 tablespoons shortening
- ½ cup molasses
- 1 teaspoon salt
- 1 package active dry yeast
- 1 cup lukewarm water
- 5 to 5½ cups all-purpose flour

In a small saucepan, whisk cornmeal into 2 cups water. Turn burner on medium. While stirring, cook cornmeal until it begins to boil. Place hot cornmeal in a large mixing bowl with shortening, molasses, and salt. Stir occasionally as it cools.

Soften yeast in 1 cup warm water. When cornmeal mixture has cooled to room temperature, add softened yeast. Stir in flour to make a dough. Knead well; let rise until slightly more than double in bulk. Punch down and shape into loaves.

Place in greased loaf pans and let rise again until double. Preheat oven to 400 degrees. Bake 15 minutes, then reduce temperature to 350 degrees and bake for 30 minutes longer. Makes 2 loaves.

Sunday Brunch Spinach Quiche

Heidi Morin • West Gardiner, Kennebec County

"My grandmother would prepare 'Morin Family Brunch' every Sunday for my family, where this spinach quiche was a staple. When I was a child, I would gather at her house with my parents, sister, aunts, uncles, and cousins. I remember we would play outside in the yard after eating."

- 10-ounce package frozen chopped spinach, thawed and squeezed dry
- 4 eggs, lightly beaten
- 1 cup grated Monterey jack cheese
- 1 medium onion, chopped
- ½ teaspoon salt
- ½ teaspoon pepper
- 1 chilled pie crust, store bought or homemade
- 3 tablespoons butter, melted
- 4 tablespoons freshly grated Parmesan cheese
- Bread crumbs or crushed butter-flavored crackers, like Ritz, for topping

Preheat oven to 350 degrees. In a medium-size bowl, combine spinach, eggs, Monterey jack cheese, chopped onion, salt, and pepper. Mix well. Spoon into pie crust and bake 30 minutes. Remove quiche from oven and dot with butter, then sprinkle with Parmesan cheese and bread crumbs or crushed crackers. Return quiche to oven and bake for 5-10 more minutes, until the topping browns up.

Pumpkin Bread

Barbie Sadler Humphrey • Bangor, Penobscot County

"One of my best friends gave me this recipe in 1984 and I've been making it ever since. It's moist and delicious and always a huge hit."

4 eggs, beaten
1 cup oil
⅔ cup water
2 cups pumpkin
3½ cups flour
1½ teaspoons salt
2 teaspoons baking soda
1 teaspoon cinnamon
2-3 cups sugar (I use 3 cups)
1½ teaspoons baking powder
1 teaspoon nutmeg
Optional: ½ cup chopped nuts or dried cranberries

Preheat oven to 350 degrees. In a large bowl, combine and beat first 4 ingredients. Add remaining dry ingredients and beat until mixed. Pour into 2 greased loaf pans. Bake 60-75 minutes, until a toothpick comes out clean. Cool in the pan for a few minutes, and then finish cooling on racks.

Popovers "Good Ones"

Cindi Annis • Monson, Piscataquis County

"My mom, Ada (Foss) Cobb, made popovers often, as it was one of my dad's, brother's, and my favorites. Over the years I've tried other recipes but when I do, I ask my self why. This one comes out great every time. Ma always used an old-fashioned egg beater to make these, and I use the same one she did. For those who don't have or maybe don't even know what one is, I'm sure you could use a regular mixer."

1 cup flour
½ teaspoon salt
2 eggs
1 cup milk
2 teaspoons melted butter

Level off 1 cup flour, and put it in a tall bowl. Add salt and stir. Add eggs, milk, and butter and beat with an eggbeaters until smooth. Pour batter in greased muffin tin or popover pan. Bake at 425 degrees for 40 minutes. Makes 8.

Zucchini Bread

Sheila Norman • Bangor, Penobscot County

"This recipe has been handed down from my grandmother, but we don't know where she got it. It is a family favorite. We freeze several 2-cup packages of grated zucchini each fall, ready to be defrosted and turned into bread. One year, I received a blue ribbon at the Piscataquis Valley Fair with this recipe."

3 eggs
2 cups sugar
1 cup vegetable oil
2 cups grated zucchini
2 teaspoons vanilla
3 cups flour
1 teaspoon baking soda
1 teaspoon salt
¼ teaspoon baking powder
3 teaspoons cinnamon

Preheat oven to 350 degrees.

In a large bowl, beat eggs until light and foamy. Add sugar, vegetable oil, grated zucchini, and vanilla. Mix well. Add dry ingredients and mix thoroughly. Divide batter in two greased bread pans.

Bake for 45 minutes to an hour, or until a knife inserted in the middle of a loaf comes out clean. Remove from pans immediately and allow to cool on a wire rack.

Ruth's Buttermilk Date Muffins

Patricia Worth • Belfast, Waldo County

"Our mother Ruth Brown Goodridge Meigs led a traditional life in many ways. She was born at home in Steuben, in 1918. After college at Gorham Normal School, she taught school in Rockland, before marrying her college sweetheart, our father. During World War Two, she lived at home with her parents and baby daughter while teaching in a one-room schoolhouse in Bucksport. Four children later, she was living and teaching at a school in the Rumford area. After our father died in 1964, she needed to earn more money, and here's where she broke out of the mold. She got a job preparing gourmet meals for several trips on the motor yacht Sea Otter out of Camden, and then was asked to cook on the Schooner Mercantile, also out of Camden. She bought her first pair of blue jeans for the job, and spent several summers off the coast of Maine in the windjammer business. In the Mercantile's galley, relying on a woodstove and icebox, she turned out her delicious downeast specialties. Her buttermilk date muffins, with scrambled eggs, bacon, and melon was one of her passengers' favorites."

- 1½ cups all-purpose flour
- 2½ teaspoons baking powder
- ¾ teaspoon baking soda
- ¾ teaspoon salt
- ½ cup packed brown sugar, or less
- ¼ cup butter or Crisco
- 1 cup raw oatmeal (regular rolled oats, not quick)
- 1 beaten egg
- 1 cup buttermilk
- ¾ to 1 cup chopped dates

Heat oven to 400 degrees. Grease or line 12 muffin cups. Mix together flour, baking powder, baking soda and salt. Stir in brown sugar. Cut in butter or shortening. Add rolled oats. Mix egg and buttermilk together and add to dry ingredients. Add dates and stir briefly. Spoon batter into muffin cups and bake for 12-15 minutes. Excellent right out of the oven with butter.

Mom's Dark Oatmeal Bread

Dean Paterson • Presque Isle, Aroostook County

"Dean Donahue, aka Geraldine Donahue, was Geraldean Paterson's mom. Clearly, I am Mom's namesake, but the spelling of our first name is different. That said, being born and raised in Presque Isle, I hail from a family of five children, growing up on homemade everything. We had a vegetable garden which yielded fabulous soups, frozen veggies, pickles, pies, cookies and other delicious desserts. Mom made most everything we ate from scratch. We had a commercial double-sided freezer in our basement and a cold-storage room for preserved/canned vegetables, jams and jellies. Beef was purchased by the 'side' and chicken was purchased by the half dozen. With five children and two adults in the house, a great deal of time was spent on food preparation, including homemade bread...white, oatmeal and Shredded Wheat. One of her specialties was to make double loaves of bread. I don't know anyone else that uses that presentation."

- 2 cups quick cooking rolled oats
- ½ cup molasses
- ⅓ cup shortening
- 1 tablespoon salt
- 2 cups boiling water
- 1 package active dry yeast
- ½ cup warm water
- 6 to 6½ cups flour

In large mixing bowl, combine oats, molasses, shortening, salt, and boiling water. Cool to lukewarm.

Soften yeast in ½ cup of warm water; add to mixture. Gradually add flour to produce stiff dough. Flour hands and knead on well-floured surface until all the flour is absorbed and the dough is smooth. Dough will be slightly sticky to touch. Place in a greased bowl, turning to grease all sides. Cover and let rise in a warm place until doubled, 1½ to 2 hours. Punch down dough, cover and let rise again for 30 minutes.

Place dough on floured surface. Divide into 4 portions. Shape into balls. Put two balls in each of two greased bread tins/loaf pans. Let rise again until doubled, about an hour. The dough should be level to the top of the bread pans. Bake in a 350-degree oven for 35-40 minutes, until golden brown. Let bread cool in the tins before removing to wire rack. I butter the tops while slightly warm to create shiny loaves.

Joan Caron's Shredded Wheat Bread

Mary Durost • Bucksport, Hancock County

"My mother, Joan Caron, led an interesting life as a Game Warden's wife in Aroostook County, starting in the late '40s. She raised four kids and fed us well. She loved submitting recipes to the local church and community cookbooks and seeing her name in print. Growing up, this was one of our favorites. Coming home to the aroma of this bread baking was such a treat. My favorite time of the year was pea season in The County. The best meal ever was fresh peas with real butter and freshly baked Shredded Wheat Bread. We didn't need anything else...."

- 3 cups milk, scalded
- 2 cups hot water
- 4 shredded wheat biscuits
- ½ cup brown sugar
- ½ cup molasses
- 2 tablespoons salt
- ½ cup melted fat
- 3 tablespoons yeast
- Flour (approximately 6-8 cups)

Combine all ingredients except flour and mix well. Gradually stir in enough flour to make a stiff dough. Turn out the dough onto a flat surface and knead, adding enough flour to prevent sticking, until you have a smooth ball (about 10 minutes).

Return the dough to a large bowl. Cover with wax paper and a towel and set in a warm place. Let rise 1 hour or until dough has doubled in size.

Punch the dough down and shape into four loaves. Put in greased bread pans. Cover again with wax paper and a towel. Let rise another hour.

Bake in a preheated 375-degree oven for about 30 minutes, until nicely brown and hollow sounding when you bop it.

Celeste's Creamy Cornmeal Cake

Ellie Markovitch • Bangor, Penobscot County

"My mom never had a cookbook. Growing up, my job was to copy all her friend's recipes into her notebook. And likewise she shared her recipes with families and friends. When I moved from Brazil to the USA to attend college, I copied her notebook with our family recipes and brought it with me. We keep my mom's recipes alive by making them, writing them, and sharing them with friends. This is one of my mom's signature Friday night bakes for the weekend. It is like magic. How is it possible all the ingredients go into the blender and then after baking we have all these amazing layers?!"

- 4 eggs
- 4 cups of milk
- 3 cups sugar (yes, you can cut back if you need to)
- 1½ cups cornmeal or corn flour
- ½ cup Brazilian cured and grated "farm cheese" (or Parmesan)
- 2 tablespoons butter, room temperature
- ½ teaspoon salt
- 1 tablespoon baking powder

Preheat oven to 350 degrees. Place all ingredients except for baking powder in the cup of a blender and blend for 3 minutes. (If your blender is small, hold back some of the milk and add that at the end.) With the blender off, add baking powder and pulse a few times. This is a liquid dough.

Grease a 9x13-inch baking dish and sprinkle with cornmeal. Pour dough into the dish and bake for 45-55 minutes, or until golden. Note that recipe can be halved and baked in a 9x9-inch pan.

Sweet Brown Bread Muffins

Cat Morrow • Kenduskeag, Penobscot County

"I'm told that my grandmother Martha especially loved the B&M canned brown bread with raisins in it. These brown bread muffins have the flavor of quintessential brown bread, but they can be made hastily, and in bulk very easily. They are wicked easy to prepare. Just one bowl, a few simple ingredients, and you've got delicious, fluffy and sweet take on the classic canned bread that is a familiar New England flavor. (Without the lengthy steaming process, or can!) Serve these anywhere you would your favorite potluck cornbread or corn muffin. For a flavorful twist, add a few teaspoons of caraway or a bit of anise seed, or substitute wild blueberries for the raisins."

Dry ingredients:

⅔ cup cornmeal
½ cup rye flour
½ cup all-purpose flour
1 teaspoon baking powder
½ teaspoon baking soda
½ teaspoon fresh cracked pepper medley (more to taste)
¾ teaspoon sea salt

Wet ingredients:

⅓ cup molasses
⅓ cup brown sugar or sucanat (optional)
1 egg
¼ cup preferred flavorless oil (such as sunflower, light olive, or avocado oil)
1 cup buttermilk, or soured whole milk (1 cup milk mixed with 1 teaspoon apple cider vinegar)
1 cup raisins or dried cranberries (optional but great with extra black pepper!)

Note: For a less sweet, more-like-the-can muffin, substitute a few tablespoons of maple sugar for the brown sugar, or skip the added sugar altogether.

Preheat oven to 350 degrees. Prepare muffin tins by lining with paper muffin cups.

In a large bowl, mix together the dry ingredients, stirring well to get rid of lumps. In a separate bowl combine molasses, brown sugar, egg, oil, and buttermilk.

Add the wet ingredients to the dry, and your raisins or dried fruit, if desired. Stir everything together until good and combined. Fill muffin cups about halfway. Bake for 20-25 minutes, or until the tops have crackled and browned thoroughly.

Turn out onto a wire rack to cool for 5-10 minutes before serving with your favorite stew or beans.

Ring-A-Lings

Paula Collier • Gardiner, Kennebec County

"My mother, Barbara Foss Herrick, is one of the five Foss Girls of Harmony. The five sisters were true 'Tee-totalers.' However, Aunt Weeza admitted to imbibing a sip of fine wine occasionally when she was ironing clothes. This bottle of Boones Farm wine lasted many years. The family laughs when we look at Louise and sister Barbara acting out in this photo. I like to think they took a sip that day. The Foss sisters and their families celebrated Christmas together every year, and it was tradition that Barbara would bring Ring-A-Lings."

Dough:

2 packages dry yeast
¼ cup very warm (not hot) water (105-110 degrees)
⅓ cup butter
¾ cup hot scalded milk
⅓ cup sugar
2 teaspoons salt
2 teaspoons grated orange rind
2 unbeaten eggs
4-4½ cups sifted flour

Filling:

⅓ cup butter
1 cup sifted confectioners' sugar
1 cup chopped hazelnuts (other nuts may be substituted)

Glaze:

¼ cup orange juice
3 tablespoons sugar

In a large bowl, soften yeast in warm water. In a separate medium-size bowl, add butter to hot scalded milk, and stir until the butter melts. Cool to lukewarm.

Add sugar, salt, grated orange and eggs to softened yeast. Stir in the butter and milk mixture. Gradually add in the sifted flour, mixing until you have a stiff dough. Work the dough thoroughly, then cover and let rise 30 minutes.

While the dough rises, make the nut filling. In a mixing bowl, cream butter. Blend in confectioners' sugar and mix thoroughly. Add nuts and mix to combine. Cover and set aside until ready to use.

On a clean floured counter or board, roll out dough to a 22x12-inch rectangle. Starting on the long side, spread nut filling onto half the dough. Fold other side of dough over the nut mixture. You will now have a 22x6-inch rectangle.

Slice the dough crosswise into 1x6-inch strips. Twist each strip 4 or 5 times. Hold one end down on a greased baking sheet, then curl strip around into a loop, tucking the other end under the dough. Cover with a towel and let rise in a warm place (85-90 degrees) until doubled in size, 45-60 minutes.

While dough rises, preheat oven to 375 degrees. Bake for 15 minutes. While ring-a-lings are baking, combine orange juice and sugar to make a glaze. Brush tops of rolls with glaze and return to the oven for 5 minutes longer, until they're a deep golden brown. Remove from baking sheet to cool.

Mam's Crêpes

Alex Gayton • Orono, Penobscot County

"My grandparents are French Canadian and crêpes are one of the breakfast foods we grew up with and love! Here's the simple recipe, straight from the source. We always used maple syrup as our filling of choice and ate slices of fruit on the side, but you can make crêpes sweet or savory. This recipe is easy to multiply because the main ingredients are a 1:1:1 ratio—our family always has to make at least a triple batch because we love having leftovers. The recipe is very flexible, and can be made vegan or gluten-free."

1 cup milk
 (or your favorite non-dairy alternative)
1 cup all-purpose flour
 (can use wheat or alternative)
1 whole egg (or can use egg replacer)
1 teaspoon cinnamon, optional
1 teaspoon vanilla extract, optional
Filling of choice: maple syrup, butter
 and sugar, jam, Nutella

Oil a large pan and place it over medium-high heat.
In a mixing bowl, combine all ingredients and mix thoroughly. If the batter is too thick, add additional milk. Note: Crêpe batter should be thinner than pancake batter.

Ladle batter onto the pan, tilting the pan in a circular motion so the batter spreads into a thin layer. Cook about 2 minutes, until the bottom is light brown. Flip and cook on the other side. Spread with your filling of choice, and roll before serving. Makes 5 servings.

Gluten-Free Pizza Crust

Caitlin Shetterly • Freeport, Cumberland

"Back in 2013, when our family went gluten free because it turned out neither my husband nor I could eat it, at first we thought we would never eat pizza again! And that made us sad!!! We tried all kinds of things like cauliflower crust and eggplant crust and some weird crackery thing. Nothing was any good. So I started, slowly, experimenting with my own flours and recipes and...one day I came up with a pizza crust we loved. Now, we have pizza every Friday night.

In the old days, before the pandemic, my boys and I would go to the library every Friday on the way home from school. We'd get easily 150 books, spread out on three library cards, each Friday and then each kid would pore over their stack. This started with our youngest when he was about six months old. I'll never forget him sitting up in his high chair and going page by page through picture books and then doubling back to something that jogged his memory or he wanted to figure out. And meanwhile, our oldest would literally fall into the books. I mean—gone; in an alternate reality. They learned so many things over the years in all those books. I am so grateful to our library because thanks to all those books my kids teach me new things every day.

So, while they were quiet with their books, I'd make pizza crust. It was such a celebration of books and pizza every Friday and we looked forward to it. These days it's a little harder to go from school to the library and home with masks and people and all the stress. But I try to go up alone with a big bag, and we still have the pizza."

1 cup organic millet flour
1 cup organic tapioca starch
1 cup organic brown rice flour (or white rice or sweet rice, depending on what you can find)
½ cup ground flax meal (you can omit this, but it gives the crust a nutty, whole wheat flavor.)
1 teaspoon salt
1⅔ teaspoons dry yeast
½ teaspoon psyllium powder
2½ teaspoons xanthan gum
1⅔ cups water
1½ tablespoons honey (or more, I do a big glob!)
¼ cup olive oil, plus more for drizzling
Corn meal or gluten-free bread crumbs, for sprinkling

Note: I use all organic flours for my crust. My reasons are twofold: the first is that I do believe that organic tastes better and just works better, too, in my recipes. The second reason is that I am increasingly concerned about the chemical load we are asking of our fields, plants, soil, and water sources.

In the bowl of a stand mixer fitted with the whisk attachment, combine all the flours, then whisk in the salt, yeast, psyllium powder, and xanthan gum. Switch mixer attachment to the dough hook.

In a small saucepan over low heat, warm the water, honey and olive oil on the stove until it's lukewarm, 105-110 degrees. Drizzle it in and mix on the lowest setting until dough comes together. If it's too watery, add more tapioca starch until the dough becomes a nice big ball that is soft and pillowy to the touch. When you reach the right consistency, drizzle more olive oil on top and put a glass lid on top of the bowl to keep it really warm and damp—gluten free is all about moisture. Let it rise for about 45 minutes or so—I aim for longer if I can.

While the dough is rising, prepare two pizza pans. I put olive oil all over them and then sprinkle with either some organic corn meal or gluten-free bread crumbs. Split the dough into two balls. Take the first one and plop it on the prepared pan. From the center of the ball outwards, push the dough out with your hands until you reach the edges of the pan. Try to keep it thick enough that it doesn't break. I do it for each one, and I make a nice rolled crust on the sides. It's really easy...once you've done it a couple of times. Top with a mix of cheeses and your favorite goodies—my kids love turkey bacon and pineapple, fried mushrooms, olives, spinach, and onions. Bake at 450 degrees until done.

Puffets

1906 • The Orono Cook Book

The Ladies of the Methodist Episcopal Church • Orono, Penobscot County

A small, rectangular tea cake, the puffet has gone through many changes in the last two centuries. Earlier versions used yeast until the modern baking soda became more readily available. And later versions use puff pastry and sometimes stuff the little bite-sized treats with fruit, vegetable, or meat fillings. Whichever version you prefer, making puffets is a great excuse to use the old cast-iron gem pan. —DL

Take 1 quart flour, ½ teaspoonful salt, butter the size of an egg, 2 eggs, 2 tablespoonfuls of white sugar, 1 pint of milk, and 3 teaspoonfuls of baking powder. Rub butter into the flour, beat the eggs separately, adding the whites last. Bake in gem-pans in a hot oven.

Ma Dudley's Caramel Rolls

Avis E. Dudley • Castle Hill, Aroostook County

This recipe appears in Avis Dudley's 1977 cookbook, *Ma Dudley's Secrets of the Dudley Homestead*, reprinted with permission.

Dissolve 1 cake of household yeast in 1 quart warm water (wrist temperature). Sift 1 quart unsifted flour, 1 cup sugar, and 1 tablespoon salt into the liquid. Mix together and let rise ½-¾ hour.

Add 1 cup melted oleo and 2 quarts flour. Mix well. Sprinkle a little flour on the board. Put dough on it and knead with a circular rotating upward motion toward you. Continue to knead until it has a smooth elastic texture, about 10 minutes. Then put back in dish to rise. Cover it while rising. If you have the large plastic garbage bags, these are excellent to put the dough in to raise. The bag keeps the dough at an even, moist, warm temperature.

When it is double in bulk, punch it down then proceed to put it on the pans. Put a piece of the dough 1 inch thick, 6 inches wide, and 12 inches long on the board. Then stretch the dough until it is ½ inch thick. Spread a thin layer of brown sugar over it, then begin at the side nearest you to roll the dough into a roll about 2 inches across and 16 inches long. Roll it good and tight so it will stay together. Now cut off pieces about 1 inch thick and you will have an uncooked roll.

You sort of float melted oleo over the bottom of the pan. I do not crowd the rolls in the pan. I lay them across the pan with the rolls touching each other. Continue to put layer by layer in the pan until the bottom is covered.

I like to set these on the white part of my electric stove until they are at least double in bulk. If you see these are not going to be raised enough when you have to put them in to bake in a 350- to 375-oven, set the pan of rolls in a pan the same size with about 1 inch of hot water. This will really boost them up. You can even put them in the oven still in the pan of hot water for about 5 minutes. If you do, lay a piece of aluminum foil over the top of the pan the first 10 minutes and you have a more pleasant texture. Then remove the foil and continue baking them. Set the timer for 25 minutes then test them for doneness.

ROSEMONT
Market &
BAKERY
Cultivating Meaningful Relationships Between Local Farms and our Communities so that We can all Access and Experience Joyful Food
Photograph by Zack Bowen of South Paw Farm in Freedom, Maine

Wicked Joe®
ORGANIC COFFEES
ORGANIC
FAIR TRADE
RESPONSIBLY GROWN
WICKEDLY ROASTED
MAINE ROASTED
learn more at
WICKEDJOE.COM
USDA ORGANIC
Certified B Corporation
FAIR TRADE CERTIFIED
NON GMO Project VERIFIED
nongmoproject.org

Since 1974, we've proudly served over 25,000 injured and disabled Mainers.
"Let's settle this one with a cup of Joe!"
LAW OFFICES OF
JOE BORNSTEIN
PERSONAL INJURY ATTORNEYS
207-CALL-JOE

NOW YOU'RE COOKING
Everything you need to make an apple pie just like Grandma's
Now You're Cooking
49 Front Street in Historic Downtown Bath, Maine
acooksemporium.com | 207-443-1402

Jelly

Put crabs on boil
take off & turn in
bag & drain over
night. Take juice &
boil about 1/2 hr.
measure juice such
as 6 cups juice to
4 cups sugar,
boil 20 min.

Mustard pickle

cut up, peel & seed
6 qts. cucumbers,
fron, over-night.
put 1 cup salt
over them. drain
next morning. cut 1 1/2
qt. onions cook together,
til tender then ~~drain~~
with part Vin. & water.
drain.
2 qt. vinegar
2 1/2 cups sugar
1 " flour
1/4 box mustard
1 tea-sp turmeric

Mince Meat

7 cups of sugar
1 can of nut meg
1/2 " " cinnamon
4 pkg. raisins
6 lb. meat
4 times as much apple as
meat.
1/2 lb. suet.
about 1/4 cup. salt.

Pepper Relish

12 red peppers (hot)
12 green "
14 small onions
put through food chopper
Pour boiling water
over and let stand 20
minutes then drain
add 2 1/2 cups of sugar
3 tablespoons salt
1 qt. vinegar.
Cook 1/2 hour, seal
up hot.
Remove seeds of
peppers

PICKLES & PRESERVES

Photo: Pages from the handwritten recipe book of Amy Frost of Eastport include recipes for jelly, mustard pickles, and pepper relish. Her recipe for Eastport Fish Chowder, submitted by her granddaughter Faye McNall, can be found on page 74.

Grammie Tripp's Beet Relish

Allison Marcoux • Madison, Somerset County

"My grandmother, Irene Olive Collins, was born in Flagstaff in 1904. She married Cecil Tripp, and they raised their eight children, including my father, in New Portland. My grandparents didn't have much financially, and relied heavily on their garden, raising animals, and hunting in the Maine woods. This was one of my grandmother's many recipes, and it's a family favorite. There are other beet relish recipes out there, but my grandmother upped the horseradish, a food she was fond of. My grandparents had horseradish root growing on their property. My grandmother lived a full 92 years, and maybe the health benefits of all that horseradish contributed to her long life of good health."

1 quart chopped fresh cabbage
1 quart cooked chopped beets
1 cup grated fresh horseradish root
1 tablespoon salt
1 cup sugar
2 cups cider vinegar

In a large bowl, combine cabbage, beets, horseradish, and season with salt. In a separate large pot, dissolve sugar in vinegar and bring to a boil. Add beet mixture to vinegar, and bring to a gentle boil. Pack into hot sterilized pint-sized jars, leaving ¼ inch headspace, and process as you would any relish.

Candied Grapefruit Peel

1916 • The New Rutherford Cook Book

Ladies' Aid of South Bristol • South Bristol, Lincoln County

South Bristol's Mrs. Tracy knows how to write a good recipe. Candymaking needs a steady hand and precise measurements, which she provides here. But she's also practical, and clearly fun, which we know from her opening salvo, "Eat the grapefruit!" —DL

Eat the grapefruit! Wash skins and remove any remaining pulp. Cut in squares, cover with water and let it come to a boil. Pour off water, and cover with water again, cooking into tender. Drain, measure and for each cup of peel take ¾ cup sugar. Put peel and sugar on stove again and cook ten or fifteen minutes or until the syrup is quite thick, care being taken not to let it burn. Remove and put it into a strainer to drain. Roll each piece in sugar while hot and put on plates to stand 24 hours, when it can be put into jars to keep from becoming hard. — Mrs. Tracy

Pickled Cucumbers and Onion

Margo Rowen • Stetson, Penobscot County

"As kids we loved to eat cucumbers right out of the garden. My mother had a hard time getting a cuke back to the house as we would eat them so fast. She made up this concoction with all the little, small, and misshaped cucumbers in the garden so that they were all appreciated and put to use. My favorite recipe at this time of year when things are winding down in the garden."

¼ cup sugar
¼ cup vinegar
⅛ cup water
4 to 5 medium cukes, sliced
1 large vidalia onion, sliced and quartered
Salt and pepper, to taste
Parsley flakes
1 teaspoon celery salt

Mix everything together in large tight-lidded bowl. Refrigerate, and shake the bowl often. Other veggies can be added too, if you like. These pickles are great with a meal!

Peach Delight

1951 • Cooks Tell How
V.F.W. Auxiliary Capt. Frank W. Hulett Post • Auburn, Androscoggin County

I had assumed this cookbook's handsome oil-cloth wrapper decorated with apple branches had been added by a careful owner to preserve the little book from the perils of the kitchen. But I found another copy of the book, also with an attractively decorated piece of oil-cloth (but with a different design) for its wrapper. It turns out the members of the V.F.W. Auxiliary were issuing the book with wrappers made from leftover fabric, an example of the D.I.Y. approach taken by community groups to get their cookbooks published at lower costs. —DL

3 lbs. peaches (mashed)
3½ lbs. sugar
Juice of 2 oranges
1 large bottle of maraschino cherries with juice

Cook one hour and seal. —Mrs. Laura Humphrey

A Two Relish Family

Mary Bagley • Veazie, Penobscot County

"Ours is definitely a two relish family. Hot dogs - fried, steamed, grilled or over the campfire - are always served with Bea's Canada Pickle Relish. And if hamburgers are on the grill, Grammie Bagley's Sweet Tomato Picallili is on the table. The two are rarely switched! My Great Aunt Bea Doane was a kind, gentle woman and a wonderful cook. I have many happy memories of watching her at work at her Hoosier cabinet. And I have loved this relish since I was a little girl. My mother-in-law, Barbara Bagley, was another wonderful woman and great cook. Her relish is a terrific way to use up the last of the green tomatoes after the frost. This relish goes very well with baked beans, too!"

Bea's Canada Pickle Relish

- 1 quart whole onions (I use two pounds), trimmed and peeled
- 6 very large cucumbers
- ¼ cup salt
- 1 teaspoon celery seed
- 1 tablespoon dry mustard
- 1 teaspoon turmeric
- 3 tablespoons flour
- 2 cups white sugar
- 1 pint cider vinegar

Grind the onions and cucumbers together. Cover with water and the salt. Let stand over night, then drain. In a large pot, mix together the spices, flour, and sugar. Add the vinegar and cook until thick (about 10 minutes), stirring frequently. Add the drained onions and cucumbers. Bring mixture to a boil. Take off heat. Pack into hot sterilized jars and seal according to manufacturer's directions.

Grammie Bagley's Sweet Tomato Picallili

- 2 quarts ground green tomatoes, drained
- 1 pint ground onions
- 2 red peppers, ground
- 2 green peppers, ground
- 3 cups white sugar
- ¼ cup salt
- 1 pint cider vinegar
- 2½ tablespoons pickling spice, wrapped in cheesecloth bag

In a large pot, cover the ground tomatoes with cold water and bring to a boil. Drain and add all the other ingredients. Cook on medium heat for 30 minutes, stirring often. Pack into hot, sterilized jars and seal according to manufacturer's directions. Makes about 7 pints.

Refrigerator Pickles

Deborah Hayden • Brunswick, Cumberland County

"My Aunt Ruth Holmes Marks was the daughter of Norwegian immigrants, born in 1918 in Wisconsin. Her father was a minister who got his degree and was ordained in Chicago and then worked in a church in Wisconsin for a few years. Next he was offered a job at a Scandinavian church in Portland. He accepted the post and arrived with his wife and five children in the early 1920s. He loved Portland harbor because it reminded him of his home in Bergen, Norway, and he lived out the rest of his life in Portland. The family has remained in close touch with each other and their heritage. I first tasted these pickles at a family gathering at Aunt Ruth's summer camp. I asked for the recipe and she mailed it to me. That was about 40 years ago. The recipe was handwritten and said that the kind of jar that was needed would be 'like the one Grammy Holmes used for Christmas cookies.' These pickles stay crisp no matter how long they are in the jar. They are mild and crispy. Just keep adding new vegetables throughout the season. Peppers, green tomatoes and such also work. You will need a very big jar and room for it in the fridge for the whole summer. Actually, sometimes, I have adjusted the liquid and used a smaller jar."

- 10 to 12 cucumbers, sliced ⅛ to ¼-inch thick
- 4 large sliced onions
- ½ cup pickling salt
- 4 cups white vinegar
- 5 cups sugar
- 1 teaspoon turmeric
- 1½ teaspoons celery seeds
- 1½ teaspoons mustard seeds

Prepare your vegetables. Combine and stir thoroughly everything except the veggies. Do not heat this mixture. Layer onions and cucumbers in the jar. Pour in the brine. It should cover everything. Refrigerate for about 3 days before using. Keep adding onions and cukes all season. Enjoy!

Lady Ashburnham Pickles

Marianne Pinkham • Nobleboro, Lincoln County

"The recipe for Lady Ashburnham Pickles was originally published in a 1960s *Maine Rebekahs Cookbook*. The recipe was passed on to my family by our neighbor and friend Shirley Bailey when she discovered that rather than zucchinis, my father's vegetable garden was filled with an abundance of ripe cucumbers: those big, chunky, yellow cucumbers that are rarely seen in today's market place where misfits are not allowed. This recipe is a perfect sweet and savory foil for cucumbers that are left to ripen after the green cukes that are used in salads or for bread and butter pickles have been picked. Now, some 60 years later, if I can find a garden patch with cucumbers that have been left on their vines to ripen fully I continue to make a batch of Lady A pickles to share with friends and neighbors. It makes a holiday gift with a bright yellow smile."

26 large ripe cucumbers (skins have started to turn yellow)
2 quarts yellow onions
½ cup pickling salt
Cold water

Dressing (Brine):
4 pints hot cider vinegar
12 tablespoons all-purpose flour
4 tablespoons dry mustard
4 tablespoons turmeric
4 tablespoons celery seed
8 cups granulated sugar

Prepare the vegetables: Clean, scrub cucumbers. Peel, cut in half, remove seeds and then cut cucumbers into small pieces and chunks. Clean and remove the skins from the onions. Cut into fine pieces. Place cucumbers and onions in a large, pottery crock. Sprinkle the pickling salt over the cucumbers and onions. Cover with cold water. Place lid on top of the crock and let sit overnight. In the morning, transfer the cucumber mixture into a large colander and drain. Once drained, place the cucumber mixture in a large, heavy-bottom stock pot.

Prepare the dressing: In a separate bowl or container combine and mix together all of the dressing ingredients.

To make the pickles: Pour the dressing over the cucumber mixture and mix all of the ingredients together. Bring to a slow boil. Reduce the heat and cook, stirring occasionally, until the cucumber chunks are translucent, about a half hour.

Ladle (pack) the hot cucumber mixture and liquid into hot, sterilized glass canning jars (pints or quarts) leaving ½ inch headspace. Process as you would any pickle. After making sure that the jars lids have sealed, label and store in a cool place.

Curried Green Tomato Relish

Gail D'Agostino • Dover-Foxcroft, Piscataquis County

"This recipe came from my Aunt Doris (Landford) Stevens from Newburyport, Massachusetts, whose family extended to Farmington, Maine. Doris' children were close with their cousins, aunts and uncles from Farmington. Doris' nieces and nephews in Maine revered her, and we still make her recipe today. Our extended family exemplifies a true blend of Maine and Massachusetts."

- Sliced green tomatoes, to fill roasting pan
- 4 large sliced yellow onions
- ½ cup kosher salt
- 2½ cups sugar
- 1 tablespoon curry powder
- 6 cups cider vinegar
- 1½ teaspoons turmeric
- ¼ teaspoon mustard seeds

Fill a giant roasting pan full of sliced green tomatoes and sliced yellow onions. Sprinkle with kosher salt. Let stand overnight, or at least 8 hours. Drain and lightly rinse.

In a large pan, combine sugar, curry powder, cider vinegar, turmeric, and mustard seeds. Bring to a boil, and then add drained tomatoes and onions. Stir together, and boil mixture for 10 minutes. Pack into hot sterilized pint-sized jars and seal according to manufacturer's directions. Makes 10 pints.

RHUBARB

Photo: Rhubarb girls: Marika Kuzma, Lesia Sochor, and Joann Robbbins at Sochor's rhubarb patch in Brooks in the mid-1970s.

Marion's Rhubarb Coffee Cake

Rachel Freedman • Portland, Cumberland County

"For many, sharing food, sitting around a communal table, and cooking and baking together are traditions that illustrate who we are. Over food, we connect and bond; we laugh, tell stories, listen and taste the incredible creativity, love, and ingenuity of the people who cook for us. Food, like traditions, is best when shared. At Wayside Food Programs, bringing people together over food is a critical part of our food security work. Food is an essential resource for connecting people to their families, their friends, and their communities, which is why Wayside is not only dedicated to connecting people with food, but also using food as a tool for connecting people with each other. We also believe that giving community members space and opportunities to share their gifts is fundamental to strengthening our community. When you prepare and share food with our community, you have an opportunity to express pride in your culture and your origins. Almost every week for 30 years, Wayside volunteer Marion starts her Thursday by coming to the kitchen at Wayside and sharing her time and baking skills with our community by preparing delicious desserts for our Community Meals program. This recipe is a favorite of staff who can all be found congregating in the kitchen when the timer goes off; fellow volunteers who started as strangers and are now friends who enjoy a coffee break together every week, and community members who share food at our meals. We hope you enjoy it with some good company."

2 cups flour
1¼ cups sugar
1 teaspoon baking soda
1 teaspoon salt
1 teaspoon cinnamon
¼ teaspoon cloves
¼ teaspoon allspice
2 large eggs
½ cup salad oil
⅓ cup milk
2 cups fresh rhubarb (can use frozen in a pinch), unpeeled and cut into small pieces

Topping:
1 tablespoon butter
⅔ cup flour
½ cup light brown sugar
¾ cup coconut (optional)
¼ cup chopped nuts (optional)

Preheat oven to 350 degrees. Sift dry ingredients into a large bowl. Mix eggs and oil together in a separate bowl. Add egg and oil mixture to dry ingredients, and blend in the milk. Fold in the rhubarb. Pour batter into a greased 9x13-inch pan.

Make the topping by blending together the butter, flour, and brown sugar. Add coconut and chopped nuts to the mixture, if using. Sprinkle the topping over the unbaked cake batter. Bake for about 50 minutes, until a toothpick inserted in the center comes out clean.

Brownie's Rhubarb Pudding

Millie Stewart • Brunswick, Cumberland County

"Mildred 'Brownie' Schrumpf of Orono was a renowned cook of northern and eastern Maine who wrote a wonderful food column for the Bangor Daily News for many years, starting in 1951. She was a 1925 graduate of the University of Maine with a degree in home economics, which she put to great use helping families across Maine make the best use of what they had to work with in their ancestral and newly planted gardens. Rhubarb was certainly available on every farm at least. This recipe appeared in her cookbook, *The Flavor of Maine*, published in 1976 as a tribute to the U.S. bicentennial. At my house, this was a well-loved recipe welcoming spring after a long, cold winter. Easy and inexpensive to make!"

3 tablespoons quick cooking tapioca
4 cups sliced rhubarb, about ½-inch thick
1 to 1¼ cups white sugar
½ teaspoon salt
½ cup water
2 tablespoons butter

Preheat oven to 350 degrees. Butter a 1½ quart casserole. Add tapioca and rhubarb. Mix sugar and salt together, and add to the casserole, with the water. Stir briefly to mix. Dot with butter. Bake uncovered for 10 minutes, then cover and continue baking until rhubarb is soft, 20 to 25 minutes. Serve hot or cold. Serves 6.

Rhubarb-Ginger Crostata with Whipped Mascarpone

Peggy Grodinsky • Portland, Cumberland County

"When I bought my house in Portland, Tom Atwell, who has written the gardening column for the Portland Press Herald for many years, brought me a gift for my new garden (at that time mostly lawn) from his well-established one: several rhubarb plants. He knew—perhaps from an article I'd written on the subject—how much I adore rhubarb. My patch is now well-established and keeps me on my toes every May and June as I try to keep up with its many stalks. This free-form pie is easy to make, uses plenty of rhubarb, looks very pretty and tastes wonderful. The recipe originally came from Food & Wine several years back, and while I'm an inveterate recipe tinkerer, it's spot-on just as it is. Do make your own pie crust – the one I use for this uses both butter and lard; good pie crust is essential here. Yes, blueberry pie, who could ever say anything against blueberry pie? But rhubarb pie feels pretty classic Maine to me, too."

1 cup granulated sugar
¼ teaspoon salt
2 tablespoons cornstarch
1½ pounds rhubarb (about 6 cups), sliced into ½-inch pieces, divided
¼ cup chopped candied ginger
Zest of 1 orange
Pastry for generous single crust pie, chilled
Egg wash of 1 egg mixed with 1 tablespoon water or milk
Turbinado sugar, for sprinkling

Whipped Mascarpone:
1 cup mascarpone
3 tablespoons confectioners' sugar
2 tablespoons heavy cream

Whisk together the sugar, salt, and cornstarch in a medium saucepan. Add 2 cups of the rhubarb. Cook, stirring, until the sugar has melted and the rhubarb is beginning to break down, about 8 minutes. Continue to cook until the mixture thickens slightly. Take the sugared rhubarb off the heat, let it cool slightly, then add the remaining raw rhubarb to the mixture. Add the candied ginger and orange zest, as well, and let the fruit cool completely. (You can make the filling ahead.)

Preheat the oven to 425 degrees. Roll out your pie crust on a lightly floured counter. Move the crust to a baking sheet. Spread the cooled filling over the crust, leaving a border of a generous 1 inch. Fold up the borders over the filling, in casual pleats. Brush the crust with the egg wash. Sprinkle the crust with turbinado sugar (it makes for a nice crunch).

Bake 30 to 35 minutes until the crostata is nice and golden brown. (Not too pale! Color equals flavor here.) Serve just slightly warm with ice cream or whipped mascarpone, which has a nice tang that echoes the sour pucker of the rhubarb.

To make the whipped mascarpone: Whip together mascarpone, confectioners' sugar, and heavy cream until light and fluffy, about 1 minute.

Piquant Rhubarb Sauce

Kate Huntress • Yarmouth, Cumberland County

"This unusual recipe is especially delicious with bean burgers or lentil cutlets."

- 1 tablespoon water
- 1 large onion, finely chopped
- 3 cups washed, trimmed rhubarb stalks, cut into 3-inch pieces
- ½ cup turbinado sugar
- 2 tablespoons red wine vinegar
- Salt and pepper, to taste

Heat the water in a saucepan, add the onion, and cook slowly for 10 minutes, making sure the onions don't brown. Add the rhubarb to the cooked onions and stir in the sugar, vinegar, and salt and pepper, to taste. Simmer 20 minutes with the lid on the pan, until the rhubarb is soft. Remove the lid and continue simmering until thick. Sauce keeps in the refrigerator for 3 days.

Rhubarb and Pineapple Marmalade

c. 1910 • The Home Cook Book

Congregational Church of Madison, Women's Association • Madison, Somerset County

A nice blend of the local with the exotic (at least for the time and place), rhubarb and pineapple make a fine marmalade. It's interesting to imagine the journey of the pineapple from the tropics to Maine, and to compare it with that of the rhubarb, which may have been a walk of just a few feet from the kitchen door. —DL

7 lbs. rhubarb; 7 lbs. sugar; 1 large pineapple grated; juice of a lemon. Stir over moderate fire until sugar is dissolved. Simmer 1 hour. Pour into jelly tumblers and seal. — Mrs. George Flint

Rhubarb Squares

Susan Hall • Hampden, Penobscot County

"Since I love rhubarb and like to grow it even more, I cook with it every spring. My neighbor and I watch for the first sign of it sprouting up with a sigh of relief that winter is just about behind us. I have probably made these rhubarb squares over one hundred times over the years. The recipe originally came from the Eddington School Cook Book 1987-88. Surprisingly, it was submitted by my father-in-law's wife. They are always requested at family gatherings, loved at the snowmobile club bean suppers, and at church gatherings, not to mention the first dessert when the rhubarb is ready! I sometimes cut the squares larger as a 'fork' dessert with ice cream or whipped cream, or cut smaller sized squares for a 'finger food' dessert. Note: I make the rhubarb mixture well ahead so it can cool."

- 3 cups diced rhubarb
- 1½ cups sugar
- 1 teaspoon vanilla
- 2 tablespoons cornstarch
- ¼ cup cold water
- 1½ cups flour
- 1 cup firmly packed brown sugar
- ½ teaspoon baking soda
- 1 cup butter or margarine, chilled
- ½ cup chopped walnuts

In a large pan, mix together rhubarb, sugar, and vanilla. In a smaller bowl, combine cornstarch and cold water, stir, and add to the rhubarb mixture. Cook over medium-low heat until rhubarb is tender, stirring constantly while mixture thickens. Set aside to cool.

In a medium-size bowl, mix together flour, brown sugar, and baking soda. Cut in cold butter or margarine, and add nuts. Pat ¾ of the mixture into a greased 9x13-inch pan. Spread rhubarb mixture over the base, and sprinkle remaining ¼ of the crumbs over the top. Bake at 350 degrees for 40 minutes. Serve warm or cold.

Roque Bluffs Sour Cream Rhubarb Squares

David Lewis • Buxton, York County

"My parents bought our summer house in Roque Bluffs in the late 1960s, and inherited a lovely rhubarb patch with it. Our soon-to-become-dear-lifelong-friends next door also had a lovely rhubarb patch. Every year, whichever family arrived at Roque Bluffs first for the season would welcome the other with a fresh pan of these rhubarb squares and a welcome-home note. This tradition continues today, among the children and grandchildren of these families that have been so close for so many decades—over 54 years."

Gram Soule's Rhubarb Squares

DACF Commissioner Amanda Beal • Warren, Knox County

"My grandfather was an epic rhubarb grower, tending to his plants growing in the salty air on the shore of Casco Bay in Freeport. His plants would grow so large that figuring out what to do with all of that rhubarb was an annual challenge. My grandmother would make batches of these rhubarb squares throughout the spring and summer, which we all loved, and therefore earned rhubarb its place as a favorite plant in my garden today."

Squares:
1 cup packed brown sugar
½ cup butter, softened to room temperature
1 egg
2 cups flour
1 teaspoon baking soda
½ teaspoon salt
1 cup sour cream
1½ cups rhubarb, cut into ½-inch pieces

Topping:
½ cup sugar
½ cup chopped walnuts or pecans
1 tablespoon melted butter
1 teaspoon cinnamon

In the bowl of a stand mixer, cream together brown sugar, butter, and egg. Sift together flour, baking soda, and salt in a separate bowl. Add flour mixture to butter mixture alternately with sour cream; beat together thoroughly. Mix in the rhubarb pieces with a spoon, and scoop batter into a buttered 9x13-inch baking pan.

Combine the topping ingredients in a separate bowl and then spread evenly across top of batter. Bake at 350 degrees for 45-50 minutes. Cut into squares and serve warm or cold.

Stewed Rhubarb

Jane Legard • Bath, Sagadahoc County

"One of my memories from childhood is having stewed rhubarb and rhubarb pie. My family had huge gardens and we had our own rhubarb patch. We recently sold our home on Water Cove where we had lived for over 25 years and moved to Bath, where we have a lovely 'cottage' looking out at the Kennebec River. I still have sources for rhubarb and continue trying new recipes and enjoying the ones I've made for years—I even freeze some for use throughout the year. One of our family Christmas traditions is to have a Yankee Swap. One year I baked a rhubarb pie for my gift to swap. It was difficult to keep track of who had the pie as everyone wanted it! Stewed rhubarb is good as a breakfast fruit or as a dessert. This is an easy recipe to make especially if you are doing other things in the kitchen and can work this into your morning. It's nice to put a sauce dish of rhubarb at each place for dinner in place of a salad. Or you might try it over a little ice cream for dessert. This is a basic, old fashioned recipe!"

1 quart cut-up rhubarb
¼ teaspoon salt
Scant cup sugar

Cut off leaf and root ends of rhubarb. Wash the rhubarb and cut into 1-inch pieces, without peeling. Measure 1 quart, and place pieces in top of double boiler. Add salt and pour sugar over top of rhubarb. Cover and place over boiling water. Cook over low heat for 1 hour, stir when half done to mix the fruit with the sugar. Remove from heat; when cool, place in refrigerator. Serves 6.

Edith and Margaret's Rhubarb-Raisin Pie

Linda Alperin • Topsham, Sagadahoc County

"This recipe was original by way of my maternal grandmother, Edith (Stanton) Gray. My mother's sister, Margaret (Gray) Legate, baked this pie every June, using rhubarb grown in her Shelburne, Massachusetts garden. Margaret had a friend, Lenita Butler, who lived in Blue Hill whom she visited every summer. This pie traveled to Maine via Margaret to be enjoyed during these annual visits. I carry on the tradition of baking this family favorite pie. Being prepared with raisins rather than the traditional strawberry-rhubarb combination makes it unique—and equally tasty!"

Pastry for double crust pie
1 cup white granulated sugar
¼ cup brown sugar, packed
3 heaping tablespoons flour
A good pinch salt
4 cups fresh, raw rhubarb; sliced but not peeled
½ cup raisins
Several pats butter

Preheat oven to 425 degrees. Roll out both pie crusts; place one crust in pie plate.

Mix white and brown sugars, flour, and salt together in a bowl. Sprinkle ⅓ of this mixture over the bottom of the pie crust. Continue as follows: Sprinkle in ½ of the rhubarb and raisins, followed by another ⅓ of the sugar mixture. Sprinkle in the other ½ of the raisins and rhubarb and then top with the remaining ⅓ of the sugar mixture. Dot with several pats of butter. Cover filling with the remaining pie crust, vent the crust with slits and seal edges.

Bake for 15 minutes at 425 degrees. Turn down heat to 350 degrees and bake for another 30 minutes, longer if necessary for a bubbly filling. Allow pie to cool before serving. Store, covered, in the fridge. It's best to prepare the pie a day ahead of serving to allow filling to become firm. Serve pie warmed in microwave or at room temperature—this pie tastes fine even when served cold from the fridge!

CLASS OF
2023
N
WARRIORS
N

APPETIZERS, SAUCES, & DIPS

Photo: Students from the Cooking Club at Nokomis Regional High School in Newport prepare their Warrior Bruschetta, near the school garden in which they grow and harvest many of their ingredients. Their recipes for the bruschetta and Cooking Club Salsa can be found on pages 64 and 65.

Nuts & Bolts (Homemade Chex Mix)

Sydnia (Welch) Czarnecki • Gouldsboro, Hancock County

"My maternal grandmother, Grace Vague, lived in Bangor on the corner of the Pushaw Road and the Church Road. She and her daughters—my mother, Glennice Welch, and my aunt, Elsie Betters—always made this treat at Christmas time. I have carried this on with my own children. I usually start at about Thanksgiving and end up making five or six batches by the time Christmas rolls around! When my daughter was vegetarian, I would make a couple of batches substituting butter or margarine for the bacon fat, but I'd add a dash of Liquid Smoke. This is delicious with eggnog!"

- 1 box each Wheat Chex, Corn Chex, Rice Chex, and plain Cheerios
- 1 bag of thin pretzels sticks or shapes (use fun pretzel shapes if you can find them!)
- 1 pound mixed nuts
- ¾ cup bacon fat
- ¾ cup butter or margarine
- 1 teaspoon celery salt
- 1 teaspoon garlic salt
- 1 tablespoon Worcestershire sauce
- 1 tablespoon Tabasco sauce

Mix together the cereals, pretzels, and nuts in 2 large roasting pans.

In a small saucepan, melt together the bacon fat and butter or margarine. Add the spices and sauces to pan and mix together.

Pour the bacon fat and butter mixture over the dry ingredients, stirring as you go to make sure all the dry ingredients get covered. Bake at 200 degrees for 2 hours, stirring every ½ hour.

Kelp & Crab Dip

Susan Lewis Baines • Spruce Head, Knox County

"When you're married for 41 years to a commercial fisherman, you learn how to cook with good, fresh seafood of all kinds. Lobster is Bob's main fishery in the summer and fall, scallops in the winter, and now we've diversified further and have become kelp farmers. We seed in November, it grows through the winter, then the kelp is harvested in May. We are learning about this amazingly healthy and delicious sea vegetable and I am having a great time coming up with recipes, dishes, and creative ways to incorporate kelp in our diets."

- 8-ounce tub fresh Maine crabmeat, picked through
- ¼ cup mayonnaise or full-fat sour cream
- ¼ cup Atlantic Sea Farms Ready Cut Kelp
- 1 teaspoon Old Bay Seasoning, plus more for serving
- Juice and finely grated rind of 1 lemon
- ½ shallot, finely minced
- Salt and white pepper, to taste
- Finely minced red bell pepper, for serving
- Finely chopped chives, for serving

In a large bowl, mix together crabmeat, mayo, kelp, and Old Bay Seasoning. Fold in grated lemon rind, and add half the lemon juice. (Reserve remaining lemon juice for serving.) Fold in minced shallot, and add salt and white pepper, to taste. Chill for at least 1 hour.

To serve, prepare your serving dish or crock with a rim of Old Bay. Place reserved lemon juice on a shallow plate, and sprinkle Old Bay Seasoning on a separate plate. Invert your serving dish onto the lemon juice to wet the rim, then invert the dish again onto the plate of Old Bay. The seasoning should adhere to the rim.

Carefully spoon crab dip into prepared dish or crock, then sprinkle top with minced red bell pepper and finely chopped chives. Serve with crackers and chilled, cooked shrimp.

Cooking Club Salsa

Nokomis Regional High School Cooking Club • Newport, Penobscot County

"Every Thursday a diverse and passionate crew of students at Nokomis Regional High School come together to cook. We cook everything from pumpkin pies to bruschetta, which tastes great on a baguette. The meals we cook are greatly enjoyed not only by the cooking club members, but by parents and lucky teachers that happen to be nearby. We incorporate the vegetables and herbs from our garden into everything we prepare. The new Nokomis Garden has been up and running for only a year, but Nokomis students and staff have made it possible. Many students built the boxes and greenhouses where the vegetables grow and help to take care of the plants we use and enjoy. In our weekly cooking club, we learn and use skills such as different ways to cut and prepare, cook, and roast vegetables, and learn how to work as a team with fellow club members. Any extra food is sent home with those who have done the work so that they can share the bounty with their families." —Mackenzie Jones and Roland Kitchen, Class of 2023

4 ripe tomatoes, diced
1 lime, juiced
A handful of finely chopped cilantro
1 Poblano or pepper of choice, diced
(we grew 7 varieties of hot peppers!)
1 red or sweet onion, diced
A pinch of salt

Mix together and enjoy!!

Warrior Bruschetta

Nokomis Regional High School Cooking Club • Newport, Penobscot County

"It was a bright and sunny Thursday afternoon when we took our ingredients and supplies and headed to the picnic table. We had no cutting boards and dull knives, but we made do with what we had. We used pieces of wood leftover from making raised beds for our cutting boards and passed around the one sharp knife to cut. We had people slicing our beautiful Striped Roman Tomatoes and our fresh basil, and we had onions and garlic from a local farm that were being chopped as well. We mixed it all up with olive oil and balsamic vinegar and a pinch of salt, and now all we had left was to slice up our baguettes and enjoy some beautifully fresh bruschetta." —Jacob Redwine, Class of 2025

6 ripe tomatoes, chopped
1 garlic clove, minced
½ red onion, chopped
Fresh basil, chopped roughly
Balsamic vinegar reduction
(purchased or reduced at home)
Extra virgin olive oil
Sliced baguette, for serving

Toss tomatoes, garlic, onions, and basil in a bowl. Add a pinch of salt and pepper and a generous swirl of both the olive oil and the balsamic vinegar reduction. Stir once or twice and spoon onto slices of baguette.

Members of the Nokomis Regional High School Cooking Club

Emma Brown, Aleigha Bryant, Allison Carroll, Kolby Collins, Eliyahna Coover, Harley Fuller, Alexis Greeley, Brice Hewins, Amarah Howell, Bailey Jones, Mackenzie Jones, Brieonna Kidwell, Keira King, Roland Kitchen, Hayden Ludden, Erickson Mills, Cassie Nicholson, Anthony Piantodosi, Sara Pomeroy, Jacob Redwine, Makayla Salley, Cloey Sharon, Kylee Sprague, Cody Stevens
Staff: Jenine Olson, Anne Dailey

Cheese Ball

Craig Littlefield • Pittsfield, Somerset County

"When my mother, Norma Foss Littlefield, was alive, my cousins would all call her to ask for cooking advice. During her working years, she generally did something involving food: working in the kitchen at Unity College, running concessions at Eaton Mountain in Skowhegan, and working the concessions in the pit at Unity Raceway. She would bring her cheese ball to our family parties, and it was always a favorite!"

- 8-ounce package of cream cheese, softened
- 1 cup cheddar cheese, shredded
- ½ cup blue cheese, crumbled
- 2 teaspoons Worcestershire sauce
- ¼ cup onion, minced
- Crushed walnuts or pecans, for rolling

Blend cheeses, Worcestershire sauce and onion together in a mixer until fluffy. Form into one or two balls, whichever size you prefer, and roll in crushed walnuts or pecans. Chill. Serve with crackers.

Betty Carr's Famous Cranberry Relish

Karen Bustillo • Orono, Penobscot County

"We used to make my mother's cranberry relish recipe when we were very, very small, with a hand crank meat grinder that we would attach like a vice to the dining room table. The extra juice would drip down the parts of the grinder into a pan on the floor and made a wonderful juice treat at the end!"

- 12-ounce bag cranberries
- 1 cup sugar
- 1 navel orange, unpeeled
- 1 apple, peeled and cored

Grind all ingredients together in a food processor. Refrigerate overnight.

Boursin at Home

Carol Tanner • Falmouth, Cumberland County

"I've enjoyed growing garlic and herbs for many years and combined them to make this concoction for family gatherings. It is welcomed by garlic lovers any time of year and makes enough to serve a crowd."

2 large cloves garlic
Two 8-ounce packages cream cheese, at room temperature
½ cup (1 stick) butter, softened
¼-½ teaspoon freshly ground black pepper
½ teaspoon each salt, thyme, basil, oregano, dill, marjoram

Drop garlic into a food blender to chop. Set aside. With a mixer, blend and whip the cream cheese and butter until soft and creamy. Add the finely chopped garlic, black pepper, and herbs to the whipped cream cheese and butter mixture. Mix until thoroughly incorporated. Refrigerate overnight. Serve with crusty French bread or crispy crackers.

Zucchini Appetizer

Jack McAdam • Springvale, York County

"My wife, Ellen, and I are the seventh generation to run McDougal Orchards, in Springvale, with the eighth generation, Matthew and Polly, working to push us into retirement. My mother-in-law, Pat, made this appetizer on a number of occasions. I'm not sure where she got it. Recently our daughter asked my wife to make it. Great way to use up some of your zucchini."

- 4 eggs
- 3 cups grated zucchini
- ½ cup oil
- ½ cup chopped onions
- 2 tablespoons chopped parsley
- 1 clove garlic, minced
- ½ cup Parmesan cheese
- ½ teaspoon salt
- 1 cup Bisquick or 1 cup flour mixed with 2 teaspoons baking powder
- ½ teaspoon dried oregano (optional)

Mix together all ingredients in a large bowl, and pour into a greased 9x13-inch pan. Bake at 350 degrees for 25-35 minutes. Cut into squares and serve warm.

Raw Onion Sandwich

c. 1940 • Cook Book

Portland Society of Arts & Crafts • Portland, Cumberland County

The Portland Society of Arts & Crafts had been established in 1890, and was operating a shop on Congress Street next to the Public Library when this little cookbook was published around 1940. We don't know who contributed the recipes, but the selection is a bit eccentric, as with this little sandwich which is either simple or avant-garde. —DL

One small onion, one hard boiled egg, one small bottle stuffed olives, one snappy cheese. Chop together and spread.

Native Maine, Local You Trust

The folks here at Native Maine are proud that we were able to continue supporting our customers through the challenges that 2020 and 2021 brought. Here are a few of our most proud moments...

- In three short months, Native Maine packed and delivered 125,127 USDA Farmers to Families Food Boxes throughout ALL 16 Counties with the help of more than 170 food pantries, schools, and churches throughout the State.
- We serviced more than 700 independent restaurants.
- We delivered to more than 500 schools across Maine & New Hampshire.
- Sourced local products from over 80 farms and businesses.
- We sponsored an educational orchard in a local school through the non-profit ReTreeUS
- Donated more than 4,000 cases of fresh fruits and vegetables over the peak of Covid
- We were proud to have serviced and helped keep our community safe by delivering more than 2,000 home deliveries throughout Southern Maine.

Briggs Farm Beef
(Somerville)

MAINE HARVEST
FEDERAL CREDIT UNION

Nomad Pasta
(Belfast)
and Briggs Sausage

Financing for farms and food producers with deposits from those sharing our mission

www.MaineHarvestFCU.coop

- For lending inquiries, please contact Lending@maineharvestfcu.coop
- For deposit inquires, please contact Info@maineharvestfcu.coop

NCUA

A Dinner on Malaga Island: A *Re.Past*

By Myron Beasley

Entertaining the Missionary—Sunday on Malaga Island

On July 12, 2018, I curated *Re.Past Malaga* a public memorial in the form of a dinner to remember the legacy and families of Malaga. The story of Malaga Island is a forgotten chapter in Maine's history. The 41-acre island located at the mouth of the New Meadows River, and just two miles off the coast of Phippsburg, was once inhabited by a fishing community of black, white, and mix-raced people. The yellow journalism of the moment described the community as "degenerates," "peculiar," and the island "disgusting." The discourse surrounding the community reflected the confluence of the racist eugenics movement in the United States, the towns along Maine's coast becoming summer destinations, and economic retribution. Then-governor Frederick Plaisted drafted a declaration to have the more than 45 inhabitants forced off the island by July 1912. The homes were leveled, the one-room schoolhouse was removed, and the graves were exhumed and reburied as a mass grave inland. Many of the children were committed to the Maine School for the Feeble-Minded (now Pineland Farms) in New Gloucester. Today the island sits abandoned. Despite years of petitioning the state of Maine to write a formal apology, not to mention recent attention from published academic research and museum exhibitions, it was not until 2012 that Governor John Baldacci acknowledged the horrific event and issued an official state apology to the descendants of Malaga. In 2017, Governor Paul LePage oversaw the placement of a commemorative marker at the Pineland Farms gravesite.

A repast is a meal to commemorate the loss and celebrate the living and the cycle of life. Within African American cultural tradition, the repast is as important as the church liturgy. It was forbidden by law in the United States to hold funerals for the enslaved. Death became associated with "homecoming," a release from the horrors of slavery. The communal meal, the repast, became an integral and meaningful way to remember the dead and acknowledge life and the living. A performative meal uses food items to draw attention to a particular social and political issue. From archeological and historical records, we know that Malaga was a fishing community with access to provisions from the mainland. The residents relied on the water and sourced fish such as herring and groundfish; they also gardened and grew vegetables, including corn, potatoes, beans, and berries. In a repast, the food is served to comfort and invoke the memory of those lost and to nourish the soul of the living.

Included in the menu was Salmon & Salt Cod Chowder chowder. Chowder is a dish associated with New England. The word is Cornish from *jowter* as in a peddler of fish. According to food scholar, Scott Barton, chowder is like a gumbo having influences from Native American (first nations corn soup), French, English, and even African cookery.

It's also believed French soldiers who had been shipwrecked around the Maine coast were short of supplies and used all they had salvaged from the ship to survive. Into the boiling chaudière, (a cast-iron pot with a strong handle) that was either hung over a fire or set into hot coals they added clams they had gathered and cooked them with pork, crackers and potatoes.

In 2018, forty-seven guests, representing the forty-seven evicted residents, engaged in the Re.Past, a performative dinner honoring the people of Malaga. It not only remembers them, but just as importantly respects and celebrates them. It also serves as an admonition to us that the past is never dead. It's not even the past.

Myron Beasley, Ph.D. is Associate Professor of American Studies at Bates College, where he also serves on the committee of Gender and Sexuality Studies. His ethnographic research includes exploring the intersection of cultural politics, material culture, and social change.

THE MENU

The menu served at *Re.Past Malaga* was drawn from local cookbooks and historical and archeological artifacts.

Dry Hopped Cider

Nezinscot Farm Sun Tea

Salmon & Salt Cod Chowder

Chow Chow

Marfax Beans with Salt Pork Belly

Summer Berry Pudding

Abenaki Corn Molasses Bread

The recipe for Malaga Island Salmon & Salt Cod Chowder can be found on page 84.

Fish ChowDER FAYE
CROCK-POT

CHOWDERS, SOUPS, STEWS, & BEANS

Photo: Faye McNall, aka "Fish Chowder Faye," stands at the ready during the chowder contest at (formerly) Sample's Shipyard in Boothbay Harbor in 2012. Her grandmother's recipe for Eastport Fish Chowder can be found on the next page.

Eastport Fish Chowder

Faye McNall • Boothbay, Lincoln County

"My Nana, Amy, was born in Eastport in 1898, one of five girls and two boys in a family that struggled to put food on the table. She learned how to cook by watching her mother making meals on a wood stove. She kept a handwritten notebook of recipes she had learned to make and was rightfully proud of her cooking ability. She could do everything from pies and cakes to bread and rolls on a wood stove. When I was seven years old she showed me how to make a fish chowder, just as she had learned as a child. I recall standing on a stool so that I could see into the pot as she explained how the fish broth with potatoes and onions simmering in it should look pearly and opaque as the starch cooks into the briny broth. Thickening a chowder with flour or cornstarch was a cardinal sin! A supper of hot chowder, little puddles of butter and oyster crackers on top, is worthy of serving to company. Here in Boothbay, I've earned the nickname 'Fish Chowder Faye' because I serve this to so many of my guests."

- 1 pound haddock
- 2½ cups water
- ½ cup peeled and diced red potatoes
- ¾ cup chopped onion
- 1½ cups light cream
- ½ stick (4 tablespoons) butter
- Salt, pepper, and Old Bay Seasoning, to taste

Note: Aleppo pepper can be substituted for black pepper, if you wish.

Place fish fillet and water in heavy soup pot so that the water just covers the fish. Leave pot uncovered and bring to a boil. Turn heat down and simmer fish for 10 minutes. Using a slotted spoon, remove fish from broth, and set aside.

Place potatoes and onions in fish broth and return to a boil for 15 minutes. Potatoes should be very tender and broth should be pearly and opaque. Remove from heat, return fish to the pot, and add light cream and butter. Season to taste with salt, pepper, and Old Bay Seasoning. Warm gently without boiling.

Turn heat off and cool chowder to room temperature. Chill overnight in the refrigerator before reheating to serve.

715 Hammond St. Potluck Vegetarian Chili

Jamie Gordon • Bradley, Penobscot County

"I work in a Bangor dental office that has a break area with access to a kitchen. Multiple times a year, usually during the fall and winter months, someone in our work family will say 'we need to do a chili.' Knowing what that means, we choose a date, which normally is a day in the middle of the week, as there are always leftovers. Everyone signs up to bring whatever ingredients are on hand in their pantry or refrigerator. This all goes into a slow cooker first thing in the morning and by lunchtime we have a hot, healthy meal. Our chili is a bit different every time, but it always tastes good to us. This tradition started when our former employer and friend, Dr. Al (Alison Poulin) was with us. Dr. Al passed in July 2020 and we think of her often, but especially on our chili days!"

Onions
Green peppers
Garlic
Carrots
Celery
Corn
Zucchini and summer squash
Two 28-ounce cans diced tomatoes
2 cups vegetable V-8 juice
Three or four 15-ounce cans various beans, combination of your choice
Chili powder
Oregano
Salt and pepper
Spinach
Cooked, diced sweet potato

For serving:
Shredded cheese of choice
Sour cream
Avocado slices
Black olives
"Heat" sauce or spice

In a crockpot, combine whatever amounts of chopped, raw, crunchy vegetables are desired with canned tomatoes and V-8 juice. Cook on high for at least 3-4 hours, then add the canned beans and spices. An hour later, add the fresh spinach and cooked sweet potato, still cooking on high. The actual cooking part of this recipe usually takes at least 5 hours on high to get the vegetables thoroughly cooked. Serve with shredded cheese, sour cream, avocado, black olives, and hot sauce or seasoning.

Trout Chowder

Ayana Green • Caribou, Aroostook County / Mi'kmaq Homeland

"The Mi'kmaq Fish Hatchery began in 2015, with many thanks to the US Fish and Wildlife Service and Maine Community Foundation's support. It began as a conservation project to alleviate pressures on wild brook trout populations from multiple stressors including land use impacts from pollution but also drought and warming waters from climate change. The project also served to reconnect Wabanaki people with their culture and a food source that they have been connected to since time immemorial. Eastern Brook Trout were once a staple to native people, but because of mercury fish consumption rates (that apply to every river in the state of Maine) this brain-healthy staple is no longer able to provide sustenance as a wild caught fish. And so the Mi'kmaq Nation (previously the Aroostook Band of Micmacs) began raising brook trout utilizing clean groundwater in their environmentally sustainable Recirculating Aquaculture System (RAS). The hatchery is co-located with their farm, Micmac Farms, and together the farm and hatchery share a vision of providing healthy food to the local community and food pantries. The vision is for food sovereignty, food access, and environmental sustainability in food production for the local community and the tribal members. The hatchery can hold up to 20,000 pounds of fish, and all trout are raised without harsh chemicals or antibiotics, something we take a lot of pride in!"

3 pounds sweet onions, diced
1 pound celery, diced
1 pound carrots, diced
1 head garlic, minced
4 tablespoons olive oil
1 pound red potatoes, washed well and diced (skin on)
8 cups vegetable stock
2 bay leaves
1 tablespoon kosher salt
1 tablespoon freshly ground black pepper
⅛ cup dill weed
4 tablespoons butter
½ cup flour
1 cup half-and-half
2 pounds trout, skinned, deboned, chopped into pieces

Place the onions, celery, carrots, and garlic into a large stock pot with the olive oil, toss around to coat the vegetables, and cook on medium heat for about 10 minutes. Add in diced potatoes and cook for an additional 10 minutes. Add enough vegetable stock to cover vegetables. Stir in bay leaves, salt, pepper, and dill weed. Cover and turn heat down to a simmer. Cook until potatoes and carrots are tender, about 1 hour.

In a separate pot, melt butter on medium heat. Add flour and mix well. The consistency should be like a paste. Cook, stirring, until you get a nice golden color, about 5 minutes. Vigorously whisk in half-and-half, and quickly add the mixture to the large stock pot. Add in the raw trout and let cook for 10 minutes. Remove from heat and serve immediately, preferably alongside homemade biscuits.

Beans Tricky

Patricia Cote • Greenville, Piscataquis County

"These beans were the result of unexpected drop-in guests, and not much in the house to serve. So this dish was all ad lib! Nobody expected it to be so good, but it was a big hit. Hence the family addition of the word 'tricky.'"

1 tablespoon vegetable oil
1 large onion, diced
1 medium green pepper, diced
1½ pounds 90% hamburg (also works well with venison or moose meat)
2 quarts cooked beans
14-ounce can stewed tomatoes
½ cup sliced green olives
¼ cup Frank's hot sauce (optional)
Parmesan cheese, for serving

In a large, heavy-bottomed pot, set over medium-high heat, heat vegetable oil and sauté onion and pepper until crisp tender. Add the meat, and cook, stirring, until crumbly with a few small to medium-size pieces. Reduce heat to low, and add all remaining ingredients. Cook it slowly and serve hot, topped with Parmesan cheese and sourdough bread and coleslaw.

Tri-County Tomato Soup

Roberta Bailey • Vassalboro, Kennebec County

Sponsored by Maine Organic Farmers and Gardeners Association

"In the early years of MOFGA, there were many active local chapters around the state. The Tri-County chapter consisted of farmers and gardeners from Penobscot, southern Aroostook, and Washington counties. We gathered monthly for meetings. Few of us had telephones. To set a meeting, we would send out postcards which would arrive the next day, then the recipients would respond by postcard, another day's time, and a meeting date could be set 'quickly.' In the summer, we had work parties, clearing pasture or

shingling a new out building, building a grape arbor, making lighter work of the big projects. In winter, we had guest speakers who taught us to graft trees, or save seed, we watched movies sent from the Maine State Library, and compiled co-operative seed orders, pre-order food co-op orders, and soil amendment orders. There was always a potluck meal, time for a general catch up on farm life and local news and the weather. We were neighbors, like-minded friends often 40 miles apart, a long-distance community of support. We shared music, work, stories, food and recipes. We shared this recipe, and each of us adjusted it to our own taste preferences, less celery, more basil or garlic, etc. You can as well. It is a great recipe for using up surplus tomatoes. It is great to have the immediate option of a warming bowl of soup waiting for you on your pantry shelf. You can taste the summer sunshine."

50 medium tomatoes
2 to 3 green peppers
3 large onions
4 to 8 cloves garlic
10 to 15 leaves sweet basil
5 stalks celery
5 to 10 sprigs parsley
6 tablespoons organic cornstarch
6 tablespoons hot water
3 tablespoons salt
¼ to ½ cup honey
3 tablespoons vinegar or lemon juice

Cook tomatoes, skin and purée them, or put them through a Victorio strainer. Add the vegetables and herbs and cook until soft. Purée all.

In a bowl, mix together the cornstarch, hot water, salt, and honey. Add to the puréed soup. Stir in the vinegar or lemon juice and adjust seasonings to taste. Freeze the soup, or can it.

Martha's Tomato Bisque

Kris Lape • Portland, Cumberland County

"My sister Martha was the creative mind behind Vaughan Street, the popular and joyful food center in the West End for over twenty-five years. Soups, sandwiches, chilis, muffins, salad and so much more were her creations. Though she died in 2018, her gifts live on through her food, and her recipes are still cooked and loved. This is a beloved recipe that my sister made for numerous family events. It was the comfort after a loss, the warmth after the cold, and the deliciousness to move us forward."

- 1 large onion
- 1 teaspoon butter
- 28-ounce can diced tomatoes
- 3 cups chicken broth
- 3 ounces hot salsa
- 1 pound cream cheese
- 2 cups cream
- ½ teaspoon lemon juice
- 1 teaspoon Tabasco
- Chopped cilantro, for garnish

In a stock pot, sauté chopped onion in butter. When soft, add the tomatoes, chicken broth, and salsa. When hot, remove a cup of the liquid and blend it with the softened cream cheese until fairly smooth. Add back to the pot with the cream, lemon juice, and Tabasco. Top with chopped cilantro, if desired.

Oma's Goulash

Jennifer Kreckel • Rumford, Oxford County

"Goulash was a mainstay in my husband's family growing up, and it became one in ours as well. My husband's childhood friend Jack used to say if there was goulash for dinner at the Kreckels', it was Thursday. This recipe was one of the first things I learned to cook from my mother-in-law, who was a fabulous cook. She always served it with cucumber salad. It is a nice hearty meal for the fall and winter. Now, my granddaughter, Avery, makes sure that I make it whenever she comes to visit."

- 3 tablespoons bacon fat
- 2 pounds beef stew meat, cut into 1-inch cubes
- 1 onion, diced
- 1 small can petite diced peeled tomatoes
- 1 tablespoon spicy brown mustard
- 1 teaspoon dried thyme
- 6 cups beef bone broth
- 1 tablespoon salt (or to taste)
- 1 teaspoon black pepper (or more, if you like it spicier)
- ½ cup sliced mushrooms
- 1 cup instant flour (I use Wondra), to thicken

In a large stew pot, heat bacon fat over high heat until sizzling. Add stew meat and cook, stirring often, until the beef is well browned. Add diced onions, stirring constantly until translucent and glassy. Continue cooking at high heat and add the diced tomatoes. Pour in ⅓ can of water to deglaze the pan, scraping up the browned bits at the bottom. Continue cooking over high heat, stirring occasionally, until the mixture boils down, 3-5 minutes.

Once the mixture has cooked down, stir in another can of water and scrape up any more browned bits. Stir in the mustard and thyme. Boil down again, stirring occasionally, another 3-5 minutes. Add one more can of water to deglaze the pan, and boil the mixture down one final time. It should be thick, like a rich gravy.

Add the bone broth to the beef mixture, and stir well to thoroughly incorporate. Add salt, pepper, and mushrooms. Bring to a boil over high heat, then turn down to low and simmer, covered, for 4 -5 hours, or until meat is tender. Sample the gravy and adjust seasonings to taste.

Combine instant flour with 1 cup of water, and mix until smooth. Pour mixture into the pot, stirring vigorously to avoid lumps. Add more instant flour if it is not thick enough for your liking. Serve goulash with rotini noodles, bread dumplings, or spaetzle.

Maine Fish Chowder

Nancy Harmon Jenkins • Rockland, Knox County

"My mother, a 13th-generation Downeast Yankee cook at ease in her kitchen in Camden, always started her chowder by 'trying out,' as she put it, diced salt pork. That old English term means to render. You try out pork fat, just as you do whale blubber, to separate the liquid part from the solid. When the bits of pork were crisp and the fat was runny in the bottom of the heavy chowder kettle, she strained out the pork bits and set them aside, then added chopped onions to the fat. 'Not too hot, now,' she said, because you don't want the onions to brown but rather to melt. Once the onions were soft, she stirred diced potatoes into the oniony fat, added water just to cover, and cooked the potatoes until they were soft. Finally the fish, a meaty slab of haddock cut into chunks, was set on top of the potatoes. Just when the fish changed color, going from translucent to opaque white, she added milk — rich whole milk enhanced with extra cream, a little salt, and a lot of pepper. Once the milk began to simmer, she covered the kettle and put the whole thing to set — not sit, but set — on the back of the stove, invariably mentioning that 'down home' (meaning back in Thomaston, where she came from a line of sea captains) they let the chowder set on the warming shelf of the cookstove for an entire day before it was considered sufficiently mature to be consumed. And then just before it was served, she stirred in the crisp pork bits she had tried out so many hours before, together with a good big lump of butter.

There were and are variations. Sometimes she threw in a couple of bay leaves with the onions, and once in a while she sprinkled paprika over the top — just for color, since the paprika she used had no discernible taste. I have started chowder with diced slab bacon when good salt pork wasn't available and liked the slight smokiness it lends the dish. I have also, following the footsteps of Boston's master seafood chef Jasper White, used finnan haddie instead of haddock, which gives a decidedly smoky flavor — delicious if you like that sort of thing. But the basic preparation remains the same and it makes an excellent dish, one hearty enough to serve as a main course, which chowder almost always was, along with a couple of sour cucumber pickles for contrast."

Harvest Time Borscht

LouAnna Perkins • Penobscot, Hancock County

Sponsored by Maine Farmland Trust

"I have adapted this recipe from one in my mother's box of family favorites. The partially grated, partially julienned veggies are a traditional touch, but the 'throw in whatever the garden offers' reflects my own style, developed once I became a gardener. It was in Alaska that I first tried using moose meat (terrific!). After that, I began experimenting with whatever meats came along. (It's great to have a family of game harvesters!) Never the same twice, this borscht begs to be tinkered with—herbs, seasonings, bone broth, wild mushrooms...whatever. It's also good as a pot pie with biscuit topping."

- Approximately 1 pound meat, cut into small cubes (any kind of meat will work, venison is terrific, but then, so is beef, pork, chicken, rabbit...)
- 2 teaspoons salt, divided
- 2 medium carrots
- 2 medium beets
- 2 medium potatoes
- 2 each turnips, parsnips, onions, whatever else is in the garden that wants to come in!
- 2 celery ribs
- Quarter of a medium cabbage
- 1 tablespoon olive oil
- 2-3 garlic cloves, pressed
- 8-10 paste tomatoes, diced, or 4 tablespoons tomato paste
- 1 bay leaf or 3 sage leaves
- 2 cups (more or less) chopped beet greens
- ¼ cup chopped parsley
- Sour cream and sourdough bread, for serving

In a large pot, combine the meat, 1 teaspoon of salt and 10 cups of cold water. Bring it to a boil over medium-high heat, skimming off the scum for clearer stock. Then reduce heat to medium and simmer until tender, 45 minutes to 2 hours, depending on the meat.

Grate 1 carrot and 1 beet on a large grater, and julienne the others. (I like the different treatments of beets for texture and color.) Cube or julienne the potatoes and other veggies, and cut celery into small pieces. Thinly slice the cabbage.

When the meat is almost tender, add potatoes and bay leaf or sage. Meanwhile, heat the olive oil in a large skillet over medium-low heat. Add grated carrots along with pressed garlic. Sauté the carrots until nice and fragrant. Add beets and cook for 2 minutes, stirring. Then stir in the tomatoes or paste and cook for another 8 minutes, stirring frequently.

Add sliced cabbage, beet greens and celery into the stock and cook for 5 minutes. Stir in the sautéed vegetables and cook until heated through, about another 5 minutes. Add salt if needed, add pepper or pinch cayenne, if desired.

Stir in parsley and serve immediately with sour cream and sourdough bread, OR, let cool and keep refrigerated till time to serve, then reheat, stir in parsley, and serve with sour cream and sourdough.

Clambake Chowder

Daria Walton • Chelsea, Kennebec County

"My family used to have clam bakes every summer, and the next day I'd make a batch of chowder using the leftovers. It's best with seafood cooked the traditional way, in wood with seaweed, but it's also great when everything has been cooked indoors on the stove. This can be adjusted to accommodate whatever leftovers you have —if there are more, add more milk. If your potatoes are cooked, use less clam juice. Chowder is versatile and you can make it about what you like best!"

- ¼ cup butter
- ½ cup chopped onion
- 1 cup chopped potatoes
- 2 cups clam juice
- Salt and pepper, to taste
- 1 cup picked lobster meat
- 1 cup clams and/or mussels, shucked
- 1 cup sweet corn, removed from cobs
- 2 cups milk or half-and-half (fat-free half-and-half
- ¼ cup sherry
- Oyster crackers, for serving

In a large, heavy-bottomed pot, set over medium heat, melt butter and sauté onion until translucent. Add potatoes and clam juice. Season with pepper and a little salt (be careful—clam juice is salty!). Simmer until potatoes are tender. Add in lobster meat, clams and/or mussels, and corn, and stir for a moment until heated through. Stir in milk and sherry. Adjust seasonings and add pepper and a bit of salt, to taste. Serve with oyster crackers.

Malaga Island Salmon & Salt Cod Chowder

Myron Beasley • Lewiston, Androscoggin County

This chowder was served at *Re.Past Malaga* in 2018, a public memorial in the form of a dinner to remember the legacy and families of Malaga Island. You can read about the tragic history of Malaga, and the dinner, in the essay "A Dinner on Malaga Island: A Re.Past", which can be found on pages 70-71. —MH

- 6 tablespoons unsalted butter
- 2 large yellow onions, chopped
- 3 stalks celery, chopped
- 1 box salt cod, soaked overnight in tap water (no need to refrigerate)
- 6 cups fish stock
- 2 pounds small new potatoes, unpeeled and chopped into bite-size pieces
- Three 5-ounce cans pink salmon
- 4 cups light cream
- 2 cups heavy cream
- 3 tablespoons chopped dill
- 1 tablespoon chopped chives
- Salt and pepper

Melt the butter in a good-sized soup pot and sauté the onions and celery until translucent, about 8 to 10 minutes. Test the salt cod for salt level. If it seems too salty, drain, add fresh tap water, and slowly bring to a boil. Test again and if it is still too salty, repeat this process using fresh water, repeating until desired level of salt is reached. Then drain, flake the salt cod, and add it to the onions and celery.

Add the stock and potatoes. Cook over medium heat for an hour or until the flavors are melded. Add the salmon and cream and cook for 20 more minutes. Finish with herbs, and add salt and pepper to taste. Serves 6 as an entree or 8 for an appetizer.

Parsnip Stew

Date Unknown • The Sorosis Cook Book

Chelsea Grange no. 216 • Chelsea, Kennebec County

There's nothing like the welcome honesty of a recipe that tells you to start dinner at "half past nine in the morning." Sarah Calden has given us a simple recipe but one which depends upon a long, slow cook. A word of warning: The recipe writer has inverted the order of two of her instructions, which is a common enough mistake in community cookbooks (and traditionally published cookbooks too!). It's a reminder to read twice and cook once. —DL

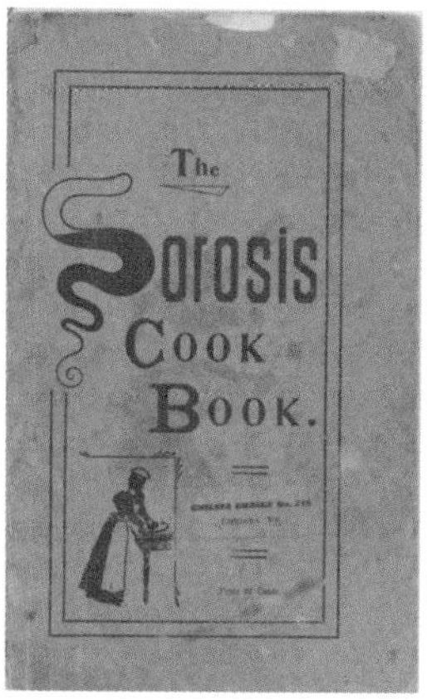

About half past nine in the morning, fry out three or four slices of pork. Then lay on top of the pork layers of parsnips and potatoes. Scrape the parsnips, cut lengthwise two or three times then crosswise. Slice the potatoes, cover with water and boil slowly. Set back on the stove to keep warm. Season with pepper and salt. —Mrs. Sarah L. Calden

Elephant Stew

Edythe (Bray) Gervais • Skowhegan, Somerset County

"My father, Edward Bray, sent this recipe to one of our daughters for her bridal shower."

- 1 elephant
- Salt and pepper
- 2 rabbits (optional)

Cut elephant into bite-size pieces. This should take about two months. Add enough brown gravy to cover. Cook over kerosene fuel for about 4 weeks at 465 degrees. This will serve 3800 people. If more are expected, two rabbits may be added but do this only if necessary as most people do not like to find hare in their stew.

Ukrainian Borsch

Zhenya & Schelene Shevchenko • Gray, Cumberland County

"Borsch is a staple in many households from the former Soviet Union. It seems like each family has their own recipe passed down through the generations. This recipe came from Zhenya's grandmother and her old Soviet cookbook with some modifications through the years. Schelene lived in Ukraine, where we met, and also learned to make borsch from her host exchange family. As we were writing this recipe submission, we were arguing about which way is best. Zhenya would tell you to skip the beef broth and to boil the meat. Schelene would tell you to use some beef broth as a base and lightly fry the meat. If you look on the internet, you'll find hundreds of variations of this recipe! Any way you slice it, this recipe is amazing and you won't regret trying it. PS - Schelene does not like beets, but LOVES borsch."

1 quart beef broth
2 pounds stew beef
Olive oil, or another oil if you prefer
3 medium or 2 large onions, diced
2 or 3 tomatoes, diced
4 to 5 potatoes, peeled and cubed
3 medium or 2 large beets, diced or shredded
3 or 4 carrots, diced or shredded
Half to full head cabbage (or package of shredded cabbage)
2 tablespoons tomato paste, optional
Bay leaf
Salt and pepper
Sour cream, for serving
Parsley, for serving
Garlic, optional

Combine beef broth in the pot with another quart of water. You have two options to add the meat: 1) you can put the raw stew beef into the water, boil and skim the foam, or 2) you can lightly fry the stew beef in olive oil and add to the water, which creates less foam.

While the meat is simmering, prep the vegetables. Dice onions and tomatoes, cube potatoes. We typically peel and shred carrots and beets, but you're also welcome to dice these. (Beware—the beets will stain, so use something that washes easily!) You can shred cabbage, but you can also use a small bag of shredded cabbage from the grocery store if you want to cheat.

Lightly fry onions in olive oil until translucent, then add carrots, fry for another minute then add beets and tomatoes. Fry for another 5 minutes on medium heat and then add to pot.

Add potatoes and cabbage to pot and continue to simmer. Add tomato paste if desired (creates stronger tomato base), bay leaf, and salt and pepper to taste. It's easy to go back and add more salt/pepper later if needed! Cover pot and let simmer until potatoes are soft. Then let cool with the lid on. Borsch gets better as it sits, we promise!!! Day 2 is always a richer flavor.

When you're ready to serve, we recommend a dollop of sour cream, and you can garnish with parsley if you like.

Feeling daring? Try peeling a clove of garlic, take a small nibble and follow with a spoonful of borsch. It's like a flavor explosion!

Cock-a-Leekie

Karen Walker • Veazie, Penobscot County

"This recipe was found in my Grandma Day's hymnbook. It has been in the Day family for over 300 years, and was translated in 1868 from Scottish to new English by our great, great, great, great-grandmother, Mehitable Grover Day, who was born between 1770 and 1780, and lived in Leeds, Maine. She gave the recipe to her granddaughter-in-law, Josephine Guptill Day, who passed it on to her own granddaughter-in-law, Alda Mae. The Day Family Association is proud to share it, with modern adaptations, so that it may continue into the new millennium."

- 5 cups chicken broth
- 2 leeks (about 1 pound), rinsed well and sliced
- 3 carrots, cut into ¼-inch slices
- ⅓ cup quick cooking barley
- 1 bay leaf
- ½ teaspoon black pepper
- 1 pound boneless, skinless chicken breast, cut into 1-inch chunks
- ½ cup pitted prunes, coarsely chopped

In a large pot set over high heat, bring chicken broth, leeks, carrots, barley, bay leaf, and black pepper to a boil. Reduce heat to low, cover, and simmer 10 minutes, or until the vegetables and barley are tender.

Add chicken and prunes and return to a boil. Reduce heat, cover, and simmer 10-15 minutes, or until the chicken is cooked through and no longer pink in its thickest part. Remove bay leaf before serving.

Swedish Fruit Soup (Fruktsoppa)

Janet Erickson • New Sweden, Aroostook County

"This recipe was my grandmother's, Anna Nelson Anderson, who came from Sweden in 1899. It is very good."

- 1 pound prunes, washed
- 1 pound raisins, washed
- Dried apricots, if desired
- 4 apples, peeled and sliced
- ½ teaspoon salt
- 1 cup sugar
- 2 teaspoons cinnamon
- ½ teaspoon nutmeg
- 8 cups cold water
- ½ cup orange juice
- 2 teaspoons grated orange rind
- 3 tablespoons cornstarch, mixed with equal amount water
- 15-ounce can peaches
- Cherries and bananas, if desired

Mix dried fruit, apples, salt, sugar, spices, water, and orange juice and rind in a large pot and simmer for 4 to 5 minutes. Mix cornstarch with water and add slowly to the mixture. Boil 4 minutes. When cool, add canned peaches and optional cherries and bananas.

Crockpot Bacon Corn Chowder

Edythe (Bray) Gervais • Skowhegan, Somerset County

"I grew up in Bingham, but my husband and I lived in Belgium from 1969-1971 when my husband was in the military and stationed at SHAPE (the Supreme Headquarters of the Allied Powers Europe). We moved to Skowhegan in 1975 and raised our three children here. I was a stay-at-home mom until all the kids were in school, and volunteered at school, church, scouts, sports boosters, etc. I love to read, make quilts, and work on ancestry. I've learned that I am a General Society of Mayflower Descendants member four times over. My husband and I have been married 52 years and enjoy our six grandchildren. We are now both retired and have enjoyed turning off the GPS and traveling the back roads—and eating! This crockpot chowder is one of our favorites. I like to make this in the morning and let it simmer all day."

4 tablespoons butter or margarine
1 small onion, diced
1 cup water
2 cups diced raw potatoes
2 teaspoons salt
¼ teaspoon pepper
1 can cream-style corn
12-ounce can evaporated milk
2 cups light cream
1 cup whole milk
1-2 tablespoons crumbled bacon or Bacon Bits

Melt butter in a frying pan. Add onion and cook slowly until onion is yellowed. Add water, diced potatoes, salt, and pepper. Cover, lower heat, and simmer until potato is tender, 15-20 minutes.

Pour into a crockpot and add cream-style corn, evaporated milk, light cream, whole milk, and bacon or Bacon Bits, to taste.

Cover crockpot and set to simmer. Stir occasionally until suppa time. Just before serving, I use my immersion blender and swirl it around the crockpot for 5-15 seconds to make the chowder creamier and smoother.

Grammie's BBQ Beans

Alisha Targonski • Jefferson, Lincoln County

"This recipe is from the kitchen of my grandmother, Helen (Sceggell) Bouchard. These are beans we most enjoyed growing up when we went 'down to camp' to visit Grammie and Grampy, Helen and Bob Bouchard of East Millinocket. The family camp, Camp Kwitchabichin, located on Ambejejus Lake near Mt. Katahdin, is where my family would gather every summer, us down from Aroostook and my cousins up from from Southern Maine. These beans were, and remain, a summer staple and there's something about them, they bring back so many childhood memories: summers on the lake, listening to Red Sox games, and being with my grandparents."

- 4 ounces bacon, diced
- 2 medium onions, chopped
- 2 large garlic cloves, crushed
- 1 green pepper, diced
- 2 tablespoons brown sugar
- 2 teaspoons chili powder
- 1 bottle chili sauce
- 2 tablespoons soy sauce
- 2 tablespoons balsamic vinegar
- ¼ teaspoon hot sauce
- Two 15-ounce cans each, cannellini and red kidney beans, drained

Brown bacon in a heavy-bottomed pan, then remove. In drippings, sauté vegetables until tender. Stir in remaining ingredients except beans, and bring to a boil for 5 minutes. Stir in the beans and cover. Bake at 375 for 30 minutes. These are best the next day.

We're proud to support the Maine Community Cookbook
Live here, work here, play here, bank here.
For You 24/7:
800-860-8821
CamdenNational.com
Camden
NATIONAL BANK

Rabelais Inc.
Thought for Food
Six centuries of culinary books, manuscripts, and ephemera for the cook and the collector.
Biddeford, Maine
info@RabelaisBooks.com
www.RabelaisBooks.com

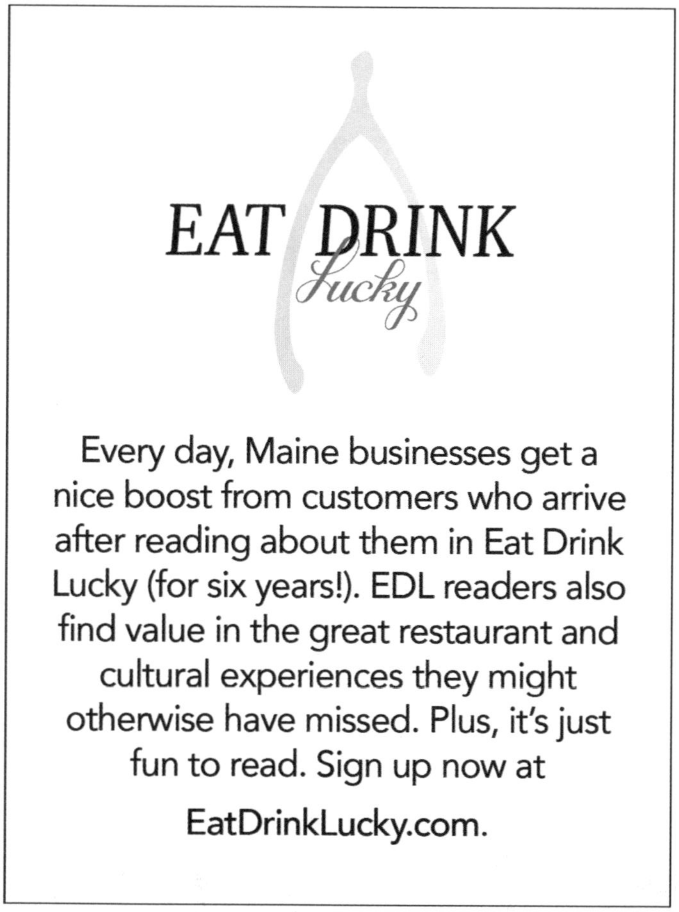
EAT DRINK
Lucky
Every day, Maine businesses get a nice boost from customers who arrive after reading about them in Eat Drink Lucky (for six years!). EDL readers also find value in the great restaurant and cultural experiences they might otherwise have missed. Plus, it's just fun to read. Sign up now at
EatDrinkLucky.com.

GAIN SKILLS FOR WORK OR LIFE
EARN YOUR DEGREE THEN TRANSFER
SOUTHERN MAINE COMMUNITY COLLEGE
PREPARE FOR A CAREER YOU'RE PASSIONATE ABOUT
IT'S TIME
for an education that meets your needs.
SHORT-TERM TRAINING • CERTIFICATES • DEGREES
www.smccME.edu
SOUTHERN MAINE COMMUNITY COLLEGE

POTATOES

Photo: Iver Soderberg surveys the fields at his potato farm in New Sweden in 2006. The family recipe for Janssons Frestelse (Jansson's Temptation) can be found on page 96.

1 2 3 4 5 Potatoes

Georgia Hansen • Spruce Head, Knox County

"This side dish has been a family favorite for years. I brought the recipe with me when I moved to Maine in 1977 and became a Maine resident instead of a summer visitor. When my aunt shared this recipe with me, she called it 1 2 3 4 5 Potatoes. Now that my husband is diabetic, I sometimes call it 1 2 3 4 NO Potatoes, and omit potatoes (which are high on the glycemic index), or I change the order and number of ingredients, starting with one potato, instead of ending with five potatoes. The beauty of the recipe is that you can use any combination of these root vegetables in any proportion."

- 1 turnip
- 2 parsnips
- 3 onions
- 4 carrots
- 5 potatoes
- Salt and pepper, to taste
- Optional: garlic and/or bay leaf
- Butter, to taste
- Parsley, fresh or dried, to garnish

Peel and dice all the vegetables. Put diced veggies in a large cooking pot with just enough water to cover the vegetables; add salt, and, if desired, a couple of garlic cloves and/or a bay leaf. When water comes to a boil, reduce to medium heat, cover and cook 15 minutes, or longer if needed, until all the veggies are soft when poked with a fork. Remove bay leaf. Drain veggies but reserve some of the cooking water. Mash right in the pot. (Alternatively, you can put vegetables through a ricer or food mill, which is what my aunt did.) Add butter, salt, and pepper to taste, then stir in enough of the reserved cooking water to make the consistency of mashed potatoes. Transfer to a serving dish, add a dollop of butter on top and sprinkle with chopped parsley, and pass the pepper grinder.

Mom's Potato Salad

Marsha Merryman • Oakland, Kennebec County

"My mom, Luella Merryman, loved to cook for her family, and she especially loved to bake. When I was in middle school she became a lunch lady as a baker at the Sugg Middle School in Lisbon Falls. She stayed there for many years, and the smell of her rolls brought teachers and staff to the door looking for warm samples! Her cookie jar was always full and she always had something to bring out for coffee time when my Uncle Winfield 'Winnie' Libby would stop by Saturday morning after his golf game. This potato salad is her invention and we always had it at our Moxie Day picnic at her house."

- 2½ pounds potatoes, peeled
- ⅓ cup white vinegar
- ¼ to ⅓ cups vegetable oil
- ½ cup grated onion (approximately 1 medium onion)
- 1 tablespoon sugar
- 1 teaspoon each garlic powder, celery salt, parsley
- Miracle Whip, to taste
- 8-10 hard-boiled eggs

In a large pot, boil potatoes until they're tender. Combine vinegar, vegetable oil, onion, sugar, and spices, mix, and pour over hot potatoes. Use a large spoon to stir and break up potatoes. Let set in the refrigerator overnight.

In the morning, mix in Miracle Whip to taste, and add at least 8—better with 10!—hard-boiled egg. Everything is flexible according to taste. Chill until ready to serve.

Janssons Frestelse (Jansson's Temptation)

Karen Soderberg Hinchliffe • Portland, Cumberland County

"My mother, Monica, was born in Stockholm, Sweden. My father, Iver, was born in Woodland, Maine and never visited his ancestral Sweden, homeland of his bride, but stood by her in recreating many Swedish traditions, including the annual making of the smelly but DELICIOUS Janssons Frestelse. They shared a love of potatoes and fish—and family and dogs who indiscriminately loved leftovers. My parents never made just one family-sized serving size but rather enough for the New Sweden Covenant Church smörgåsbord—12-15 lasagna dishes full! My mom died in October 2015. In the summer of 2017, I made Janssons Frestelse for my dad. He was delighted. The next person who visited him and opened the refrigerator thought they were doing him a favor by throwing away anything and everything that looked or smelled spoiled. My recent bake seemed to qualify—however, it was NOT spoiled! It was nonetheless thrown out."

- 8-10 Aroostook potatoes, cut into thick sticks (see Note)
- 1-2 large onions, coarsely chopped and sautéed
- 1-2 tins anchovy fillets
- 2-3 tablespoons butter (or margarine)
- 2 cups half-and-half or cream

Note: Potatoes can be peeled or not, depending on the season. If making this in June for Midsummer, then peel, but if in autumn, don't bother, as you have new potatoes and the peel is thin and wonderful.

Preheat oven to 425 degrees. Place half of the potatoes into an oven-proof dish. Layer with half of the sautéed onions and half of the anchovy fillets. Repeat with remaining potatoes, onions, and anchovies. Pour the anchovy brine over the mixture, dot with butter, and pour in 1 cup of the half-and-half. Bake for 30 minutes, then pour in remaining half-and-half and return to the oven for an additional 30 minutes.

Baked Potato Soup

Charlotte Grass Shaw • Mars Hill, Aroostook County

"As a child on cold frosty mornings in Aroostook County, I would pick potatoes and get 25 cents per barrel. When the day was done and the barrels of potatoes were stored for the day, it was time to return home and count the picker's tickets from their day's labors. After seeing countless potatoes during the day, it was always a special treat to have more potatoes on your plate for supper, whether it be baked, mashed, riced, scalloped, hash, potato salad, or potato soup—which my dad called 'Poor Man's Soup,' probably because potatoes were plentiful at our house. To this very day, one of my favorite comfort foods is baked potato soup."

- 5 large Maine potatoes
- ⅔ cup butter or margarine
- ½ cup flour
- ¾ teaspoon salt
- ¼ teaspoon pepper
- 6 cups milk
- 1 cup sour cream
- ¼ cup thinly sliced scallions
- 10 bacon strips, cooked and crumbled
- 1 cup shredded cheddar cheese

Bake and cool potatoes. When potatoes are cool enough to handle, cube them. Set aside.

In a large saucepan, melt butter. Stir in flour, salt, and pepper, and continue stirring until smooth, about 1 minute. Gradually add milk. Bring mixture to a boil and cook, stirring, for 2 minutes, or until thickened. Remove from heat and whisk in sour cream. Stir in cubed potatoes and scallions. Garnish with bacon and cheese.

Shepherd's Pie

Meg Gerritsen • Bridgewater, Aroostook County

"Potatoes are perfectly suited to Aroostook soils and climate, and have been grown up here for well over 200 years. Steadfastly, potatoes remain an important part of Aroostook's cultural identity. For farmers like us who make their living growing Maine potatoes, they are a critical part of a rich, potato-centered way of life. In Aroostook County, not only are potatoes a vital economic driver, but the countless potato fields provide community cohesion and serve as the main roadside attraction for the long-distance travel required of everyone in the sprawling Big Sky country that is Aroostook. Not surprisingly, in this land where The County honors heritage, potatoes still loom large on menus, at roadside stands, and occupy a hallowed place at Aroostook kitchen table settings. Elsewhere in New England, a fine, sunny fall day might be breezily called a 'nice day.' However, here in very rural Aroostook County, it's still universally perceived as, 'A good day to dig potatoes.'"

2 pounds potatoes
1 large onion, diced
3 large Chantenay carrots, diced
Oil or lard (about 2 teaspoons)
Celery leaves
1 pound hamburger or leftover chopped meat
Salt, pepper, sage, and thyme, to taste
1-2 cups stock
¼ to ⅓ cup flour
Leftover vegetables for color
½ cup cream, sour cream, Greek yogurt, or milk

Preheat your oven to 350 degrees. Wash, cube and boil the potatoes in enough water to cover in a covered saucepan, until tender. Set aside to cool. Potatoes can also be steamed in a pressure cooker or Instant Pot.

In a large Dutch oven or deep frypan, cook the diced onion and carrot in a little oil or lard until starting to tender. Add the celery and crumbled hamburger and fry until just browned. Leftover diced pork, beef, poultry, or venison can be used instead of burger and added after the vegetables are cooked. Season with love, and salt and pepper, sage, and thyme to taste.

At this point add a little stock from last week's roast, or what have you, about a cup or two. You can thicken this with a little flour mixed in the cold stock before adding to the Dutch oven. Whisk in. Then add any other leftover cooked vegetables you think will brighten the mix: peppers, shell beans, etc.

Drain and mash the potatoes with a masher or ricer. Remove the skins if you like, or leave them in. Blend the mash with cream, sour cream, Greek yogurt, or milk. Or it is fine just as is. Season mashed potatoes with ½ teaspoon salt and generous amount of pepper. Spread the mash over the top of stew mixture. Bake for 30-40 minutes, until bubbly and just browning on top a bit. Serve to damp-haired, wool sock–wearing chilly-but-warm-hearted family at the end of a day outdoors.

Potato Casserole

Jasen Hutchinson • Monticello, Aroostook County

"My mum, Marie Jewell Hutchinson, was raised in The County, on property that the Jewells homesteaded in Monticello about 200 years ago. My grandfather Aliston 'Al' Jewell farmed with his brother, Leon Jewell. I'm not exactly sure when my grandfather started Jewell Bros. Potatoes, but his son, my uncle, Edward 'Buz' Jewell worked with him until they both retired from farming. Uncle Leon retired before that. I still have some old receipt books of where he sold potatoes at market. And like most everyone in The County, they had pickers. Gramp and Buz never used a harvester. Their farm's picture is at the former Houlton tourist center, and also on a postcard showing two pictures of the farm in different years, when they rotated crops. The original homestead burned down in the 1940s, and my grandfather built up the property again, at Jewell's corner in Monticello."

- 10 medium potatoes
- 6 ounces cream cheese
- 1 cup sour cream
- 2 teaspoons onion salt
- ¼ teaspoon pepper
- 2 tablespoons butter
- Grated cheese, for serving (optional)
- Paprika, for garnish (optional)

Preheat oven to 350 degrees. Cook potatoes in a large pot of boiling water, then drain, and mash. Mix all remaining ingredients into mashed potatoes and beat to thoroughly incorporate. Place mixture in a 2-quart casserole dish and bake, uncovered, for 30 minutes. Garnish with either grated cheese or paprika.

Brown-Butter Gnocchi with Crispy Prosciutto and Sage

Jessica Battilana • Falmouth, Cumberland County

"When I was a kid, I'd always ask for meat loaf and mashed potatoes as my birthday meal. And these days, when I'm sick or sad, I bake myself a potato and load it with pats of salted butter. Gnocchi, which likely originated in Northern Italy, is a pasta made from potatoes, and it's really just a sophisticated form of comfort food. I've never particularly liked the combination of gnocchi with tomato sauce; the sauce masks their delicate flavor. But gnocchi tossed in nutty brown butter with crispy bits of prosciutto and sage leaves? That makes sense.

Adding too much flour to gnocchi dough can cause them to be leaden and dense, but if you don't add enough, they'll fall apart when boiled. Practice makes perfect—you're looking for a dough that is soft but not sticky, and the amount of flour that you add to each batch may change, since the moisture content of the potatoes (and flour) can vary."

- 2 pounds russet potatoes (about 3 medium)
- 6 tablespoons unsalted butter
- 1 egg
- ¼ cup plus 2 tablespoons finely grated Parmigiano-Reggiano
- 1 teaspoon kosher salt
- 1 cup all-purpose flour
- Olive oil
- 4 ounces thinly sliced prosciutto
- 5 sage leaves
- Freshly ground pepper

Preheat the oven to 400 degrees. Rinse the potatoes and place them on a rimmed baking sheet. With a fork, poke holes in each potato. Bake until tender, about 1 hour. Remove from the oven and when just cool enough to handle but still very warm, split the potatoes in half and scoop out the flesh. Discard the skin. Pass the potato flesh through a ricer onto a rimmed baking sheet and spread in an even layer.

Melt 2 tablespoons of the butter. In a small bowl, whisk together the melted butter, egg, 2 tablespoons of the Parmigiano, and the salt. Drizzle over the riced potatoes, then sprinkle about ¾ cup of the flour over. With your fingertips, gently work the mixture into a ball. The dough should be soft but not sticky; if it's sticky, add some of the remaining flour by the tablespoonful. Form the dough into a disk and cut the disk into 1-inch slices. Roll each slice into a ball.

Lightly dust a rimmed baking sheet with flour and set nearby. On a lightly floured work surface, working with one ball of dough at a time, roll into a snake about ¾ inch around. Cut each snake crosswise into ¾-inch pieces. Using your thumb and one piece of dough at a time, roll each piece across a gnocchi paddle or the tines of an overturned fork, pressing down lightly so the gnocchi curves around your thumb slightly then drops onto the prepared baking sheet. Repeat with the remaining balls of dough until all of the gnocchi have been formed. (You can make the gnocchi to this point, freeze them on the baking sheet, and then transfer them to plastic freezer storage bags. They can be boiled from frozen.)

Bring a large pot of salted water to a boil. Drizzle a rimmed baking sheet with a small amount of olive oil. When the water is boiling, add the gnocchi to the water in batches. The gnocchi will sink and then float; when they rise to the top, boil them for 2 minutes. With a spider or slotted spoon, transfer the gnocchi to the baking sheet.

Heat a large nonstick frying pan over medium heat. Lay a few slices of the prosciutto in the pan in a single layer and cook, turning once, until crispy, about 2 minutes. Transfer to a plate and repeat until all of the prosciutto has been fried. Add the remaining 4 tablespoons of butter to the pan and, when it melts, add the sage leaves and fry until crisp. Transfer to the plate with the prosciutto.

Let the butter continue to cook until it's light golden brown and has a nutty aroma. Slide the gnocchi into the pan and, with a rubber spatula, stir gently to coat the gnocchi in butter. Cook without stirring until the gnocchi are heated through and beginning to develop a golden-brown crust on the bottom, about 2 minutes. Crumble the prosciutto into the pan and stir gently with the rubber spatula to combine. Season to taste with salt and pepper, then transfer to a platter and garnish with the fried sage and remaining ¼ cup grated Parmigiano. Serve immediately.

Potatoes

1888 • Culinary Cullings: Choice Gleanings from Many Households

The Ladies of the Congregational Society • Presque Isle, Aroostook County

"The great art of cooking potatoes is to take them up as soon as they are done. Of course it is important to begin to cook them at the proper time. When boiled, baked, fried or steamed, they are rendered watery by continuing to cook them after they have reached the proper point. For this reason, potatoes to bake or boil should be selected so as to have them nearly the same size. Begin with the largest first, and continue to select the largest till all are gone. Be careful that the water does not stop boiling as thus the potatoes will be watery. Never boil them very hard, as it breaks them."

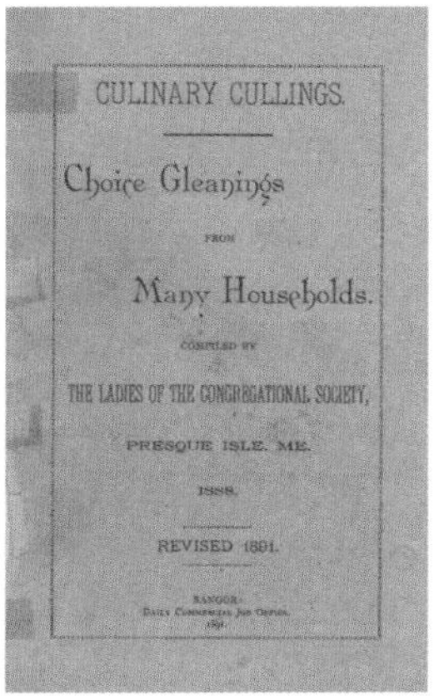
CULINARY CULLINGS.

Choice Gleanings

FROM

Many Households.

COMPILED BY

THE LADIES OF THE CONGREGATIONAL SOCIETY,

PRESQUE ISLE, ME.

1888.

REVISED 1891.

New England Doughnuts

Pamela Leone • Freeport, Cumberland County

"This keepsake recipe, handwritten, was given to me by Joan Laughlin of South Freeport. She was the quintessential garden lady and maker of Maine foods from old family recipes. Everything was heirloom, including her! Joan served as a postal clerk in the South Freeport Post Office, a small neighborhood substation. She was a lover of cats, and to this day, neighbors feed a stray that they believe was her cat accidentally left behind when she moved to Vermont under the care of her favorite niece for the last few years of her life. Joan was a dear neighbor and friend who passed away last year at 86. My boys grew up making these and now I make them with our grandchildren as this is very kid-in-the-kitchen-friendly (except for the frying). I share this recipe in memory of Joan Laughlin."

1 cup sugar
¼ cup shortening
½ teaspoon salt
2 eggs, beaten
1 cup cold mashed potatoes (nothing added)
4 cups all-purpose flour
1 tablespoon baking powder
½ teaspoon baking soda
1 teaspoon nutmeg
1 cup buttermilk or sour milk
½ cup peeled chopped apples, optional
Several cups vegetable oil, for frying

Toppings: Confection sugar, cinnamon and sugar, or Vermont style with glaze of 1 tablespoon butter, 1 cup confectioners' sugar, and 1 tablespoon maple syrup, mixed together.

In a large bowl, cream together the sugar, shortening, and salt. Add beaten eggs and stir in mashed potatoes. Into a separate bowl, sift dry ingredients. Add dry ingredients to the creamed mixture in three parts, alternating with sour milk. To make a Maine-style variation, mix into the dough ½ cup peeled chopped apples.

On a lightly floured board, quickly roll out dough to ¼-inch thickness, and cut out.

In a deep fry pan or pot, heat vegetable oil to 375 degrees. Drop doughnuts gently into the oil, and turn once as they float. Add topping of choice while doughnuts are hot. This recipe makes around 3 dozen doughnuts, plus centers.

Mom's Chocolate Potato Doughnuts

Laurie Reynolds • Windham, Cumberland County

"My mother and grandmothers were all wonderful cooks. This doughnut recipe was shared with Mom by Louise Morris, from St. Francis. It's a taste of potato country, and one of Mom's favorite doughnut recipes."

- 1¾ cups sugar
- 2 tablespoons butter, melted
- 1 cup hot mashed potatoes
- 3 eggs
- 1 cup undiluted evaporated milk, mixed with 1½ teaspoons vinegar and 1 teaspoon baking soda
- 1 teaspoon vanilla
- 2 teaspoons baking powder
- 1 teaspoon salt
- 9 tablespoons cocoa powder
- 4 cups flour
- Crisco or lard, for frying

In a large bowl, mix together ingredients in the order given and stir to form a workable dough.

On a lightly floured board, roll out dough to ¼-inch thickness, and cut out.

In a deep fry pan or pot, heat Crisco or lard to 375 degrees. Drop doughnuts gently into the oil, and turn once as they float. Tip: To make good doughnuts better, dip cooked doughnut in hot boiling water when removed from the fat.

Roasted Fennel, Potato and Green Beans

Susie Stedman • Westport Island, Lincoln County

"This wonderful side dish is dead easy to prepare and goes deliciously with my husband Adrian's Brilliant Roast Chicken."

- 2 fennel bulbs, trimmed
- 1½ pounds Yukon gold potatoes
- Malden's sea salt, to taste
- Olive oil
- Finely chopped fines herbes: parsley, chives, tarragon, chervil
- 1½ pounds thin, tender green beans (haricots verts), trimmed
- Freshly ground black pepper, to taste

Preheat oven to 400 degrees. Cut fennel bulbs into strips. Thinly slice potatoes. In a large bowl, toss fennel and potatoes with sea salt, olive oil, and herbs. Spread mixture in a roasting pan and roast for 20 minutes. Remove from oven.

Toss green beans with potatoes and fennel and return to the oven for another 15-20 minutes. Sprinkle with freshly ground black pepper and serve hot or at room temperature. Makes 4 to 6 servings.

Serve with Brilliant Roast Chicken, page 178.

Grandma's Potato Pancakes (Nagymama's Palacsinta)

Elyse Eichler • Durham, Androscoggin County

"My Hungarian grandmother made these pancakes every Thursday when I was a little girl. She would come over to watch me and my sister, while my parents had their weekly meetings at the Waldorf school we attended. One vivid memory I have is of me wanting to stay with my friends in my kindergarten's playground after school and not wanting to leave. When my mom said 'We have *palacsinta* at home that *nagymama* made,' I became highly motivated to get home to eat some! We enjoy these warm, with sour cream and apple sauce."

- 3½ pounds red or Yukon gold potatoes, peeled and cut into ½-inch cubes
- 1 tablespoon salt
- 3½ cups flour, plus extra for rolling
- 1 large egg
- 2-3 tablespoons milk, if dough is too dry
- Coconut oil, lard, or other vegetable oil for frying

Place a large pot of water over high heat and bring to boil. Add potatoes and salt, and cook until potatoes are easily pierced with a fork. Drain cooked potatoes and place them in a large bowl. Using a potato masher, mash them until no large lumps remain.

When potatoes have cooled slightly, mix in 1 cup of flour and the egg. Using a wooden spoon, continue to mix, while adding flour in ½ cup increments. Keep stirring until the dough is no longer sticky. At some point, the mixing will be easier with your hands. This may take as long as 15 minutes, but keep working the dough, adding a little milk if it becomes too crumbly.

Lightly flour a clean counter or silicon mat, and turn out the dough. Form the dough into a roll about 3 inches wide and 12-18 inches long. Cut the roll into 1-inch lengths.

Working with one piece at a time, use a rolling pin to shape the dough into a pancake about ¼-inch thick and 8 inches in diameter.

Place a large frypan over high heat and add 3 tablespoons of oil. Test the oil with a little crumb of the dough—if it sizzles, it's ready for the pancake. Using your hands, carefully lift up the rolled pancake and place it in the frying pan. Fry for 3 minutes, or until the edges begin to brown. Flip it over and cook for another 3 minutes. Repeat with each pancake, adding more oil as needed. Tent finished pancakes with foil to keep warm. Makes 10 pancakes.

Plum Dumplings

Lynne Holland • Brunswick, Cumberland County

Sponsored by UMaine Cooperative Extension

"My grandmother, Josephine Hay, was a refugee from the Austro-Hungarian Empire, coming to the United States in 1900 at the age of 4. She lived in the area that is now known as Slovenia, but she spoke German at home. She was my scrabble and jigsaw puzzle buddy. With 19 grandchildren, I always felt like I might have been her favorite since I received her recipe box and silverware. This recipe is one of my favorites."

- 2 cups hot mashed potatoes
- 2 to 2 ½ cups flour
- 1 ½ teaspoons salt
- 4 tablespoons butter
- 2 eggs, slightly beaten
- 24 purple prune plums (can also be made with fresh apricots)
- ¾ cup sugar
- ½ cup plain breadcrumbs, browned in 1 tablespoon butter
- Butter, for frying

In a large bowl, cut mashed potatoes into flour with a pastry cutter or two knives. Add salt and cut in butter. Add eggs and mix well.

On a lightly floured surface, roll out dough into a rectangle until it is ¼-inch thick. Cut the rolled dough into two dozen 3-inch squares.

Wash and pit the plums (or apricots); put a scant half tablespoon of sugar where the pit was. Put a plum in the center of each dough square and pinch the edges together to cover the fruit.

Bring a large pot of salted water to the boil. Drop each dumpling into boiling water and cover. Let boil for 10 minutes. Dumplings will be floating when done.

Remove from water and roll each dumpling in browned, buttered breadcrumbs and pan-fry. Serve hot.

Home Fries

Katherine McGee Wilson • Fort Fairfield, Aroostook County

"My grandparents, Thurber Eugene Holt and Henrietta (Bishop) Holt, owned several potato farms in Fort Fairfield. This was our Sunday morning treat, served with scrambled eggs and leftover beans. Home fries were called 'hash' when I was growing up. We'd plan ahead and bake or boil extra potatoes the day before so it came together quickly for breakfast."

4 medium all-purpose or Yukon gold potatoes, about 1½ pounds, boiled, drained, and cooled
3 tablespoons butter
1 tablespoon olive oil
½ cup diced onion
Salt and freshly ground pepper, to taste
Extras you might like to add: diced green bell peppers, bits of cooked meats, such as ham, corned beef, or cooked bacon

Peel the potatoes (or not, your choice) and cut into chunks, slices, or cubes. In a nonstick skillet, melt the butter and olive oil together over medium heat. Add the onion and cook for about 1 minute, until just translucent. Add the potato chunks. Season well with salt and pepper. Cook until heated through and turning golden brown, about 5 minutes, stirring occasionally. Add in any extras, and continue cooking until hot. Serve and enjoy!

Just Plain Hard Times

Ada Foss Cobb • Monson, Piscataquis County

"Thirty-three cents an hour on the W.P.A. building roads in the late Thirties was what Daddy earned. It seems like almost nothing but at least one could buy food, even though it was not what we really wanted. Salt pork, potatoes, canned mackerel, canned milk, rolled oats, cornmeal, and molasses were some of what we called the staple groceries.

Many meals at our house consisted of boiled potatoes, salt pork and brown gravy, hot biscuits with white oleo (if we didn't get it mixed). Breakfast was rolled oats, or cream of wheat cereal with canned milk.

Supper often was poor man's soup which was cut-up potatoes and onions cooked together with the fat after frying slices of salt pork in it. The big slices of salt pork were put into the soup, but Daddy was the only one who liked or ate it. Us kids always coaxed for the crispy pork rinds and they were divided by Dad and usually kept until after the meal and we called it our cud. Sometimes they lasted so long, and tasted so good.

My sister Norma dearly loved potatoes, and I recall her piling her plate with boiled potatoes. She'd mash and mash and moisten with milk, and sometimes she would smooth and flatten it out with her knife and cut it like pieces of fudge. It's funny why I remember those silly things.

Store-bought bread was even a treat; sometimes we would eat a whole loaf at one meal. If we had toast we would slap the bread directly on the stove top covers; one slice might be burned to a frazzle, the next one hardly warm but it tasted so good after having biscuits for days and days.

Of course we had other foods, baked and stewed beans, vegetables from the garden, but all food was hard to come by, while earning such meager wages."

Artwork: Potato Farm by Katherine McGee Wilson

A Brief Vegetarian History of Maine

By Avery Yale Kamila

Plant-based roots run deep in the Pine Tree State, and when Maine achieved statehood in 1820 vegetarians had already been living here for more than 100 years. They've continued to make Maine their home ever since. So who are some of Maine's best known vegetarians and what did they eat?

Back in 1820, Revolutionary War veteran Captain Peter Twitchell of Bethel was a new vegetarian. A glimpse of what Twitchell ate is preserved in a letter he wrote in 1844 and was later published in the "The American Vegetarian And Health Journal." Twitchell writes: "I eat no flesh or fish, or butter, nor anything like grease, eggs, or sweetning, [sic] and drink no tea, coffee, or milk; I eat bread and different kinds of sauce, and pies, except those that may have meat in them." Bread and water were the core features of the 19th-century vegetarian diet, while sauce meant cooked vegetables or peas. The temperate meals Twitchell outlines would be called vegan today.

Dr. William Alcott's influential 1838 book *Vegetable Diet* consists of medical reports about the efficacy of treating illness with plant-based foods and includes two reports from Dr. Horace A. Barrows, a Bowdoin graduate who practiced in the towns of Hebron, Leeds, Philips, Otisfield, and Harrison and adopted a full-time vegetarian diet in 1835.

In Alcott's book, Barrows reports eating "wheat meal bread, potatoes, butter, and baked sweet apples for breakfast and dinners." His only drink was cold water. In his diary, housed at the Maine Historical Society in Portland, Barrows writes about preparing whole wheat bread according to the instructions of celebrity vegetarian Sylvester Graham, whose popular 1834 lecture series in Portland provoked a riot.

Jeremiah Hacker

When the first issue of "The Pleasure Boat" cruised to newsstands in Portland in 1845, it became Maine's first pro-vegetarian publication. Jeremiah Hacker published the alternative newspaper until 1866, when its offices burned in Portland's Great Fire. Hacker, an ardent abolitionist, who regularly expressed vegetarian views, reported living on whole wheat bread and water, and he sought help through his newspaper locating rice "not watered with the tears of slaves."

Ellen Gould Harmon was born in Gorham, but grew up in Portland where she suffered a head injury as a schoolgirl. It caused seizures then religious visions, which elevated her as a prophet and led to the founding of the Seventh-day Adventist church, a pro-vegetarian worldwide Christian denomination. She married Maine preacher James White in 1846 and soon the pair were traveling across the country sharing the Adventist gospel.

In 1863, Ellen G. White experienced the first of two visions that led to the church's embrace of vegetarian food. In letters Ellen sent to James in 1865 she reveals her meals consisted of "mush, gems, and uncooked apples" for breakfast. Dinner brought "baked potatoes, raw apples, and gems," while Ellen's 38th birthday dinner that year meant a spread of "Graham mush, hard Graham crackers, applesauce, sugar, and a cup of milk." Mush was grain porridge made with cornmeal, wheat flour, or oats, while gems were hard, oven-baked, whole wheat rolls.

Ellen G. White

The Whites hired Dr. John Harvey Kellogg in 1875 to head a vegetarian water cure in Battle Creek, Michigan. Dr. Kellogg, his wife, Ella, and his brother, W. K., invented vegetarian prepared foods, including corn flakes, and mass marketed them to reduce meat consumption. In 2014, "Smithsonian Magazine" named Ellen G. White one of the "100 Most Significant Americans of All Time."

By the mid-20th century, in 1952, well-known radicals Helen and Scott Nearing moved to Harborside, and two years later published their famous book *Living the Good Life*. Its reissue in 1970 became an instant hit among the era's counterculture and drew new residents to Maine. The book advocates vegetarianism, homesteading, and organic farming.

The Nearings write in the book "lately we have largely ceased to use dairy products and have allied ourselves with the vegans." In 1980, Helen published her heavily vegan, eclectic cookbook *Simple Food for the Good Life*, where her recipes rarely exceed 10 ingredients and include dishes such as dandelion salad, stir-fried rutabaga, pumpkin shell casserole, baked soybeans, lentil pottage, Chinese thin soup, Mexican rice, and Guatemala carrots.

People who live in or have ties to Maine have published a number of vegetarian cookbooks in recent decades. Bar Harbor resident Peter Golbitz's 1998 *Tofu & Soyfoods Cookery* features recipes for tofu no-egg salad and high-protein burgers. TV host and Cumberland resident Toni Fiore's 2008 cookbook *Totally Vegetarian* (also the name of one of her PBS cooking shows) includes recipes for fettuccine walnut alfredo and tempeh cacciatore. Maine native Kenden Alfond's 2021 *Beyond Chopped Liver: 59 Jewish Recipes Get a Vegan Health Makeover* serves up baked tofu schnitzel and jackfruit brisket.

Toni Fiore

Searsport native, culinary educator, and international vegan restauranteur Matthew Kenney's 2017 vegan cookbook *Plantlab* is equal parts coffee table art book. Kenney's restaurants and academies mix raw foods with molecular gastronomy to elevate vegan dining into haute cuisine and create dishes such as farro-fennel sausage pizza with cashew mozzarella, smoked king oyster steam buns, miso ramen, and chocolate mint ice cream sandwiches. As the subtitle suggests, Kenney is among those "Crafting the Future of Food."

Avery Yale Kamila writes a vegan food column for the Maine Sunday Telegram and is working to unearth Maine's lost vegetarian history.

VEGETABLES

Photo: Habiba Salat, a farmer at Little Jubba Central Maine Agrarian Commons, stands between rows of vegetables at the farm in Wales. Her recipe for the traditional Somali Muufo Corn Bread can be found on page 24.

Spinach Doods

Nina Interlandi Bell • Woolwich, Sagadahoc County

"I don't know where my mom originally found this recipe. It was probably on the side of a box of stuffing mix or the like—you know, one of those places where all the best 'family' recipes come from. When I was a kid she always made these with boxed, frozen spinach. But you can absolutely substitute whatever dark, leafy greens you have on hand. If fresh: Gently steam until wilted, shock in cold water, and squeeze the water out. If frozen: Warm and squeeze the water out. Either way you want to start with about 16 ounces of greens and end up with about 8 ounces after squeezing the water out.

I made Spinach Doods in my 20s when I barely knew how to cook anything else. I made them in my 30s and they were a favorite even at the hippest/fanciest parties. And in my 40s, I make them for my kids who say 'This is the only way you're ever gonna get me to eat spinach.' Nowadays I even make these with a plethora of Maine wild foraged greens from my yard like dandelion, sochan, broadleaf plantain, nettles, sheep sorrel, trout lily, lambs quarters, violet, and curly dock. It's a very forgiving recipe and it's pretty hard to mess up. If you'd like some more greens, add 'em. If you want more stuffing, shove it in. And if you come upon anyone who claims to not like these, treat them with the utmost suspicion."

About 16 ounces fresh or frozen dark, leafy greens (warmed or steamed/shocked, becomes 8 ounces with water squeezed out)
3 cups stuffing mix (such as Pepperidge Farm)
2 medium onions, finely diced
6 eggs, beaten lightly
¾ cup melted, unsalted butter
½ cup grated cheese (Parmesan, Romano)
1 teaspoon minced garlic
2 teaspoons sea salt
1 teaspoon dried thyme (don't skimp on this—it's the signature flavor!)
1 teaspoon freshly ground pepper

Preheat oven to 350 degrees. Mix all ingredients together thoroughly in a bowl and then press into small meatball-sized balls. Place onto an ungreased baking sheet and bake for 20-25 minutes, or until the bottoms are crispy and the tops are a light golden brown. Delicious right out of the oven but possibly MORE delicious cold from the fridge the next day (or later that night!).

Chinese Rice Stick Stir-Fry

Kate Huntress • Yarmouth, Cumberland County

"We adopted our youngest child, Julia YunLi Beatty, in China in 2005 when she was 10 years old. One of the first dishes she ordered after we met there contained short, thick, chewy rice sticks. They looked delicious, but I had never seen them before and had no idea how to cook them. Back at home in Maine, I researched recipes online and located the rice sticks at the Hong Kong Market in Portland. I developed this basic recipe, which is easily multiplied and open to infinite variations. Our family culinary history has been greatly enriched by embracing many of our daughter's favorite Chinese dishes, including this one."

8 ounces dry or frozen rice stick cakes (found at Asian markets or online)

Sauce:
6 tablespoons soy or tamari sauce
3 teaspoons sugar or maple syrup
3 teaspoons cornstarch or arrowroot powder
1 teaspoon salt

1½ cups vegetable broth or water
2 tablespoons vegetable oil (can substitute water or vegetable broth)
1 large onion, cut into slivers
1 pound block firm tofu, drained and cubed
3 cups assorted vegetables, cut into bite-size pieces: any combination of carrots, cabbage, sweet peppers, mushrooms, bok choy, broccoli, green beans

Cook rice sticks according to package directions, or by boiling rapidly in unsalted water for 3-5 minutes and then draining in a colander under cold water. Set aside.

In a separate small bowl, mix sauce ingredients together and set aside.

In a wok or large skillet, heat vegetable oil (or use water or vegetable broth for oil-free cooking) and stir-fry the onion over high heat for 30 seconds. Add the cubed tofu and stir-fry over high heat until it begins to char at the edges. Add remaining vegetables, reserved rice sticks, and sauce mixture. Continue to stir-fry for about 3 minutes until the sauce thickens, all ingredients are coated in sauce, and the vegetables are tender-crisp. Serve at once.

Braised Collards

Craig Hickman • Winthrop, Kennebec County

"When Black people traveled north and west during the Great Migration, we carried our recipes with us. In the culinary lexicon of folks in this diaspora, your recipe for collards—how you cook collards—defines whether or not you can cook at all. Collards are on the menu at church suppers, potlucks, barbecues, picnics, and holiday feasts, no matter the season–Thanksgiving, Christmas, New Year's Eve, Easter, Memorial Day, Juneteenth, July 4th. Collards have their own special place in soul food traditions.

Every year, for as long as I can remember, my father grew the greenest, sweetest collards in our backyard garden in Milwaukee. My mother, who swore the greens could tell you everything you needed to know about how the world was doing, would read the broad leaves as she meticulously washed them, then turned the collards into heaven on a plate.

Now, collards grow like perennial weeds all over my 25-acre farm. They overwinter, flower in late spring, and self-propagate for harvesting through Thanksgiving. I read the leaves in the field. They tell me when to harvest them. Usually in the rain. I let the rainwater wash them thereafter. I swear that makes them cook more tender.

And I never remove the stems.

Collards are high in fiber, vitamins K, C and A, calcium, folate, and rich in antioxidants. Collards are commonly served as a side dish with Southern fried chicken, fish, or smoked spareribs as the main. I love collards so much I often eat them as a main course accompanied by a piece of warm cornbread, slices of fresh summer vegetables, and spoons of green tomato chow chow on the side."

5 tablespoons olive oil
2 onions, chopped
1 green pepper, chopped
1 red pepper, chopped
1 large carrot, chopped
2 celery stalks, chopped
1 tablespoon ginger, minced
6 large garlic cloves, minced
1 tablespoon curry powder
1 teaspoon turmeric
5 pounds collard greens, washed, stacked, rolled tight, and sliced into ¼-inch ribbons
8 cups homemade chicken, beef or vegetable stock, or enough to submerge the collards
1 smoked ham hock or turkey wing (optional)
5 fingerling potatoes, unpeeled and whole (optional)
1 hot pepper, chopped, or ¼ teaspoon crushed red pepper
¼ cup cider vinegar
3 tablespoons maple syrup or honey
2 teaspoons soy sauce
¼ teaspoon lemon or orange zest
Salt and pepper to taste

Heat the olive oil in a large Dutch oven over medium-high heat. Add the onions, sweet peppers, carrots, celery, and ginger. Sauté vegetables for 8 to 10 minutes or until tender. Add the garlic, curry powder and turmeric. Cook, stirring occasionally, for another 5 minutes. The spices should smell up the house.

Add the collards, stock, smoked meat and potatoes to the pot. Turn up the heat and bring to a roiling boil. Let the collards boil for 15 minutes.

Add the hot pepper, vinegar, maple syrup, soy sauce and lemon zest to the pot. Turn down the heat to medium-low and let the collards simmer, covered, until dark green and tender, up to 2 hours.

About halfway through the simmering, remove the lid and stir the pot, making sure to fold the vegetables from the bottom into the collards thoroughly. Make sure to leave the smoked meat and potatoes intact. Add more liquid to the pot if necessary. Return the lid and finish braising the collards.

Add salt and pepper and adjust spices to taste. Serve with homemade cornbread, sliced fresh okra, heirloom tomatoes and scallions, and homemade green tomato chow chow. Makes 6 to 8 servings.

County Cabbage Rolls with Marinara

Melanie Legasse • Fort Kent, Aroostook County

Sponsored by
Maine
Farm & Sea
Cooperative

"At Maine Farm and Sea Cooperative, we work to maximize the amount of local foods used in institutional foodservice operations across the state, with a focus on social, economic, environmental, and healthy dietary outcomes. Inspired by the resources of the land in Aroostook County, the school nutrition department director, Melanie Legasse, at MSAD 27 & 33, created this dish. It has delighted the students in the district, the 500+ cyclists and staff during BikeMaine 2018, and many others in the community, who have prepared cabbage rolls with their own variations. All ingredients can be found locally at the grocer or, as we did in reaching our 65% goal for sourcing ultra local, you can find your own local producers, farm stands, or CSA program to enjoy the bounty of Maine." —Dave Seddon

1 head large-leaf cabbage
3 cups of your favorite marinara sauce, plus more for serving
2 tablespoons olive oil
1 medium onion, diced
2-3 garlic cloves, chopped
1 eggplant, cut into strips or small cubes, grilled or not
½ pound mushrooms (preferably wild or locally sourced), roughly chopped
2 cups fresh spinach, destemmed and chopped, or full baby spinach leaves
2 cups long grain white or brown rice, cooked until al dente
4 tablespoons fresh or 1½ tablespoons dried parsley
3 tablespoons fresh or 1 tablespoon dried oregano
1 bunch fresh basil, roughly chopped
1 pinch dried Ancho chili powder
2 tomatoes, diced
Salt and pepper, to taste

Optional: 1 cup pulled pork, cubed cooked chicken, or any smoked meat can be added to the filling
Optional: Top with shredded mozzarella or Parmesan cheese prior to cooking

Preheat oven to 350 degrees.

To prepare the cabbage leaves: Fill a large bowl with cold water and ice to make an ice water bath. In a large pot, boil 5 quarts of water with a sprinkling of salt. Leaving the head whole, core the cabbage and place into boiling water. As the cabbage leaves turn bright green, take the leaves off one by one and place them in the ice water bath. You should have 10-12 large leaves. Dry leaves on a paper towel before use.

Coat the bottom of a 9x13-inch baking pan with 1 cup of marinara sauce and set aside.

To prepare the filling: Using a large heavy-bottomed skillet, heat olive oil over medium-high heat and add the onions and garlic. Sauté until onions are translucent, then add eggplant, mushrooms, and spinach. Cook until tender, stirring occasionally, about 5 minutes. Add cooked rice, and mix well. If adding optional meat, stir it in and mix well. Stir in herbs, Ancho chili powder, and salt and pepper to taste. Remove mixture from heat and allow to cool slightly.

To assemble the rolls: Working with one leaf at a time, spread 2 tablespoons of the vegetable filling onto each cabbage leaf. Use the largest leaves for best results. Fold the sides of the leaf around the filling and roll each leaf, tucking the ends underneath. Place the cabbage rolls seam-side down in the pan. Top with remaining marinara sauce and optional cheese, if desired.

Cook for about 40 minutes, until cabbage leaves are thoroughly cooked and marinara sauce is bubbly. Prior to serving, top with additional warmed marinara and optional Parmesan. Freeze surplus cabbage rolls for a ready-to-go meal. Makes 4 to 6 servings.

Helen Nearing's Lentil Curry

The Good Life Center • Harborside, Hancock County

This recipe appeared in Helen Nearing's classic 1980 cookbook *Simple Food for the Good Life.*

- 2 cups lentils
- 1 teaspoon curry powder
- 4 cups water
- 3 onions, sliced
- 3 tomatoes, sliced
- 1 tablespoon oil
- ¼ cup peanut butter
- ¼ teaspoon cumin seed or turmeric
- Handful of chopped parsley

Cook lentils and curry in 4 cups water till lentils are just tender. Meanwhile, sauté onions and tomatoes in oil. Stir both mixtures together. Stir in the peanut butter and cumin. Heat and serve with sprinkled parsley.

Reprinted with permission from the Good Life Center.

Mimi's Eggplant Parm

Susan Spector • Portland, Cumberland County

"Living in Portland this past year during the pandemic changed my focus on food. In essence, I found myself with a lot more free time to direct my energies towards cooking and food preparation. Meals, in particular the dinner hour, became the highlight of the day and something to look forward to in the midst of so much angst and anxiety. Experimenting with new recipes became a major 'silver lining' for myself and my family this past year. During this time, my husband and I committed to helping our two young grandsons with remote schooling two days a week. I am thankful that we were able to quickly form a pod to support and help one another. At the beginning of the week we would talk about and plan dinners with the boys. We found ourselves reverting back to 'comfort foods' and the most repeated dish was eggplant Parmesan. The beauty of this meal is that there are usually leftovers that taste even better the next day! This recipe is gluten-free friendly for my own needs, but can be revised with regular bread crumbs as well."

2 medium eggplants
3-4 large eggs
Unseasoned bread crumbs, regular or gluten-free
2 jars of your favorite marinara sauce (I use Miccuci's)
28-ounce can crushed tomatoes
1 can tomato paste
3 basil leaves, fresh if you have them
1 teaspoon each: oregano, Italian seasoning, black pepper, sugar, parsley, garlic powder, onion powder
1 tablespoon olive oil
1 sweet onion, chopped
8 ounces fresh mushrooms, sliced
2 small peppers, sliced
2 teaspoons red wine
1 pound mixed cheese, shredded: Parmesan, mozzarella, manchego, aged goat
Extra oregano, for sprinkling

Preheat oven to 375 degrees.

Peel and slice the eggplant, either lengthwise or round. Slices should be medium-cut, not too thick. Beat the eggs in a shallow bowl and set aside. Place the breadcrumbs in another bowl, preferably a flat baking dish. Dip the eggplant slices in the egg mixture and coat lightly in the bread crumbs. Place the eggplant slices on a baking sheet lined with parchment paper that is coated with olive oil or coconut oil spray. Bake in the oven 10-15 minutes on each side. Do not overcook!

While the eggplant slices bake, in a separate large bowl, combine sauce with crushed tomatoes and tomato paste and seasonings.

In a large frying pan, heat olive oil over high heat. Fry onion, mushrooms, and sliced pepper, and add red wine to mixture while cooking. Stir this mixture into your sauce.

Shred the cheese and mix together in a large bowl.

To assemble the eggplant parm: Spread a layer of sauce on the bottom of a 9x13-inch rectangular baking dish. Place a layer of eggplant, then cheese, then sauce, and continue repeating the layers up to the top of the dish. Sprinkle cheese on the top and then sprinkle a small amount of oregano over the top of the cheese. Bake for 45-60 minutes.

Mushrooms in Sour Cream Sauce

Zhenya & Schelene Shevchenko • Gray, Cumberland County

"Zhenya grew up mushroom hunting in Ukraine with his parents and grandparents. In the Soviet Union, foraging mushrooms was a way to spend time with family and friends and put food on the table. When Zhenya came to Maine in 2000, he found many of the same mushrooms that he knew from Ukraine and learned some new ones by going mushroom hunting with locals. Zhenya has shared his love of mushroom hunting with me, and our two kids Nick and Lena. Mushrooms in sour cream sauce is a very common dish in Ukraine, but it always seems to surprise Mainers!"

Mushrooms - any variety!
Onions (optional)
Butter
Sour cream
Salt and pepper, to taste

Slice mushrooms and dice onions, if using. Add butter to a frying pan, place over medium-high heat, and then add mushrooms. We typically start with a tablespoon of butter and add more if needed—it will depend on the quantity of mushrooms you have. Once mushrooms are slightly soft, add onions, if you so choose. When mushrooms are soft and onions are translucent, add sour cream. Start with several tablespoons of sour cream and add more to taste—the amount of sour cream will depend on the quantity of mushrooms. Add salt and pepper to taste.

Turn to minimal heat and let simmer a little longer, stirring as needed. This mushroom sauce is wonderful over potatoes, rice, buckwheat, or meat. We also love it rolled in a crêpe.

Vegan Crab Cakes with Caper Tartar Sauce

Betsy Harding • South Portland, Cumberland County

"This recipe has been a favorite in our family for many years and has been passed down to the next generation and friends. We make them on special occasions and it has become a tradition for my husband and I to cook together on New Year's Eve!"

Caper Tartar Sauce:

1½ cups Vegenaise (found in the cooler section in your local grocery store)
1 tablespoon capers plus 1 tablespoon caper brine
1 tablespoon nutritional yeast
1 tablespoon Dijon mustard
1 teaspoon vegan Worcestershire sauce
1 tablespoon lemon juice
½ small shallot, diced

Vegan Crab Cakes:

1½ teaspoons plus 2 tablespoons canola oil
½ cup diced red onion
½ cup diced red pepper
Three 14-ounce cans hearts of palm
14-ounce can artichoke hearts
3 tablespoons toasted nori flakes
1 tablespoon Old Bay Seasoning
1 tablespoon nutritional yeast
2 tablespoons cornstarch
1 cup seasoned bread crumbs
2 cups panko breadcrumbs (for coating and cooking of cakes)
Sea salt and ground pepper, to taste

To make the caper tartar sauce: In a small bowl mix together all ingredients, cover, and refrigerate.

To make the vegan crab cakes: Heat 1½ teaspoons of oil in a medium sauce pan over medium heat. Add red onions and red pepper and sauté until soft, about 10 minutes. Let cool.

Drain hearts of palm and pat dry. Drain artichoke hearts and squeeze all excess water from the artichokes. In a large mixing bowl, combine sautéed mixture of onions and peppers, nori flakes, Old Bay Seasoning, nutritional yeast, cornstarch, and seasoned bread crumbs, stirring to mix. Carefully add drained hearts of palm and artichoke hearts, making sure to keep chunk-size pieces of hearts of palms and artichoke intact so the mixture resembles lumpy crab meat. Set aside.

Lightly oil a baking sheet. Place panko crumbs, salt, and pepper in a bowl. Use a large tablespoon to form mixture into small cakes. Coat the small cakes with breadcrumbs. Place on the baking sheet, using wax paper between layers of stacked cakes. Cover and refrigerate for 1 hour.

Heat 1 tablespoon of canola oil in a frying pan over medium-high heat. Working in batches, cook cakes for 5 minutes to brown on one side, then flip and cook for another 5 minutes. Add another tablespoon of oil and cook remaining cakes. Serve hot with caper tartar sauce.

Sally Lincoln's "Most Requested" Eastover Jell-O Mold

Leslie Oster • Augusta, Kennebec County

"My mother, Sally Lincoln, came from a long line of fine Maine Yankee stock and was famously green-eyed and redheaded. When she married my Jewish father and raised three brown-eyed, brown-haired girls, she aspired to bring the best traditions of the Jewish and Episcopal faiths into our family. Her Uncle Ed, an Episcopal priest, even helped preside over my Bat Mitzvah. Many years later, having found friends in Maine who had similar mish-mashed families, we started an annual Easter and Passover tradition we called Eastover. When last hosted before COVID, the celebration had about 200 friends, friends of friends, kids, dogs, cows, chickens and a few barn cats. This is perhaps everyone's favorite potluck of the year; sharing favorite family Easter and Passover recipes, breaking bread (and matzoh) with friends old and new, and looking with hope to the spring and a promising growing season. And every year, since its inception, Sally Lincoln—as she is always referred to by her first AND last name—was 'expected' to bring the time-honored, oft-requested Jell-O mold! She passed in April 2020 but not before bestowing upon me her famed Tupperware Jell-O mold pan!"

6-ounce package raspberry Jell-O
3 cups boiling water
14-ounce can whole berry cranberry sauce
8-ounce can crushed pineapple with juice
Bibb lettuce leaves and fresh pineapple chunks, to garnish

Dissolve Jell-O in hot water. Stir in cranberry sauce, pineapple and juice. Pour into a ring mold that has been spayed lightly with pan release spray or PAM. Refrigerate overnight to set.

Before serving, invert gently onto serving platter. Garnish with Bibb lettuce and fresh pineapple chunks. This is also served traditionally at Thanksgiving, Christmas and Rosh Hashanah … or just as a side with roast chicken dinner.

Italian Ratatouille

Gerri Stiles • Scarborough, Cumberland County

"My Italian grandmother always had a bountiful garden. I loved helping her do the harvesting (but not the weeding!) and canning the tomatoes, peppers and mushroom, and green beans. We made pickles with the cucumbers, and jelly from the grapes and the elderberries that always seemed to be plentiful. I no longer have a garden, so now as a Senior Farm Share participant, I buy my fruits and vegetables at Flaherty's Farm in Scarborough. One of the things I like to make is an Italian Ratatouille, as it full of luscious fresh veggies and I can adapt to what's available. I give it an Italian touch by adding some pine nuts and raisins, too, in a tribute to my Nonna, who instilled in me a love of cooking at a young age that I continue to have in my senior years. I love sharing the fruits of my labor with family and friends, and just as my Nonna instilled a love of cooking for me at a young age, so I too have instilled that in my granddaughter Samantha. I would pick her up every Wednesday after school from preschool through middle school for us to spend some quality time together. She started cooking with me at the age of three, and these cooking adventures continued. She is a graduate of the culinary arts program at Southern Maine Community College and is now head baker at Tuscan Table Restaurant in South Portland."

- 3 tablespoons extra virgin olive oil
- 1 onion, chopped
- 3 cloves garlic, minced
- 3 ribs celery, sliced
- 1 eggplant, cut into ¾-inch cubes
- 1 zucchini, quartered and sliced into ¾-inch pieces
- 1 summer squash, quartered and sliced into ¾-inch pieces
- 1 pepper, sliced and cut into ¾-inch pieces
- 2 pounds fresh tomatoes, peeled and diced, or 28-ounce can diced tomatoes
- 2 tablespoons tomato paste
- ¼ teaspoon red pepper flakes
- ½ teaspoon salt
- ¼ teaspoon pepper
- 1 tablespoon fresh parsley, chopped (or 1 teaspoon dried)
- 1 tablespoon fresh basil, torn into pieces (or 1 teaspoon dried)
- 1 tablespoon golden raisins
- 1 tablespoon pine nuts

In a Dutch oven, heat oil and sauté onion over high heat until translucent, 3-4 minutes. Reduce heat, add veggies, tomato paste, red pepper flakes, salt, and pepper, and slowly simmer 25-30 minutes. (Alternatively, you can bake in the oven at 350 degrees.) Add parsley, basil, raisins, and pine nuts and simmer 5-10 more minutes. Serve over pasta topped with cheese, or eat right out of the bowl as is! Enjoy!

Aspic Salad

Lynn Young • Gardiner, Kennebec County

"The night before my first Thanksgiving with my husband's family, we had all gathered at my sister-in-law's house in Sugarloaf. There was the usual buzz of preparing, lots of wine and laughter. Then someone asked 'Who's making the aspic salad?' 'What in God's name is aspic salad?' I asked. I had never heard of such a thing. I was told that aspic salad was lemon Jell-O mixed with tomato juice and crushed pineapple. 'Great,' they said 'with a little mayo.' 'What?!' It was a recipe that was handed down from my husband's grandmother and in this family it just isn't Thanksgiving or Christmas without it. It graces the table in a cream-colored ceramic dish with orange flowers. I'd like to say that I was polite and tried the salad, but I have a few rules about eating Jell-O. First it should only be eaten when one is too ill to eat solid food. Second, it should never contain bits of fruit. And last, but not least, it should absolutely not be consumed with mayonnaise! It took me fifteen years to try it (sans mayo). Let's just say I will stick to the stuffing and green bean casserole. So why would I share this recipe when I have such strong opinions about Jell-O? Over the years we have sat at the table together and told stories. You know the ones that get told over and over again, but always make you laugh. We began to call our collection of family stories 'Aspic Salad Stories.' I love those stories. When we get together, the room warms and the air buzzes with laughter. That togetherness, the family time has taken on a new appreciation since this last year of distancing. So that shallow, cream-colored ceramic dish with the orange flowers will forever hold a place in my heart."

1 cup tomato juice
6-ounce package lemon Jell-O (or other lemon gelatin)
¾ cup boiling water
Small can crushed pineapple with juice
Mayonnaise, for serving

Mix together the tomato juice, gelatin, and boiling water, in that order. Put in fridge until set slightly, approximately 1 hour. Stir in pineapple and refrigerate until completely set. Serve with or without mayonnaise.

Gemista (Stuffed Peppers and Tomatoes)

Evan and George Zarkadas • Bangor, Penobscot County

"Both my parents love to cook, but my father especially started cooking religiously when we left Greece and moved to America. I started cooking the moment I left home for college. The number one reason for both of us to get into cooking I suspect is from our nostalgia for our home. My dad and I both try to replicate our memories through food. When my dad cooks, he remembers his motherland in Greece, and when I cook, I remember my family and I actively practice my culture. The recipe that reminds me the most of my home and Greece is gemista! It is the most refreshing and fulfilling, summery and yummy!"

3-4 potatoes
6-8 tablespoons olive oil, separated, plus more for drizzling
3 tomatoes
3 bell peppers
Salt and pepper, to taste

Filling:
1 onion, chopped
1 clove garlic, chopped
1 carrot, shredded
1 zucchini, shredded
1 tablespoon sugar
1 cup rice
1 tablespoon tomato paste
14 ounces water
1 bunch each: fresh dill, parsley, mint

Feta cheese, for serving
Oregano, for serving
Bread, for serving

Preheat oven to 400 degrees.

To prepare the potatoes: Place a large, heavy-bottomed pan over high heat and let it get very hot. Wash and scrub the potatoes, then cut them into wedges. Add 2 tablespoons of olive oil to the pan and add the potatoes. Season with salt and pepper and sauté for 4-5 minutes, just until golden. Using a slotted spoon, remove potatoes from pan, spread them in a baking dish and set aside.

To prepare the tomatoes and peppers: Slice off the bottoms of the tomatoes. Slice the tops off of the bell peppers, cutting just under the stem and paring a little off the bottom to help them stand better. Scoop out most of the inner layers of the tomatoes leaving a sturdy shell. Make sure you are careful, so you do not rip the outer shell. Chop all of the inner layers that you removed from the tomatoes and peppers. Put them in a bowl and set aside to be used for the filling. Place the hollow vegetables in the baking dish with the potatoes.

To make the filling: Place a large, heavy-bottomed pan or Dutch oven over high heat and add roughly 4 tablespoons olive oil. Add your chopped onion and garlic and sauté. Stir in the grated carrot and zucchini and sauté. Sprinkle granulated sugar over the pan, mix and sauté until the vegetables caramelize nicely. Add a generous amount of salt and freshly ground pepper. Stir in the rice and sauté for 3-4 minutes, until it turns light golden. Add the tomato paste, stir to incorporate, and sauté. Pour in the water and the reserved tomato and green pepper flesh. Let the mixture simmer for 5 minutes. Stir and remove from heat. The rest of the cooking will resume in the oven. Finely chop the parsley, dill, and mint leaves and add them to the pan. Stir.

To assemble the stuffed vegetables: Drizzle potatoes, tomatoes, and green peppers in the baking pan with a generous amount of olive oil, both inside and out and season with salt and pepper. Use a spoon to add the filling to the vegetables. Fill each cavity ¾ of the way because the rice will expand while cooking. Spoon any of the leftover filling over the potatoes to add even more flavor. Add additional water to the pan just enough to cover the potatoes halfway and drizzle with olive oil. Cover with aluminum foil and bake for about 1 hour. Check in about 30 minutes. Remove foil and bake for another 10-20 minutes, until most of the liquid has evaporated and the stuffed vegetables are cooked and golden.

To serve, drizzle with some extra virgin olive oil, and top with some oregano and a slice of feta cheese, with a slice of good bread on the side, and enjoy!

Salade Verte a la Creme (Salad Greens with Cream)

Faye Macomber • Old Town, Penobscot County

"My father, Leo Dionne of Caribou, used to make this salad. It's exactly the way he used to make it."

- 1 pound leaf lettuce
- ⅓ cup sour cream
- Sugar and salt, to taste
- Scallions, chopped

Thoroughly wash each lettuce leaf. Mix the sour cream with sugar and salt to taste in a bowl. Add the scallions and toss all together with the lettuce. Serve immediately.

Black Trumpet Mac & Cheese

Shawn Saindon • Warren, Knox County

"As an aspiring cheesemaker, I'm a fan of all things cheesy. This basic mac and cheese recipe here is a staple in our house, and is often the base for using up all kinds of veggies from the garden—some favorite combinations are butternut squash and spinach, or broccoli and zucchini, or sometimes we get real fancy and make lobster mac and cheese. It's versatile enough to experiment with lots of different additional ingredients, but this year, a bumper crop of wild black trumpet mushrooms in our neighborhood inspired this version, which I think could rival any of the mac and cheese dishes with Italian truffles I've tasted over the years (this is not meant to offend my beloved Italian friends, but it's true!)."

Mushrooms:
2 tablespoons butter
2 cups fresh black trumpet mushrooms (or other type of foraged edible mushroom; cultivated is fine, too!)

Mac & Cheese:
½ cup (1 stick) unsalted butter
½ cup flour (see Note)
4 cups whole milk
1 tablespoon salt
1 teaspoon dried, ground yellow mustard
Pinch nutmeg
3 cups shredded cheddar cheese
1 cup shredded Parmesan cheese
1 pound dried pasta (preferably penne or fusilli)
Fine breadcrumbs or panko, if desired

Note: Gluten-free baking mix can be used instead here, and gluten-free pasta works just fine with this recipe, as well.

In a skillet, melt 2 tablespoons of butter over medium heat. Add whole black trumpet mushrooms, and sauté until they start to wilt. (Note: Black trumpets are quite delicate and won't take much time to cook. Other types of mushrooms may need to be cut up and/or cooked longer, depending on their size, thickness, and other qualities.) Remove from heat and set aside while preparing the mac and cheese.

Preheat oven to 400 degrees. Start a pot of water to cook the pasta and add it when boiling.

Meanwhile, in a large, heavy-bottomed pot, melt butter over medium heat. Add flour and whisk together for a minute or so as it bubbles. Begin to add milk, about ¼ cup at a time, while whisking constantly. It will thicken up a bit each time after incorporating milk for the first few times, then relax to a thinner consistency.

Once all milk is fully incorporated, add salt, ground mustard, and nutmeg. Continue cooking and stirring until the mixture thickens enough to coat the back of a spoon. By now, your pasta may be cooked (aim for al dente) and ready to drain.

To the milk mixture, add cheese and stir until fully melted. Then add drained pasta and mushrooms and stir until evenly combined. Pour pasta into a buttered 9x13-inch baking pan. Sprinkle with breadcrumbs or panko if desired. Bake for 20-25 minutes.

Dad's "Feed Me Now I'm Starving" Spaghetti

Diane Lukac • Freeport, Cumberland County

"I grew up in a family of four and my house was where many friends gathered, especially around supper time. My father loved to cook, and he could cook anything. He was self-taught. This was unusual in my father's day in the 1940s-60s but that is the way it was in our home. Dad was the cook. Everyone loved his food, and as a result, all of his children are instinctive cooks. Male or female, we are the primary cooks in our households. When we were growing up, money was tight and we were always telling Dad that we were starving. He was constantly able to come up with delicious meals for us with ingredients on hand. This was one everyone loved, including his grandchildren. We miss him so much."

1 pound good quality spaghetti
½ head garlic
¼ cup extra virgin olive oil
2 tablespoons tomato paste
Kosher salt, to taste
Fresh basil

Cook spaghetti in large pot with plenty of boiling salted water until al dente. While spaghetti is cooking, take the garlic and separate the head into cloves. Remove the skins, and slice the cloves lengthwise into very thin pieces. Heat oil in a large skillet, add garlic, and cook until fragrant (do not brown). Add tomato paste and cook, swirling it around the pan with a wooden spoon. Add the salt and mix until it is incorporated. Once the pasta is finished cooking, use tongs to add directly to pan and mix all the ingredients together. Finally, toss in the basil and serve.

Leek and Broccoli Cheese Pie

Mona Grandbois • Biddeford, York County

"I can't honestly say that this is an old family recipe. In fact, I can't remember ever eating anything even mildly resembling quiche when I was growing up. So think of it more as a 'new and ever evolving' family recipe. Cheese pie was on the menu fairly often when my children were young. It was made with whatever leftovers were in the refrigerator—ham, broccoli, spinach, Brussels sprouts, etc. I vaguely remember once quickly dismissing a suggestion for pepperoni quiche. Today, when I make it, I try to incorporate as many local ingredients as I can and this recipe is the closest I have come to an 'all Maine' cheese pie. Thanks to the numerous farmer's markets in Southern Maine, every ingredient, except for the olive oil and pepper, is grown or made in Maine."

Crust:
2 cups grated potato
¼ cup minced onion
1 egg, beaten
Salt
Olive oil

Filling:
2 tablespoons butter
1 cup leeks, halved lengthwise and thinly sliced
1 cup small broccoli florets
½ teaspoon thyme
4 eggs, beaten
1 cup heavy cream
1 ½ cups grated cheese (cheddar and Gruyere are a nice combination, and both can be found at Maine creameries)
Salt and pepper, to taste

To make the crust: Salt the grated potato and place in a colander to drain for 10-15 minutes. Squeeze as much water out of the potatoes as possible, then combine them with the onion and beaten egg.

Generously oil a 9-inch deep dish pie plate with olive oil. Spread the potato mixture evenly on the bottom and sides of the pie plate. Bake in a 400-degree oven for 30 minutes, until set. If the edge begins to brown too quickly, cover it with a ring of foil. When the crust is set and slightly brown, remove from the oven and let it cool.

To make the filling: Over medium heat, melt the butter in a heavy-bottomed pan and sauté the leeks and broccoli florets until they are soft. Add the thyme and remove from heat to cool.

In a medium-size bowl, beat together the eggs and the heavy cream. Spread half the cheese in the bottom of the cooled crust. Top with the leek and broccoli mixture and finish with the rest of the cheese. Pour the egg and cream mixture over the filling.

Bake in a 425-degree oven for 20 minutes. Lower the temperature to 350 degrees and bake for 30 minutes more, or until a knife inserted in the pie comes out clean. Let rest for 15 minutes before serving.

Polish Pasta (aka Really Lazy Pierogies)

Amy Paradysz • Scarborough, Cumberland County

"While loving sauerkraut, mushrooms and cheese may be in my genes, making pierogies (Polish dumplings) from scratch sure isn't. Who has the time for that? Instead, I replicate the basic flavors with what my daughter and I call 'Polish pasta'—an even easier and lazier alternative to casserole-style 'lazy pierogies.' You can't really mess this up! This is our favorite immune-boosting comfort dinner."

1 onion, diced
Several fresh mushrooms (about half a box), chopped
2 tablespoons butter (or vegan butter)
1 can or jar of sauerkraut
1 pound pasta (macaroni or ditalini are a good size, but any shape is fine)
Handful of shredded mozzarella cheese or heaping spoonful of ricotta cheese (optional)
Parmesan cheese, to serve (optional)

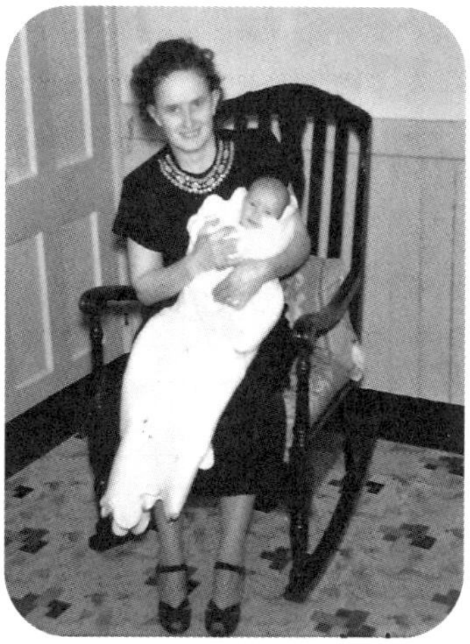

Cut up an onion and a large handful or two of mushrooms, and sauté those in a couple of tablespoons of butter (we use vegan non-dairy butter). Add the can of sauerkraut—including all the "juice"—into the saucepan with the onion and mushroom mixture and let that simmer.

Cook the pasta according to the instructions on the box. Drain cooked pasta and mix it together with the contents of the saucepan and remove from heat.

If you have any non-dairy eaters, serve them before adding a bit of shredded cheese or ricotta to the hot pasta-and-vegetable mixture (totally optional, but if cheese pierogies are your thing, go for it). Serve with Parmesan cheese. Makes 4-6 servings.

Zucchini and Corn Pancakes

Victor Trodella • Yarmouth, Cumberland County

"I created this recipe after travel to the Southwest and time spent in my garden. It's great for brunch, lunch, dinner, or a side dish—this will forever change how you see zucchini. Everyone loves it!"

1 serrano pepper, minced, seeds and pulp
1½ cups shredded zucchini (see Note)
1 cup cooked corn (sliced from cob is best, or use well-drained canned corn)
½ cup minced Vidalia sweet onion
½ cup all-purpose unbleached flour
½ teaspoon salt
½ teaspoon freshly ground black pepper
1 teaspoon baking powder
2 eggs, separated
Corn oil to cover bottom of frying pan

Note: Be sure to drain the shredded zucchini well to remove excess moisture. If you are using a Costata Romanesco zucchini, however, draining is not necessary.

Place the serrano pepper, zucchini, corn, and onion in a large bowl and and mix well. Add the flour, salt, black pepper, and baking powder, and mix well, using a spatula or clean hands. Beat the egg yolks and mix them well into the vegetables.

In a separate small bowl, beat the egg whites until they stiffen. Using a spatula, fold them gently into the vegetable and egg mixture.

Heat the oil in a nonstick skillet over medium-high heat. Use a large spoon to scoop the zucchini batter into fritters, and slip them into the hot oil. Fry until lightly browned on each side, turning once gently. Serve hot, accompanied by your favorite salsa. Serves 6.

Tomatoes Cooked Like Oysters

1910 • Woolwich Grange Cook Book

Woolwich Grange Committee • Woolwich, Sagadahoc County

The Woolwich Grange was built in 1900 and the building still stands on a bend in Route 1 across from the Montsweag Flea Market. It's also a stone's throw from the Back River, which explains why oysters were so familiar to the compilers of this cookbook. Tomatoes Cooked Like Oysters is not quite a "mock" dish, though there are others, like Corn Oysters on the same page. The recipe is instead instructions for using a familiar cooking technique (stewing oysters) with a less familiar ingredient (tomatoes). —DL

Scald and peel three large ripe tomatoes, cook till nearly done, then put in soda (as large as a pea) to make it foam, add milk, salt, pepper, butter, etc., as in an oyster stew. This is good eaten with crackers. —Mrs. Nettie Walker

Barley Waldorf Salad

2010 • Tasteful Treasures

Clark F. Miller School of Radiologic Technology Class of 2010 •
Lewiston, Androscoggin County

Community cookbooks do more than just raise funds for causes. They also help bond contributors through the enjoyable, mutual activity of sharing recipes. Radiological tech students at Central Maine Med's Miller School take a break from the academics and training to get to know each other a bit better through food, and raise money for their commencement ceremony and celebration at the same time. —DL

- ¾ cup regular barley
- 3¾ cups water
- ¾ teaspoon salt
- ¼ cup plain low-fat yogurt
- 3 tablespoons light mayonnaise or salad dressing
- ¼ teaspoon finely shredded lemon peel
- 1 tablespoon lemon juice
- ¼ teaspoon sugar
- 1½ cups seedless red or green grapes, halved
- 1 medium apple, cored and chopped
- ½ cup chopped celery
- ¼ cup chopped walnuts, toasted
- Additional seedless grapes for garnish, optional
- Lemon peel strips for garnish, optional

In a 3 quart saucepan, toast barley over medium to low heat for 4-5 minutes, or until barley is golden, stirring occasionally. Add water and ¼ teaspoon of the salt. Bring to boiling, reduce heat to medium-low. Cover and simmer for about 45 minutes, until tender. Let stand for 30 minutes to cool. In a large bowl, whisk together yogurt, mayonnaise, shredded lemon peel, lemon juice, sugar, and remaining salt. Stir in cooked barley, 1½ cups grapes, the apple and celery. Sprinkle with walnuts, and garnish with additional grapes and lemon peel strips if desired. —Shana Nowinski, *LVT, Radiology Student*

SHELLS
PLEASE

FISH & SHELLFISH

Photo: The Harmon family, Dorothy and Gilbert, with daughters Nancy and Jane, at the lobster pound at Spruce Head in 1950. Nancy's family recipe for Maine Fish Chowder can be found on page 81.

Maggie's Seafood Medley

Margaret Brandes • Portland, Cumberland County

"Sadly, I was not born in Maine, but my roots are here. My mother's family settled in Maine hundreds of years ago in the Bath, Brunswick, Harpswell area. My mother, who was a welder on the Liberty Ships in South Portland during World War II, met and married my father, who was a sailor stationed in Portland. They moved to New Jersey where I was raised. Every year we would return to Maine. Many times we would visit her uncle who was a lobsterman in Harpswell. It was during these visits that I developed my love for Maine seafood, which inspired me to create this recipe. Happily, I now call Maine 'home'."

4 tablespoons butter, separated
3 tablespoons olive oil, separated
3 shallots, finely chopped
1 clove garlic, finely chopped
3 tablespoons parsley, chopped
3 tablespoons fresh basil, chopped
4 tablespoons tomato paste
3 strands saffron
¼ cup brandy
1 cup dry white wine
1 bottle clam juice
1¼ pounds Atlantic salmon
½ pound cooked lobster meat, picked from shells
1 pound Maine sea scallops, muscles removed
½ cup cream

In a large, heavy-bottomed skillet, heat 2 tablespoons each of butter and olive oil over medium-high heat. Add shallots and garlic, and sauté until fragrant but not browned, 3-5 minutes. Stir in parsley, basil, tomato paste, saffron strands, brandy, wine, and clam juice. Reduce heat and simmer slowly for 1 hour, taking care not to burn. Remove from heat and set aside while you prepare the seafood.

Rinse and pat dry the salmon, then drizzle with remaining tablespoon of olive oil. Grill fish until almost done, but slightly undercooked. While the salmon is on the grill, cut lobster meat into medium-size pieces and sauté in remaining 2 tablespoons of butter.

Return the tomato mixture to medium heat and add the scallops. Simmer until scallops are just done, being careful not to overcook. Add the sautéed lobster and the grilled salmon, using a fork to break up the salmon as you add it. Cook over medium heat, adding more wine, if needed. Stir in the cream. Serve over pasta.

Cast-Iron Roasted Salmon Fillet with Hoisin Sauce

Chris Toy • Bath, Sagadahoc County

"This recipe is kind of a Downeast-Far East fusion dish combining Chinese BBQ hoisin sauce; the three part Chinese flavor base ginger, garlic, and scallions; Maine maple syrup; and fresh local salmon. The dish connects the Chinese cooking techniques that I learned from my mother, Grace, with the fresh, local Maine ingredients I came to love in college at Bowdoin and as a Registered Maine Guide. I now use maple syrup made with sap tapped from my own trees. This is one of my first recipes from when I started teaching cooking back in the 1970s at the Whip and Spoon in Portland's Old Port."

2 tablespoons vegetable oil
½ cup hoisin sauce
¼ cup Maine maple syrup
2 tablespoons rice wine
1 teaspoon spicy sesame oil
2 tablespoons fresh ginger, crushed and chopped
4 cloves fresh garlic, crushed and chopped
4 whole scallions, minced
2 pounds fresh salmon fillet, skin on

Lightly oil a cast-iron griddle or large oven-safe frypan. Adjust the oven rack so the griddle sits 2-3 inches under the broiler. Set the broiler to high and let it heat up for 5-10 minutes or until the oil just begins to smoke.

In a bowl mix together the hoisin sauce, maple syrup, wine, sesame oil, ginger, garlic, and scallions.

With a sharp knife make diagonal crosscuts 1 inch apart about ¾ of the way through the salmon fillet. You should have a grid of diamond shaped cuts across the filet.

Spread the mixture evenly over the fish, pressing it into the cuts.

Using one or two large spatulas slide the fish onto the hot griddle and broil it for 5-7 minutes for medium rare salmon. Add 1-2 minutes for medium, and another 2-4 minutes for well done. Remove the entire griddle from the oven and place on a heatproof tray to serve with steamed rice and vegetables.

Maine Fiddle Camp Mussels

Kate Wallace • Bowdoinham, Sagadahoc County

"The Maine Fiddle Camp kitchen is a special place. Set in the middle of the bustling music camp, it is both central to the daily rhythm of camp and also a world of its own. We wake to birdsong and smoke rising off the pond while firing up the ovens in the outdoor kitchen and drinking a morning cup of coffee. The kitchen is powered mostly by volunteers, and we make just about everything from scratch. For the weeks we are together at camp, we become a small family, banded together with the mission of feeding three meals a day to 250 to 400 hungry mouths.

One of our most beloved meals at Maine Fiddle Camp is pasta dinner, which always includes a huge batch of mussels. We get our mussels from Pemaquid Mussel Farm, founded by Carter Newell who was instrumental in the creation of Maine Fiddle Camp. Mussels are an amazing local source of protein and we are lucky to live in a place with such abundance. On what is usually a hot afternoon in August, we get a delivery of 80-100 pounds of mussels on ice, and right away we get to work on them. The kitchen is chaotic to the untrained eye—volunteers cooking and reheating pasta, stirring tomato sauces so they don't burn, chopping vegetables and roasting them on pans, and spreading garlic butter on fresh-made rolls. Hungry musicians are lining up with empty plates and big appetites. And in the midst of all this activity, we can't forget the mussels! Working in small batches with four pans going at once, we cook them as detailed in the following recipe."

2 pounds mussels
4 tablespoons butter, separated
2-3 cloves garlic
1½ cups white wine
¼ cup heavy cream or half-and-half
Handful parsley, chopped, for garnish

Pick over your mussels, removing any that are cracked or obviously dead. Rinse and beard them if necessary.

Melt 2 tablespoons of butter over high heat in a sauté pan. Add half the garlic and cook until it becomes fragrant, 30-60 seconds. Add half the mussels (1 pound) and ¾ cup of wine. Cover with a glass lid so you can watch what is happening in the pan. Observation of the bubbles is the key to knowing when the mussels are cooked. When the bubbles become small and tight, like little soap bubbles, your mussels are ready to go. This usually takes about 5-10 minutes. When the first batch is done, dump the cooked mussels into a metal bowl. Repeat with the second pound of mussels and remaining butter, garlic, and wine.

Drizzle with heavy cream or half-and-half, sprinkle with parsley, and serve right away.

Steuben Side-Walk Society Oyster Stew

Patricia Worth • Belfast, Waldo County

"My mother, Ruth Brown Goodridge (later Ruth Meigs), was born at home in Steuben in 1918. She was a great cook in the 'good plain healthy food' tradition. Once in a while on Thanksgiving or Christmas eve, she'd serve oyster stew using the Side-Walk Society recipe. I think she varied it, though, by adding whole milk and Worcestershire sauce. Delicious."

1 quart shucked raw oysters
½ pint heavy cream
3 tablespoons unsalted butter
Salt and pepper, to taste

Simmer the oysters in their own liquor over low heat. Just before they boil, remove pan from heat, then remove oysters and set aside. Skim the liquid surface well. Add the cream, butter, and salt and pepper to the hot oyster liquor. Heat carefully. Return oysters to the pot. Serve with toast or crackers.

Scalloped Scallops

Diane Mann • Lubec, Washington County

"This recipe is a family favorite, and loved at Down East potluck dinners."

1½ pounds scallops
¼ teaspoon salt
1½ cups crushed crackers
⅓ cup melted butter
3 tablespoons light cream
Dash of pepper and paprika

Preheat oven to 425 degrees. Wash and drain the scallops. Season with salt. In a medium-size bowl, toss the cracker crumbs and butter together. In a 9-inch pie plate, arrange alternate layers of crackers crumbs and scallops. Pour cream over the top and sprinkle with pepper and paprika. Bake for 30 minutes. Delicious.

Mother's Crabmeat Quiche

Geri Gay • Machias, Washington County

"My family was in the grocery business and were early Hannaford owner operators in Milbridge, Machias, and Calais. In our remote Washington County home, we had lots of dried salt fish dinners, bean hole beans, clam chowder, wild Maine blueberry pies and pancakes. And of course, lobster. My mother had a fantastic crabmeat quiche recipe, and crabmeat was readily available at several homes along the coast in Hancock and Washington counties. One summer day my mother and I noticed a sign on Route 1 that said 'Fresh Crabmeat' with an arrow pointing down a peninsula. We found the house and knocked on the door. My mother asked the woman at the door if she had any fresh crabmeat. The woman said she was out, but her daughter had some crabmeat. We asked where her daughter lived. She said, 'Go up Wyman Road, take a left onto Dyer's Bay Road and another right at Back Bay Road, another left onto Smith Creek Road and take a left by mailboxes before a steep hill on a dirt road.' We decided it sounded too complicated to drive to her daughter's house. As we started to leave she said, 'But if you want crabmeat, my daughter is here now and in the house.'"

- Pastry for single crust pie
- 8-10 ounces crabmeat
- 1 cup grated cheese or mixture of cheeses
- 1 onion, chopped
- 3 eggs
- 1 cup half-and-half or heavy cream
- ¼ teaspoon salt
- ¼ teaspoon dry mustard

Preheat oven to 350 degrees. Line a 9-inch pie tin with pastry crust.

Sprinkle crabmeat, cheese and chopped onion into the bottom of the pie crust.

Next, make the custard. In a medium-sized bowl, lightly beat eggs and whisk in the cream, salt, and mustard. Pour custard mixture over crabmeat.

Bake in preheated oven for about 40 minutes, or until mixture is lightly browned and the custard is firm in the center. Allow quiche to settle for 15 minutes before serving.

Artwork: Crab Fisherman in pencil and watercolor by Geri Gay

Broiled Pesto Oysters

Jim Birkett • Nobleboro, Lincoln County

"At one point a family member was instructed for medical reasons to avoid raw seafood. It seemed cruel for the rest of us to pig out on raw oysters while she sat quietly by. That was our introduction to Oysters Rockefeller and all its variations. This recipe differs from those you might find elsewhere by adding a preliminary blanching step that turns raw oysters from amorphous blobs into discrete entities which you might actually want to eat."

As many oysters as you want
Pesto sauce (see Note)
Bread crumbs
Grated Parmesan cheese

Note: For the pesto sauce you can use your favorite family recipe, store bought, or the Kelp Pesto recipe found on page 152.

Shuck oysters into a small saucepan with their liquor. Place the lower shells, bowls facing up, on a broiler pan. Lightly poach the oysters in their own liquor, cooking for no more than 2 minutes. Drain oysters onto paper toweling and replace them in their shells. Put a heaping teaspoon of pesto sauce on each oyster, then sprinkle generously with bread crumbs. Top with grated Parmesan cheese. Broil until bread crumbs are browned, cheese is melted and pesto is bubbling, roughly 4 to 6 minutes. Serve immediately, but remind guests that shells are very hot!

Cod Sounds and Tongues

Joan Gregoire • Nobleboro, Lincoln County

"My grandmother, Lydia Ford Keene, grew up in Bremen, and was a teacher at Lincoln Academy in Newcastle. In 1899, she sailed from New York to San Francisco as a tutor for the captain's daughter on the *John R. Kelly*, a wooden ship of 2,364 tons, built in Bath. Her Sailing Diary from that voyage contains this entry, from April 15: 'Near Equator. It is cool enough for me to eat. The food is so different from what I thought it would be, I am going to write our bill of fare...Breakfast, 8 o'clock: Oatmeal, eggs, fried potatoes, bacon, tongues and sounds, cold graham bread, hot rolls, fritters, and coffee.'

We were curious about 'Sounds and Tongues.' Cod sounds are the swim bladder, and the tongues are a muscle taken from the back of a cod's neck. Both were considered delicacies at the time. This recipe was in my grandmother's Blue Ribbon Cookbook, attributed to Mrs. Frances Curry."

Soak, scrape, and boil, as many cod sounds as required. Drain them, and put them into a stew-pan with sufficient white stock to cover them; season the sauce with salt, pepper, and powdered mace, thicken it with a lump of butter rolled in flour, and, just before serving it, squeeze in the juice of a lemon. Serve with egg sauce.

Clam Fritters

1912 • Cook Book "Something Good for Company"

The Ladies' Wesleyan Society of the Park St., M.E. Church • Milo, Piscataquis County

This is an example of a community cookbook issued by a local ladies' society within a church but produced elsewhere. Except for the title and the advertising on the covers, all of the content of this book was supplied by the Amherst Cook Book Co. of Amherst, Mass. This very same Clam Fritter recipe can be found in identical community cookbooks produced in Sparta, Wisconsin; Granite Falls, Minnesota; and Dover, New Hampshire. Despite its origins elsewhere, this recipe made its way into homes in Maine. —DL

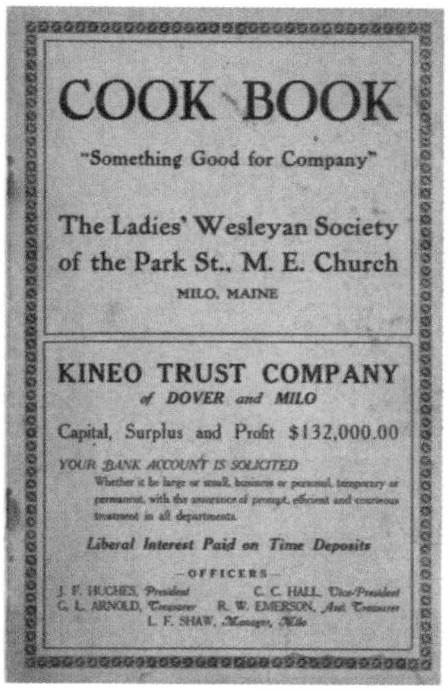

COOK BOOK

"Something Good for Company"

The Ladies' Wesleyan Society of the Park St., M. E. Church

MILO, MAINE

KINEO TRUST COMPANY

of DOVER and MILO

Capital, Surplus and Profit $132,000.00

YOUR BANK ACCOUNT IS SOLICITED

Whether it be large or small, business or personal, temporary or permanent, with the assurance of prompt, efficient and courteous treatment in all departments.

Liberal Interest Paid on Time Deposits

—OFFICERS—

J. F. HUGHES, *President* C. C. HALL, *Vice-President*

G. L. ARNOLD, *Treasurer* R. W. EMERSON, *Asst. Treasurer*

L. F. SHAW, *Manager, Milo*

One egg, one cup milk, 1 and one half cup flour, one teaspoon baking powder, salt. Squeeze black from clams, chop rims, and add to batter. Fry by spoonfuls in deep fat.

Fish Balls

Matt Dunlap • Old Town, Penobscot County

"Maine's state seal shouts out how important the sea and the land were to our early economy, with a farmer—'husbandman', according to the 1820 committee report recommending the device—on one side, and a seaman on the other. While the land and sea still say a lot about who we are, they use a somewhat different language.

Henry Cleaves, governor of Maine in 1895, stated the situation regarding farming's place in our economy bluntly in his inaugural address: 'When we consider that there are sixty-five thousand farms in Maine, containing 6,552,578 acres...we can fully appreciate that this great interest should never have a secondary place in our efforts to advance the prosperity of the Commonwealth.'

Henry Cleaves

But the world was changing under Governor Cleaves' feet, and over the next eighty years, Maine lost something like 90% of its farming capacity. Changing technologies—how we obtain, preserve, and prepare foods—allowed for the globalization of food production that we use today.

As Maine's farms disappeared, state government leapt into action. During the Depression, when Maine's towns lost 50% of their tax valuation, Governor Louis Brann declined a salary, and the Legislature slashed the state budget by nearly 70%, the Economic Development Commission used scarce tax dollars to produce a series of lovely cookbooks to promote Maine produce and seafood. One, *The State of Maine's Best Seafood Recipes*, was released just at the end of World War II.

To tell this story, the Maine State Archives invited me to host a cooking demonstration using some of these old recipes. I selected fish balls partly because it contains most of the elements of fish chowder presented in an entirely different way, but also because the dish was a favorite of the Speaker of the U.S. House of Representatives Thomas Brackett Reed of Portland, known as 'Czar Reed' for his ferocious governance of Congress. He noted in his diary that he 'love(d) fish balls, although they make me fat.'

Thomas Reed

Like many old recipes, this is elegant in its simplicity. At the cooking demonstration, generously hosted by the R. M. Flagg Kitchen School in Veazie, one of the news cameramen remarked to me that his grandmother had made the recipe when he was a kid. 'These taste just like hers,' he smiled. Another recipe for fish balls calls for an 'egg-milk sauce', which is effectively a bechamel with chopped up hard-boiled eggs; I think that was also to cut the bite of the salt cod. The beauty of this simple recipe is that you can experiment with different elements and make it your own. The recipe that follows is from the original cookbook, with my notes."

6 or 7 medium-sized potatoes
1 pint finely picked salt fish (salt cod can be found in many grocery stores)
2 eggs
Grated onion (in the original, this is not listed as an ingredient, but is noted in the method)
1 tablespoon melted butter or butter substitute
Pepper, to taste
Flour or cracker crumbs

Pare the potatoes and put in a kettle with salt fish on top. (Another recipe calls for soaking the salt cod for several hours or overnight in water to extract much of the saltiness; I recommend this procedure.)

Cover with boiling water and boil one-half hour. Drain and mash together potatoes, fish, beaten eggs, butter and pepper to taste. Add grated onion to taste. Beat all together until light, and cool slightly. Make into balls and roll well in flour or cracker crumbs. Fry golden brown in very hot (385 degree) fat. Do not crowd when frying; be sure fat is thoroughly heated. This makes fourteen small balls. (For an authentic demonstration, I used hot lard; but that may contribute to Speaker Reed's lament about these making him fat!)

When canned or packaged fish are used in this recipe, add the fish directly to the hot potatoes and mash together with seasonings until light. These fish balls may be mixed in advance and prepared, even to crumbing, to fry at the last minute.

From 2005 to 2011 and 2013 to 2021, Matt Dunlap was Secretary of State of Maine, a role that involves overseeing the Maine State Archives, recipes included.

Gram Strout's Macaroni Salad

Brian Stanley • Portland, Cumberland County

"My grandmother, Ava Waterhouse Strout, was a lifelong registered nurse and the administrator of the small community hospital in Milo. She and my grandfather, George Strout, Sr. loved Milo dearly and did what they could to give back to the community and make it better. My grandmother was not the world's best cook, by any stretch of the imagination, but she used to make this macaroni salad every summer. One bite of this salad brings me back to their house in Milo, the sound of the Red Sox on the television in the background and the smell of fresh cut grass blowing in through the open windows. This recipe brings them back to me for a brief moment."

2-pound box elbow macaroni
1 large green pepper, diced into small pieces
1 large yellow onion, diced into small pieces
4-5 radishes, diced into small pieces
1 large seedless cucumber, peeled, quartered, and sliced
6 large eggs, hard-boiled, cooled, and cut into small pieces
2-3 cans baby shrimp, drained and mashed with fork
2 tablespoons white vinegar
3 tablespoons French's yellow mustard
1 cup Hellman's mayonnaise
Salt and pepper, to taste

Note: This recipe makes a fair amount of Macaroni Salad. I find that none of the amounts of ingredients are exact and this is truly a recipe that should be amended and tweaked to suit you and your family's personal taste. A diced red pepper can be added, if desired. Picked Maine lobster or drained canned white tuna can be used in place of the baby shrimp.

Boil the macaroni and then drain and rinse with cold water to cool. I sometimes let the macaroni sit in a bit of cold water for a bit before assembling the salad.

In a quite large mixing bowl or large pot, mix the veggies together. Mix the cut up eggs gently in with the veggies. Add the mashed baby shrimp to this mixture. At this point, I generally dump one of the tablespoons of white vinegar into the mixture.

If you have left the macaroni in its cold water bath, drain and gradually mix it in with the mixture of veggies, eggs, and the baby shrimp. Add the mustard, mayonnaise, as well the remainder of the white vinegar. Add the salt and pepper, to taste, and mix together. Refrigerate and enjoy!

LOBSTER

Photo: 101-year-old lobsterwoman Virginia Oliver at the helm of her son Max's lobster boat, "Virginia." Her late husband, Bill, who fished and lobstered until he was 90, named the boat after her. Virginia's recipe for Lobster Thermidor can be found on page 150.

Lobster Thermidor

Virginia Oliver • Rockland, Knox County

At 101 years old, Virginia Oliver is the state's oldest licensed lobster harvester. When she was a child, she hauled wooden traps with her dad. Now, more than nine decades later, she and her 78-year-old son, Max, go out on the same water, with Virginia piloting her late husband's 34-foot boat, also called *Virginia*. Rockland has changed a lot over the course of her life, but lobstering hasn't—except that there are now more women on the water, and fewer lobsters to be found. Also unchanged is Oliver's love of lobster; she still cooks it at least once a week. —MH

- 2 tablespoons butter
- 2 tablespoons chopped onion
- ½ cup sliced button mushrooms
- 2 tablespoons flour
- ¼ teaspoon salt
- ⅛ teaspoon pepper
- ⅛ teaspoon paprika
- ½ cup cream
- ½ cup chicken broth
- ½ teaspoon Worcestershire sauce
- 1 egg yolk
- 2 cups cooked lobster meat, cut into pieces
- 3 tablespoons finely crumbled butter crackers or dry bread crumbs

Preheat oven to 450 degrees. In a large skillet, melt the butter and sauté onion and mushrooms. Sprinkle in flour and seasonings, and stir to blend. Cook over low heat until bubbly.

Remove pan from heat and stir in cream, chicken broth, and Worcestershire sauce. Bring mixture to boil, stirring constantly. Boil 1 minute. Stir in egg yolk, then add lobster.

Place mixture in a casserole dish and sprinkle with butter cracker crumbs or dry bread crumbs. Bake 5 minutes.

Lobster Salad with Lemon-Basil Mayo and Fresh Tomatoes

Mindy Fox • Portland, Cumberland County

"I've loved lobster for as long as I can remember. My parents, avid cooks, boiled it for butter-dunking, creamy risottos, paellas, chowders and stews. When I was old enough to cook it myself, I boiled mine too, never questioning the popular technique. Later, as a young line cook at a trendy Asian-fusion restaurant in Cambridge, Massachusetts, I learned to cook lobster tempura-style—split live to order, the flesh side battered and pan fried. A highlight of my career (and lifetime!) was making that dish for Julia Child, when she unexpectedly dropped in for dinner and afterwards joined us starstruck cooks in the kitchen to thank us for her meal!

When I later moved to Maine with my husband Steve, a Little Deer Isle lobsterman and his two ace lobstering kids let me in on a secret: the simplest and quickest way to cook lobster, and the path to the sweetest and most tender meat, is to steam rather than boil. That's been my method ever since, whether I'm setting the table with bibs, crackers and picks, or making this salad, which comes from a cookbook I once wrote. As soon as tomatoes hit their sweet peak and for as long as the season lasts, I make this recipe for family and friends. With corn on the cob and a warm fruit cobbler as bookends, it's one of my favorite meals."

- ⅓ cup finely chopped red onion
- 2 lemons, zest from both lemons grated, plus ¼ cup juice
- ½ teaspoon kosher salt
- ⅓ cup mayonnaise
- 2 tablespoons thinly sliced basil plus ½ cup loosely packed torn leaves
- Freshly ground black pepper
- 1¼ to 1½ pounds cooked lobster meat, cut into ½-inch pieces
- 1½ tablespoons extra virgin olive oil, plus more for drizzling
- 1½ pounds cherry tomatoes, halved
- Flaky sea salt

In a large bowl, combine onion, lemon zest, lemon juice, and kosher salt. Let stand 10 minutes. Whisk mayo, two tablespoons sliced basil, and ¼ teaspoon pepper into onion mixture. Fold in lobster.

In a second bowl, gently toss together tomatoes, remaining basil leaves, and oil. Season to taste with flaky salt and pepper.

To serve, spoon tomato salad onto plates. Top with lobster salad. Drizzle juices from both bowls over top. Top with a drizzle of oil and pinch flaky salt and pepper.

Luke's Lobster Tails with Kelp Pesto

Luke Holden • Cape Elizabeth, Cumberland County

"When we started working with the Maine-based kelp processor and grower Atlantic Sea Farms in 2021, we realized it was a perfect partner for lobster. Not only does kelp farming provide an additional revenue stream for the same lobstermen we buy our lobster from, but the two also pair perfectly on a plate. The sea vegetable earns top marks for nutrition and sustainability— it's packed with vitamins, minerals, and nutrients, and it mitigates the effects of ocean acidification. We also love its versatility. Its umami-rich, briny flavor complements our favorite crustacean in a wide variety of dishes. This recipe is a simple preparation combining our lobster tails with a classic pesto recipe that gets punched up with kelp, in the form of a puréed kelp cube. Our lobster tails can be grilled, broiled, roasted, or seared, but here we opt for the indoor version with a nice pan-sear on the stovetop."

Kelp Pesto:
2 Atlantic Sea Farms puréed kelp cubes, thawed
4 cups fresh basil leaves
½ cup extra virgin olive oil
⅓ cup pine nuts, toasted
2 garlic cloves
½ cup freshly grated Parmesan cheese
1 teaspoon kosher salt

4 Luke's Lobster Tails
2 tablespoons unsalted butter

To prepare the kelp pesto: Combine the kelp cubes, basil, olive oil, toasted pine nuts, and garlic in a blender until a paste forms, scraping down the basil when needed to incorporate. Add the Parmesan cheese and salt, and blend until smooth. Transfer to a bowl.

To prepare the lobster: Split the lobster tails lengthwise through the shell with a sharp knife. Melt the butter in a large skillet and pan sear the lobster tails, shell-side down first, then flip the tail and lightly brown the meat side until the meat is opaque. Top the cooked lobster tails with pesto and enjoy!

Pro tip: This recipe would also be great with grilled lobster tails. To grill, prepare the raw lobster tails in the same way by splitting them in half lengthwise, then skewer them with wooden skewers that have been soaked in water so they don't burn on the grill. Brush melted butter on the meat, and place them shell-side down on a hot grill until the meat becomes opaque white and the shell turns bright red. Turn the tails over so that the meat side is facing down on the grill. Cook until brown grill marks appear on lobster meat, about 30 seconds. Serve immediately with kelp pesto!

Lobster Noodle Salad with Sweet and Sour Sauce

Chenda Chamreoun • Portland, Cumberland County

"When I first came to the United States from Cambodia in November of 2013, I had no familiarity with cooking, having relied on my grandmother and mother for my meals growing up. When I arrived in Maine with my husband on that fall day over 8 years ago, I quickly realized I would need to learn how to cook the favorite meals that reminded me of home—my attempt at stir-fry and sweet onions just wouldn't cut it! I started by researching on YouTube, then turning to friends for more cooking tips. After some practice, I came up with my own collection of new recipes and old favorites to make for my family here in Portland. Sweet and sour sauce with noodles, while not a traditional Cambodian dish, has roots there and in Vietnamese cooking, and in Cambodia, everyone knows how to make it. I serve it over vermicelli noodles and lobster meat, and it's the perfect dish to remind me of my two homes in Cambodia and Maine."

Sweet and Sour Sauce:

4 cups cold water
2 cups sugar
1 cup fish sauce
1 cup vinegar
½-1 cup Asian sweet sauce (optional)
1 carrot, shredded (optional)
½-1 cup chopped peanuts (optional)
Sliced chilies (optional)

1 package rice vermicelli noodles
1 pound Luke's Lobster Meat (cooked knuckle and claw meat)
1 cucumber, sliced
2 cups lettuce, torn into bite-size pieces
Mint, for garnish (optional)

To prepare the sweet and sour sauce: Combine water, sugar, fish sauce, vinegar, and sweet sauce in a bowl and thoroughly mix together. If using, add shredded carrot, chopped peanuts, and chilies.

Cook the noodles by placing them in a large heat proof bowl. Boil enough hot water to cover, and pour it over the noodles. Let the noodles soak for 3-5 minutes, then drain off the hot water and shock the cooked noodles in a bowl of cold water for 3-5 minutes to stop the cooking. Once the noodles have cooled, drain and place them into a bowl. Separate noodles using a fork or your hands.

Pour the sweet and sour sauce over the noodles, and toss in the remaining ingredients: lobster knuckle and claw meat, cucumber, torn lettuce, and optional mint for garnish. Makes 4 servings.

Tom Andrews' Wicked Good Maine Lobster Chili

1994 • Out in the Kitchen

Maine Won't Discriminate • Portland, Cumberland County

The social causes addressed by community cookbooks change as times change. This statewide fund-raising cookbook raised money to fight discriminatory anti-LBGTQ legislation. Tom Andrews' detailed lobster chili recipe is chock full of herbs and spices, including some surprises, such as cilantro and jalapeño peppers. Andrews served Maine as a member of the U.S. House of Representatives, and is currently the United Nations Special Rapporteur on human rights for Myanmar. —DL

- 1 pound dried black beans
- Meat from 4 lobsters, cooked, picked and roughly chopped
- 4 dried red chili peppers, finely chopped
- 3 green jalapeño peppers, coarsely chopped
- 4 cups fish broth
- 4 tablespoons olive oil
- 4 medium-size shallots, finely chopped
- 2 medium-size garlic cloves, finely chopped
- 28-ounce can crushed tomatoes
- 1 tablespoon dried leaf oregano
- 1 tablespoon dried leaf basil
- 1 teaspoon dried leaf thyme
- 1 bay leaf
- ¼ cup unsalted butter, melted
- 1 tablespoon sweet paprika
- ⅓ cup finely chopped fresh chives
- ⅓ cup finely chopped cilantro
- Salt and pepper to taste
- Chili powder to taste

In a large saucepan, cover beans with cold water. Bring to a boil over high heat; boil briskly 5 minutes, then remove from heat and let soak 1 hour. Drain and rinse under cold running water. Set beans aside.

In a blender or food processor fitted with the metal blade, put dried chilies with ½ fish broth. Purée and set aside. In a saucepan, heat oil over medium heat. Add fresh chiles, shallots, and garlic; sauté until shallots are transparent, 2 to 3 minutes.

Add drained beans, remaining fish broth, puréed red chiles, tomatoes, oregano, basil, thyme, bay leaf, salt, and pepper. Bring to a boil; reduce heat and simmer, covered, until beans are tender, 1½ to 2 hours, adding a little water if necessary to keep beans barely covered. Sauté cooked chopped lobster in butter with paprika, adding chives, cilantro, chili powder, salt, and pepper. Add lobster to beans ½ hour before serving. Makes 6 to 8 servings. —Tom Andrews

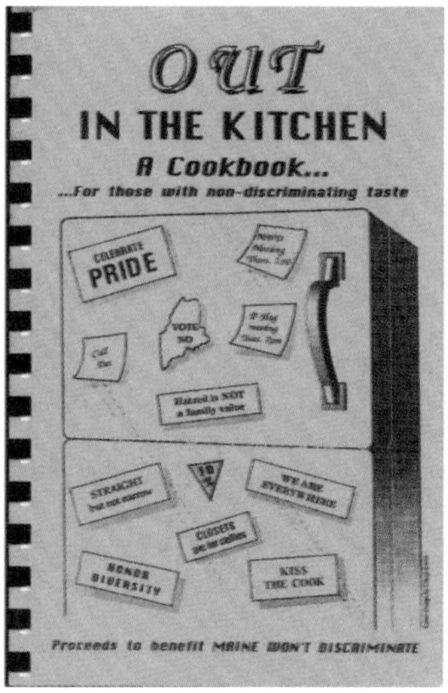

Mary Peterson's Baked Stuffed Lobster

Karen Jennings • Wells, York County

"When I was first married (37 years ago) and newly relocated to Maine, my husband and I were invited to have dinner at a significantly older friend's home. Much to my surprise, the menu was baked beans, brown bread, and hot dogs, something neither my husband nor I had ever had in combination before. This friend and his wife told us stories of other traditional Maine foods and when we professed our love of lobsters this recipe came up. The wife, Mary, offered to teach me how to make them and not long afterward had us back for this mind-blowing lobster dinner. I remember my first bite as if it were yesterday, one of the best things I had ever tasted, and still is to this day. Whenever I make it for friends it is so fun to sit back and watch them revel in this incredible dish."

- 6 large (1½-2 pound) lobsters
- ¾ cup (1½ sticks) unsalted butter
- 3 large cloves garlic, minced
- ⅓ cup Worcestershire sauce
- Juice of half a lemon
- ½ cup chopped flat leaf parsley
- Freshly ground black pepper
- 1 box Keebler onion crackers, crushed
- Lemon wedges, for serving
- Melted butter, for serving

In a steamer basket or metal colander set over a couple of inches of water, partially cook lobsters, steaming just until no longer gelatinous, about 10 minutes. Cool lobsters enough to handle, and remove meat completely from 2 lobsters. Remove tail meat from the remaining 4 lobsters by splitting the tail lengthwise down the middle from belly side, being careful to leave tail shell intact when removing meat. Chop all meat into bite-size pieces and set aside.

Take the 4 whole lobsters and remove sac from each by pushing finger up through the belly cavity into the head to find the squishy round mass, pull it out, and discard. Drain off excess juices from lobsters and place belly up on a large foil lined sheet pan.

Prepare the stuffing by melting the butter in a large heavy-bottomed sauce pan over medium-low heat. Add garlic, Worcestershire sauce, lemon juice, parsley, and several grinds of black pepper. Bring to a simmer and cook 5 minutes to combine the flavors. Remove from heat and stir in crushed crackers and chopped lobster, mixing gently until all ingredients are combined.

Preheat oven to 350 degrees. Divide stuffing among the 4 lobsters, filling each tail and belly cavity. Cover lobsters with foil and bake in preheated oven 15 minutes. Uncover lobsters and bake for another 15 minutes. Serve with lemon wedges and melted butter.

Scotian Lobster Chowder

Sam Hayward • Bowdoinham, Sagadahoc County

"This is Sam Hayward's Christmas chowder, which he claims he learned to make way, way Down East in Nova Scotia, hence the name. Sam might be embarrassed to hear it, but he is widely recognized as the dean of Maine chefs, the one who's always invoked as an authority even as he brushes off any claim to expertise. He has spent his considerable career at the helm of restaurants in Brunswick, Freeport, and Portland, where Fore Street, under Sam's influence, consistently wins major awards. More important than restaurants, however, has been Sam's tireless commitment to the good food of Maine's farmers, fishers and foragers and his unsparing effort to bring that food to all of our tables, professional or not. Farm to table? Sam gets it! I love the combination of lobster and corn but if you can't find shoepeg corn, use a good brand of frozen corn. And in summer of course, cut the kernels off a couple of cobs of fresh corn and simmer them a little longer, just until done. This makes 6 to 8 portions, especially if served, as it should be, as a main course." —Nancy Harmon Jenkins

6 live pound-and-a-quarter lobsters
3 to 4 ounces good smoky bacon, diced
4 tablespoons butter, preferably unsalted, separated
4 or 5 medium russet potatoes, peeled, quartered, and sliced
2 medium leeks, diced
8-ounce box frozen shoepeg corn
2 cups heavy cream
Sea salt and black pepper

Put about 2 inches of water into a kettle or lobster pot, one big enough to hold all the lobsters. Set the kettle over high heat and bring to a rapid boil. Add the lobsters to the boiling water and cover the pot. Return to the boil and cook for about 4 minutes. Have ready a pitcher of cold water and as soon as the time is up, turn off the heat and add the cold water to stop the cooking. Drain the lobsters and immerse them in a basin of cold water to chill down until they're cool enough to handle.

While the lobsters are cooling, combine the bacon dice and 2 tablespoons of the butter in a heavy 3- or 4-quart soup pot or chowder pot and set over low heat. Fry the bacon in the butter until it yields up some of its fat and starts to turn crispy on the edges. Stir in the sliced potatoes and the diced leeks. Add about 1¼ cups of water and bring to a simmer. Cover the chowder pot and simmer until the potatoes are tender (10 to 12 minutes), then remove from the heat.

By this time, the lobsters should be cool enough to handle. Set a fine-meshed sieve over a large bowl, and break open the lobsters over the sieve, letting all the body liquids drain through into the bowl. Break off the claws and tails and pull apart the body sections. Remove any red coral or greenish tomalley from the carapace, and use a wooden spoon to force this through the sieve, stirring it into the liquid. Add the contents of the bowl to the potatoes in the chowder pot and set over low heat to bring to a gentle simmer.

Crack open the claws and tails and extract the meat, cutting it into chunks. Add to a skillet with the remaining butter and set over medium-low heat, stirring the lobster pieces until the meat becomes opaque, then scrape the meat and all the butter into the chowder pot. Cover, and continue to simmer very gently for 20 minutes.

Add the frozen corn and simmer about 2 minutes, just until it's hot. (If using fresh corn, let it simmer for 8 to 10 minutes or until the kernels are tender.) Now add the cream and bring to a simmer again. Let the chowder simmer for just a few minutes to bring all the flavors together, then add a good pinch of sea salt and some freshly ground black pepper. Ladle into warm bowls and serve hot, with another dab of butter on top as a garnish.

Fiddlehead Lobster Quiche

Cindy Eves-Thomas • St. Albans, Somerset County

"This recipe uses two Maine favorites: lobster and fiddleheads. I make this quiche on those rare occasions in the late spring when I have leftover lobster and fiddleheads. It's become a favorite supper or breakfast dish for family and guests."

- Pastry for single 9-inch pie crust
- 1¼ cups cooked Maine lobster meat, cut into bite-size chunks
- 1½ cups shredded Swiss cheese
- 1¼ cups cooked fiddleheads, trimmed and blanched
- 3 eggs
- 1¼ cups light cream or half-and-half
- Freshly ground black pepper, to taste

Preheat oven to 350 degrees. Line a 9-inch pie plate with pastry crust.

Fill pie crust with lobster meat, shredded cheese, and fiddleheads.

In a medium-size bowl, whisk eggs, light cream, and pepper together until well blended. Pour egg mixture over the lobster, cheese, and fiddleheads in the pie crust. Bake in a preheated oven for approximately 50 minutes or until the quiche is set. A knife inserted in the center should come out clean. Cool for 10 minutes before serving. Makes 6 to 8 servings.

Deviled Lobster Manicotti with Tarragon Cream Sauce

Cathy Billings • Brewer, Penobscot County

Sponsored by
Oakhurst Dairy

"I worked at the Lobster Institute at the University of Maine for over 20 years, and believe me, I've had lobster served countless ways. Never too much, though! Lobster = Joy! When you're enjoying a traditional lobster feast, it's hard to leave any meat for leftovers, so we buy extra just for this dish. It's become a family favorite. I call it comfort food with a flare!"

Mannicotti:

8-ounce package cannelloni or manicotti pasta (about 12 shells)
1 cup whole milk ricotta cheese
½ cup grated Parmesan
½-1 cup chopped cooked lobster meat
1 egg yolk, beaten
1 tablespoon yellow mustard

Sauce:

5 tablespoons unsalted butter
½ cup all-purpose flour
2 cups Oakhurst whole milk
1 cup Oakhurst heavy cream
½ teaspoon salt
1-2 teaspoons dried tarragon, or more to taste
½ cup grated Parmesan, for sprinkling
Paprika, for sprinkling

Preheat oven to 375 degrees.

Bring a large pot of lightly salted water to a boil. Add manicotti shells and cook for 8 to 10 minutes, until al dente. Do not overcook. Drain.

In a medium bowl, stir together the ricotta, Parmesan, lobster, egg yolk, and mustard. Spoon mixture into the cooked manicotti shells. Place in a buttered baking dish.

To prepare the sauce: In a medium saucepan, melt the butter over medium heat. Add the flour and whisk until smooth, about 2 minutes. Gradually add the milk and cream, whisking constantly, until the sauce is thick, smooth, and creamy, about 10 minutes. Do not allow the sauce to come to a boil. Remove from the heat and stir in the salt. Put the tarragon in the palm of your hand and rub until powdery, then stir into the sauce. Pour sauce over the stuffed manicotti, sprinkle with grated Parmesan and lightly dust with paprika.

Bake uncovered for 30 minutes. Let stand for about 5 minutes before serving.

Connor's Lobster Mac & Cheese

Connor Cote • Sanford, York County

"My son Connor is 11 years old and has loved to cook and bake since he could walk. We call him Chef Connor Onion because of his love to cook and his love of onions! He loves going to Wells Beach and then coming home to make us all our favorite meal. Connor has severe eczema and allergies, along with speech issues, but he's so resilient. He finds a peace and sense of self in cooking. Connor is always experimenting in the kitchen, and he adapted this lobster recipe from his favorite creation, Connor's Mac-a-Cheez-It!"—Stacy Cote

Lobster!
1 pound of your favorite type of pasta
½ cup (1 stick) unsalted butter
½ cup flour
4 cups milk
Spices, if desired (nutmeg, dry mustard)
3 cups shredded cheese
Breadcrumbs

Preheat oven to 350 degrees.

Cook your lobster. Cool and pick the meat. Chop lobster meat and set aside.

In a large pot of water, cook your pasta. Drain and set aside. In the pot, make a roux by melting butter and stirring in the flour. Cook for 3-4 minutes, then slowly pour in your milk. Stir until your sauce thickens. Stir in spices, if you like. Add your favorite cheese and stir to melt and combine. Mix in your pasta and then your chopped up, cooked lobster. Spread mixture in a buttered 9x13-inch baking pan. Top with breadcrumbs. Bake for 15-20 minutes. Enjoy!

Poor Man's Lobster (aka Haddock)

Carol Brown • Phippsburg, Sagadahoc County

"Lobster has always been a part of my life. In 1945, the year that I was born, my family built a camp on Winnegance Bay in Phippsburg. Every summer thereafter we moved from our home in Bath to our camp for the summer. Our small and rustic camp had no running water, no bathroom, no telephone, and no television. We did have an outhouse and a few electric lights. The milk man delivered to our area weekly and brought blocks of ice for our ice box to keep our food cold. We were poor!

While my father went to Bath to work at the Bath Iron Works each day, my mother and I tended a vegetable garden, carried water from the spring, foraged for berries, fished for flounders, dug clams and went swimming. After a long day at work, my father fished lobster traps from a small skiff powered by a 5 horse-power outboard motor. He pulled his wooden lobster traps by hand while I stabbed the fish used for bait with the bait needle so that he could then string the dead fish onto the bait string to lure more lobsters into the trap. We had great weekend gatherings eating all the lobster we wanted. The lobsters were cooked outside in a very large pot over an open wood fire. The small lobsters always tasted the best.

As my father aged and no longer lobstered, my husband Mike and I took over the summer camp. Mike had a larger boat and he took up the lobstering. Our son got his first lobster license at age eight and fished two lobster traps from a small boat powered by two oars. Again, we ate lots of lobster.

Way back in the early 1900s, before they were eaten by folks along the shore, lobsters could often be picked up by hand at low tide and were considered food for the poor. Lobsters were fed to prisoners because they were plentiful and cheap. Now lobster has become a delicacy for those with a limited food budget; it's a special treat. A few years back, I facilitated a gourmet cooking class at Bailey Evening School in Bath. It was fun and relaxed, and participants shared recipes that they often cooked. One gentleman shared this recipe for a dish called 'Poor Man's Lobster.' Ironically, the dish has no lobster in it!"

- 1 pound haddock fillets
- 1-2 tablespoons lemon juice
- ½ cup mayonnaise
- 1 teaspoon prepared mustard
- ½ cup grated Parmesan cheese
- Paprika, for sprinkling

Preheat oven to 400 degrees. Lightly butter a glass baking dish. Place fillets in a single layer, and sprinkle with lemon juice. In a small bowl, mix together mayonnaise, mustard, and cheese, and spread over the fish. Dust lightly with paprika. Bake for about 20 minutes, or until fish flakes easily. Makes 2 to 3 servings, depending on appetites.

The Right to Food

By Craig Hickman

Food is water. Food is soil. Food is light. Food is nourishment. Food is medicine. Food is life.

Our ancestors ate wild turtle soup, steamed snails, fried grasshoppers, fire-roasted grubs, raw fish eggs, and lived to tell about it. Our ancestors figured out how to make hog intestines, pig feet, beef tongue and brains, chicken hearts, thymus glands, oxtails, and pork belly taste good.

And lived to tell about it.

Fast forward several centuries. During my childhood in Milwaukee, the government agencies that were supposed to ensure food safety didn't seem to care much about the quality of the meats available in the neighborhood grocery stores. For the exchange of our food stamps and our hard-earned money, the only chicken available would be so yellow with age and degradation, my mother would soak it overnight in vinegar and lemon water to kill whatever might live on it, then stew it for hours in a pressure cooker to kill anything else. Twenty minutes or so before dinner, she would drop dumplings in the savory potlikker and build a part of heaven smack dab in the middle of our kitchen.

We lived to tell about it.

The only beef steaks and pork chops available at the same store were so gray, we felt safe to eat them only after they were charred past well done in the oven's bottom broiler and then smothered in skillet gravy and sautéed wild mushrooms we foraged on weekend camping trips.

We lived to tell about it.

When yellow chicken and gray beef steaks were among the only animal protein choices available to us at the store, it was no surprise, then, that my father would go hunting with the other fathers in our neighborhood to harvest opossum, raccoon, squirrel and rabbit, all of which went into the pressure cooker with his garden-grown carrots, potatoes, celery and onions to create a wild game stew so good I could never eat enough. Or he would catch perch or trout in Wisconsin's pristine lakes and slow cure the fish, sometimes whole, sometimes fileted, in his backyard, hand-built smoker for longer keeping.

We lived to tell about it.

Food is *life*.

Back in 1888, Supreme Court Justice Stephen Field argued:

"I have always supposed that the gift of life was accompanied with the right to seek and produce food, by which life can be preserved and enjoyed, in all ways not encroaching upon the equal rights of others... [The] right to procure healthy and nutritious food and to manufacture it, is among those inalienable rights, which no state can give, and no state can take away.... It is involved in the right to pursue one's happiness."

More than 75% of the people's representatives and senators in the Maine Legislature concurred—and came *together*—to provide a once-in-a-lifetime opportunity for the people of Maine to ratify and enshrine a constitutional Right to Food, the most fundamental of our natural rights. And so, with 61% of the vote, the people of Maine said YES.

Where I come from, you don't grow up dreaming that someday you'll be in a position to inscribe your own words on the pages of a constitution.

But I am here to tell about it.

Constitution of Maine. Article I. Declaration of Rights. Section 25. Right to Food. All individuals have a natural, inherent, and unalienable right to food, including the right to save and exchange seeds and the right to grow, raise, harvest, produce and consume the food of their own choosing for their own nourishment, sustenance, bodily health and well-being, as long as an individual does not commit trespassing, theft, poaching or other abuses of private property rights, public lands or natural resources in the harvesting, production or acquisition of food.

As the author and original sponsor of this amendment in 2015 and again in 2019, as a farmer, poet and chef, I am most humbled that the Legislature, under the leadership of lobsterman and state representative Billy Bob Faulkingham, and the people of Maine, informed by the wisdom of farmer and amendment co-author Heather Retberg, reflected back the independence and love for freedom and self-sufficiency that brought me twenty years ago to this place I call heaven.

True to our motto, Maine is the first of the United States to enshrine the Right to Food in our Constitution, the original right of all living beings, reaffirming that all power is inherent in the people.

Thank the Lord.

Right to Food means food self-sufficiency that engenders food security. Right to Food means self-determination that uplifts human dignity. Right to food means individual liberty that promotes personal responsibility.

Right to Food makes manifest resilient community, protects our traditional foodways in perpetuity, and undergirds a sturdier foundation for our laboratories of democracy.

Let us build.

And so, without further ado, Right to Food must now become one of the highest considerations for policymakers at all levels of government in crafting public policy that uplifts the dignity and worth of every human personality.

Exactly the way life should be.

Let us begin.

Craig Hickman is an American writer, farmer, and Democratic politician from Winthrop currently representing Maine Senate District 14. He served in the 126th Maine House of Representatives as the representative for Maine's 82nd district from 2012 to 2018. He has received a Gertrude Johnson Literary Award, the James Baldwin Award for Cultural Achievement, and a Spirit of America Foundation Award.

FLESH & FOWL

Photo: Doukas sisters, Virginia, Aphie, Mildred, Despina, and Stella line up behind the family matriarch, Marego, at their home on Sherman Street in Portland in 1944. The family's recipe for Greek Braised Lamb Shanks can be found on page 172.

Toy Len Goon's Beef with Peppers and Tomatoes

Doris Wong • Portland, Cumberland County

"My mother, Toy Len Goon, was 1952's American Mother of the Year. She successfully blended East and West cooking after arriving in 1921, helping her husband Dogan run a hand laundry in Portland, bearing him eight children, and cooking delicious meals. Because she didn't have ready access to a lot of Chinese foods and ingredients, she learned to improvise. One of Mother's dishes that was enjoyed by all was a steak, pepper, and tomato dish which contained Chinese salted dried black beans. No recipe was ever written down. It came together from her head and heart."

- 1 heaping tablespoon Chinese salted dried black beans
- 1 large garlic clove, finely chopped
- 6 thin slices fresh ginger root, cut into strips
- 3 tablespoons olive oil
- 1 pound flank steak, cut in short strips
- 2 tablespoons soy sauce
- 1 large green pepper, cut into medium pieces
- 3 large ripe tomatoes, cut into wedges
- Mixture of equal parts cornstarch and water, for eventual thickening of finished dish

In a small bowl, mix together salted dried black beans, garlic, and ginger.

Heat a large skillet with half of the olive oil. Add half of the black bean mixture and stir. When ingredients have lightly browned, add the steak. Stir quickly, as the steak will cook quickly, then add half the soy sauce. Remove seasoned cooked steak to a plate and set aside.

Add the balance of the oil to the skillet, along with the remainder of the black bean mixture. Once the mixture has lightly browned, add the peppers and cook for 1 minute. Add the tomato wedges, and stir together for an additional minute. Add the remaining tablespoon of soy sauce and 1 cup of water. Cover the pan and let steam for about 5 minutes.

Stir in the cooked flank steak, and add cornstarch mixture to thicken, starting with 1 tablespoon and adding as desired. Serve over boiled white rice.

Trash Can Turkey

Paula Smithson • Gray, Cumberland County

"We camped years ago with a large group of friends. Ted Pierce, from Gray, showed us how to make this fun way of cooking turkey, and we have shown many people since then. It was an annual tradition at Littlefield Beaches in Greenwood. No matter the season, everyone brought all the fixings for a Thanksgiving dinner."

12 pound turkey
3 strips bacon

Equipment:
Galvanized metal trash can, with lid
25-pound bag of charcoal
Lighter fluid
Matches
1 package heavy duty aluminum foil
1 turkey stand
Square-pointed shovel
Heat resistant gloves

Place trash can lid upside down on the ground and pour charcoal into it. Soak with lighter fluid and light. Don't blow your head off!

Cover turkey stand with foil so that it's completely covered. If you are constructing it yourself, do not use pressure-treated wood for the stand.

When charcoal is ready for cooking (very hot), lay two strips of foil approximately 4 feet long on the ground, side by side. Place covered turkey stand in the center of the foil. Place the turkey on the stand. Lay 3 strips of bacon over the neck area, and then cover that with enough aluminum foil to just hold it on. Place cylinder of trash can upside down over the turkey.

Use the shovel to place half the hot coals around the base of the can, folding the foil up around the charcoal to make a collar that will hold the coals snuggly around the can. Place the remaining hot coals on the top of the upside-down can. Cook turkey 2 to 2¼ hours. After turkey has cooked, scoop charcoal off the top of the can and away from the base. Lift the can with heat-resistant gloves. Avoid burning yourself—the can will be extremely hot! Enjoy the turkey. It is delicious and a rare treat!

Grammy Kay's Wild Rice and Sausage Stuffing

Robert Bernheim • South China, Kennebec County

"Sweatshirt weather in late August is a harbinger for Grammy Kay's Wild Rice and Sausage Stuffing. My grandmother, Katherine Ross Brooks, would make this dish to accompany her roast chicken for Sunday dinner, and she always made it with her Thanksgiving turkey. Despite the deep Vermont roots of my grandmother, this recipe continues to succeed with a combination of Maine-based ingredients. It's an ideal dish when you have access to Northern wild rice from the Kennebec Estuary in September."

1 cup Northern wild rice (quick wild rice will also work)
1 large sweet onion, diced
½ cup fresh wild mushrooms, stems removed and diced
3 tablespoons butter (preferably Casco Bay Butter)
1 teaspoon thyme leaves
1 teaspoon dried marjoram
1 teaspoon ground sea salt
1 tablespoon Bernheim Original Kentucky Straight Wheat Whiskey (or similar whiskey), optional for flambé
¾ pound breakfast sausage (Mailhot's "Downeast," if you can find it)

Rinse wild rice, then bring 3 cups cold water to a steady boil in a large sauce pan. Follow the directions on the package to boil the wild rice until it "pops." (If using foraged Northern wild rice, be sure to consult the forager for their best practices in preparing the wild rice.) Once the rice is fully cooked, fluff with a fork and set aside, covered.

Dice the onion. Rinse, dry and dice the mushrooms. Mix together in a bowl. Using a heavy-bottomed frying pan, melt the butter until it is just foaming. Quickly add the onions and mushrooms. Sauté and add the herbs and sea salt. Stir gently. When the onions and mushrooms have turned translucent and are beginning to brown, add whiskey to the pan, and quickly flambé, if you would like. Scrape the onions and mushrooms into a bowl and set aside, covered.

Using the same pan from the onions and mushrooms, fry the breakfast sausage, breaking it up into small browned bits as you go. Set aside.

In a large serving bowl, thoroughly mix the wild rice, onions, mushrooms, and sausage. Keep warm in the oven or serve immediately with poultry. This stuffing can be made ahead and used to stuff the chicken or turkey, or it can be reheated and served along with the poultry. Serves a hungry family of six.

Mark's Glop

Karen Prouty • Scarborough, Cumberland County

"My husband, Mark Rollins, and I grew up in Central Maine, but have lived in the Portland area since 1986. We have been married 35 years, and have adhered to the traditional roles wherein the husband is responsible for yard work and the wife prepares meals. I still enjoy cooking after all these years, but I do appreciate those occasions when we dine out or he prepares an evening meal. This Italian inspired concoction was devised by my husband after I nagged him that I needed a break from cooking. I actually named the dish 'Glop' since I was not initially a fan, but his Orono aunts lauded it as a 'gourmet' delight, and after a few modifications (e.g., inclusion of the sausage), I no longer complain when he prepares it for dinner. It is actually tasty and easy to prepare. However, there is one note of caution: This recipe should be served immediately, otherwise it will turn into GLOP."

- 3 or 4 Italian-style sausages, cooked and cut up into bite-size pieces
- ½ pound fettuccine pasta
- 1 large container fresh baby spinach
- 1 pint container cherry tomatoes
- ¼ to ⅓ cup olive oil
- ½ to 1 cup grated Parmesan cheese
- 3 tablespoons dried basil
- Garlic powder, to taste
- 4-6 ounces kalamata olives, halved
- Black pepper and/or red pepper flakes, to taste

Prepare sausage and set aside. Bring a large pot of salted water to a boil and cook pasta until al dente, adding the spinach and tomatoes during the final few seconds of cooking. Remove from heat, drain the pasta and vegetables, and return to the pot. Add ingredients in this order, tossing after each addition: olive oil, Parmesan cheese, dried basil, garlic powder, olives, sausage, and black pepper and/or red pepper flakes. After a final toss, serve immediately.

Grammy Morse's Stuffing

Angel Jamison • Bath, Sagadahoc County

"My mother Donna, the youngest of eight children, grew up with limited financial resources, but as she often commented, 'not as poor as my older siblings.' Raised solely by her mother, Madeline Morse, she often shared that despite their economic situation, and not having a father figure present, she never felt these losses due to the pure strength of her mother. I have heard stories of them buying lobster bodies for 5 cents each, as they could not afford the whole lobster, and to this day—when I eat lobster, you bet I eat the whole thing and I think of that story every time. For Christmas 1996, my mother compiled a small binder of favorite family recipes. Twelve years later my mom would pass, and that binder of recipes would become cherished even more. Within that binder is 'Grammy Morse's Stuffing,' a family recipe that my mother made frequently. For Thanksgiving dinner, straight into the cavity of the bird it went, using the heel of a loaf of bread to secure it all. This stuffing is unlike any stuffing I have ever had. It is absolutely as delicious as it is unique, like the women who made it. They loved their families with all of their hearts, and brought us together, from the blueberry fields, to the stove, to the table."

Broth:

Turkey innards: neck, liver, heart, gizzards
1 onion, chopped
3 celery stalks, chopped
Salt and pepper, to taste

Stuffing:

2-3 packages of saltine crackers, crushed while still in the package
1 onion, chopped
3 celery stalks, chopped
Salt and pepper, to taste
Ground sage or poultry seasoning, to taste
3 tablespoons butter
2 eggs

To make the broth: Rinse the turkey innards, place in a small pan, and cover with water. Add all of the remaining ingredients and boil until tender. Reserve the broth and keep it hot. Cut up or pull off the meat from the neck and reserve for the stuffing.

To make the stuffing: Combine crackers, onion, celery, and seasonings in a large bowl. Put the butter on top and pour the hot broth, over the mixture. The broth will melt the butter. Mix thoroughly, then add the eggs and stir to combine. The stuffing will be moist. Add the meat from the neck to the stuffing. Place in a greased casserole dish and bake at 350 degrees until done, about 30 minutes. This stuffing can also be used inside of the turkey, with a slice or the heel of a loaf of bread at the opening of the cavity to keep all in place.

Baked Spam

Jayne Farrin • Presque Isle, Aroostook County

"My mom, Myrtie Foss Farrin, was the middle sister of the five Foss sisters from Harmony. She and her sisters were all excellent cooks. My mom passed in 2008, and I wish I could remember the last time I ate a piece of her apple pie. She didn't use a recipe for her crust as it was done only by 'feel' using Robin Hood Flour and Crisco. The apples were Macs and flavored only with nutmeg.

Occasionally Mom would whip up baked Spam for supper. Probably there wasn't much for meat remaining in the house when she served this. Mom would also serve it pan fried, or grind it and mix it with relish and mayonnaise, or grind it and add it to egg salad. Baked was one of my favorites, but honestly, I liked every way she prepared Spam."

- ⅓ cup brown sugar
- 2 teaspoons flour
- ⅔ teaspoon dry mustard
- ⅓ cup water
- 1 tablespoon apple cider vinegar
- 1 can Spam
- Whole cloves

Mix brown sugar, flour, dry mustard, water and apple cider vinegar together. Score top of Spam in a diagonal pattern and repeat scoring diagonally in the opposite direction to create a crossing pattern. Insert whole cloves at the crossings. Pour brown sugar mixture over Spam and bake at 350 degrees for 30 minutes.

Sweet and Sour Substitution

Lisa Colburn • Orono, Penobscot County

"I visited my mom for lunch one day many years ago. The main course featured a delicious sweet and sour chicken dish. Impressed, I asked for the recipe. She handed me a recipe that she'd clipped from a magazine. 'Well,' she said, 'I didn't have the soy sauce they asked for, so I substituted Worcestershire sauce. I didn't have orange marmalade, so I substituted strawberry jam. I didn't have vinegar so...' By the time she was done telling me how she prepared the dish, the only thing she used from the original recipe was the chicken! She was an imaginative cook!"

Greek Braised Lamb Shanks

William Doukas • Portland, Cumberland County

"All four of my grandparents came to the United States as teenagers in the 1920s. They came from Gytheio and Kotronas, Greece, and in the 1940s, they supported their families as candy makers and chefs, while other family members served in the Second World War. During the war, within Portland's Parkside neighborhood, one side of my Greek family operated Bill's Cafe. From what I understand, they fed a lot of Victory shipbuilders. I would like to think that braised lamb, a traditional Greek dish, was on the menu. Bill's Cafe burned to the ground in June of 1945, a few months before V-J Day. It required a challenging rebuilding effort, and eventually reopened as Longfellow Restaurant. My own memories of lamb consumption go back to the early 1960s, when my Greek grandparents, maternal and paternal, served it many Easters. Upon inheriting their cookbooks and examining old photographs, I could tell the recipes were handed down well before I entered the scene. Note: The best things take time! Allow yourself 3 ½ hours to make this delicious dish."

Shanks:

- 4 lamb shanks, 1½ to 2 pounds each
- 4 tablespoons olive oil
- 8 tablespoons salt (Kosher, Morton's or Crystal Diamond)
- 4 tablespoons black pepper
- 4 teaspoons Aleppo pepper (red pepper flakes are a good substitute)
- 4 tablespoons oregano
- 4 tablespoons Hungarian paprika
- 4 teaspoons ground coriander
- 4 teaspoons thyme

Sauce:

- 2 large sweet or yellow onion, chopped medium to fine
- 4 tablespoons minced garlic
- 4 tablespoons concentrated tomato paste (one 4-ounce can)
- 2 apples, cored and cut into eighths
- 2 pears, cored and cut into eighths
- 2 mangos, seeded and cut into eights
- 2 lemons, quartered
- 2 tablespoons salt
- 1 tablespoon black pepper
- 8 bay leaves, broken in half
- 1½ cups beef broth
- 28-ounce can chopped tomatoes
- ½ cup honey
- 2 cinnamon sticks
- 4 teaspoons ground rosemary

To prepare the lamb shanks: Rinse shanks, pat dry, and trim all visible fat and remove silver skin halfway up on the bone portion. To remove silver skin, make a cut all the way around the bone and slip a sharp knife underneath, angling it slightly upward, and move blade back and forth on the membrane, then pull off with thumb and forefinger. If the tissue is slippery and hard to grip, use a paper towel.

Evenly sprinkle salt, black and Aleppo pepper, oregano, paprika, coriander, and thyme on all sides of the shanks.

Preheat oven to 300 degrees, and set the rack to lower middle position. In 2 large uncovered Dutch ovens or heavy, deep skillets set over medium flame, heat olive oil until it shimmers. (If only a single Dutch oven is available, take turns browning two at a time, and place in a deep large pan.) Place 2 shanks into each pan and turn every 2-3 minutes, browning on all sides. The pieces should not be crowded while browning. Remove meat and set aside.

Combine onions and garlic with the drippings in the Dutch ovens, and stir for 3-4 minutes before reducing heat to low. Mix in tomato paste, fruit, salt, pepper, and bay leaves, and cook for 5 minutes on the stove top.

Add beef broth, tomatoes, honey, and cinnamon sticks, and mix gently. Cook for 5 minutes, then nestle lamb shanks into the mixture. Grind rosemary over the shanks and transfer uncovered Dutch oven(s) into the preheated oven. Braise for a total of 2½ hours, turning over halfway through. Cover meat for the final 45 minutes. Lamb should be tender, and a fork should slip easily in and out of meatiest portion.

Using tongs and a large spoon, gently place tender lamb shanks on a platter to rest for 15 minutes, spooning a little sauce over each and loosely tenting the platter with aluminum foil.

Transfer the remaining sauce to a bowl and discard lemon wedges, cinnamon sticks, and bay leaves. Strain sauce through a medium mesh strainer, and then use a fat separator to pour off extra fat. Discard liquid fat, but keep vegetable solids that are caught in the strainer.

Allow the strained liquid to set for 5 minutes, then pour it into a blender. Add the solids and process for a minute. Return lamb shanks to Dutch ovens and pour the blended sauce around them, then simmer on the stove top for 10 minutes, spooning sauce over the meat while it simmers. Serve each shank with a cup of sauce over the top. Makes 4 servings.

Sachmon Cha Kreurng (Chicken Stir Fried in Kreurng Seasoning)

Chhom Yay • Kennebunk, York County

"My mother, Chhom Yay, came to America in 1986, escaping the war-torn country of Cambodia, and fell in love with the quaint small towns in Southern Maine. It wasn't long after settling into life in the U.S. that she found herself struggling as a single parent with three children, all under that age of 6. She came to the U.S. in hopes of a brighter future for her and her family and she wasn't about to let any obstacle keep her down. Much like most immigrants, she worked multiple jobs to ensure that her family could survive and make the most out of the land of opportunity. With the hardships of life, raising a family, and working nearly 50 hours a week, my mom somehow still found a way to cook traditional Khmer foods for her family. She found solace and comfort in cooking. It reminded her of Cambodia, her family (many of whom were lost to the war), and the culture that was ripped away from her. We chose this recipe to share with our Maine neighbors and friends because it's a great dish to tease your tastebuds of what Cambodian dishes have to offer. The dish highlights the great balance of sour, tangy, umami savory-ness that many Cambodian dishes are known for. My mother held back on the level of chili spice, to not overwhelm the overall newcomers that might want to try this recipe." - Savy Kuch

Kreurng paste:

2 stalks lemongrass, finely minced
¼ cup sliced galangal root
¼ cup turmeric
¼ cup minced ginger
¼ cup minced Thai chili pepper
¼ cup minced garlic

Chicken stir fry:

¼ cup canola oil
¼ cup minced shallots
¼ cup minced yellow onion
4 pounds boneless chicken, white and dark meat, roughly chopped
Chicken broth, if necessary
5-6 pieces fresh Thai lime leaves
¼ cup shrimp paste
2 tablespoons clam juice
2 teaspoons garlic powder
2 teaspoons onion powder
2 tablespoons brown sugar
1 tablespoon squid sauce
½ cup water
16 ounces mushrooms, roughly chopped
16-ounce can cooked quail eggs
32-ounce jar young tamarind leaves
4-6 ounces fresh mreah prov (also called tulsi or holy basil)
½ cup fresh Thai basil or ¼ cup fresh sage leaves

To make the Kreurng paste: Combine all ingredients in the bowl of a food processor or blender and purée until the mixture becomes a thick paste. Set aside.

To make the chicken: In a large wok over medium heat, drizzle about ¼ cup of canola oil. When the wok and oil are hot and ready, toss in the shallots and yellow onion to sauté and lightly brown. It will brown quickly, if the oil is hot enough.

Start to add the chopped chicken pieces into the wok. Toss and break up the chicken while it's cooking. Cook chicken until slightly firm but not completely done; just enough to render out all the liquid. Scoop out the chicken, leaving the broth in the wok. (The chicken will finish cooking, in the sauce, later.) Set chicken aside.

Turn the heat up to high and bring the broth to a boil. Spoon out half of the broth, to use later. There should be 1-2 cups of broth in the wok. Add more, if necessary. Let the liquid simmer, and add ¾ to 1 cup of the Kreurng paste. Stir and mix, as it simmers. Add the whole Thai lime leaves, shrimp paste, clam juice, garlic and onion powders, brown sugar, squid sauce, and water. Let mixture come to a simmer. Add a cup of the reserved chicken broth. Let the sauce get to a bubbling simmer. Add the mushrooms and the liquid from the can of quail eggs. Let sauce simmer.

Return to the reserved sautéed chicken, making sure to break up the chicken bits, as it has probably cooled down into one solid whole piece. Add the chicken pieces back into the wok with the sauce. Heat on low, tossing the chicken to thoroughly coat it in the sauce. Add the remaining reserved broth (there should be 1 cup left). Let simmer on medium-low heat, covered, for about 5-6 minutes.

Remove cover from the wok, then add the young tamarind leaves and mreah prov (tulsi) leaves and Thai basil or sage. Toss mixture well.

Add the quail eggs at the end and toss lightly to mix into the sauce, being careful not to break the delicate eggs. Cover and let simmer for another 5 minutes.

Remove from heat, when done. Stir-fry is best served over a warm pile of steamed jasmine rice.

Bun Filling

Craig Sipe • Orr's Island, Cumberland County

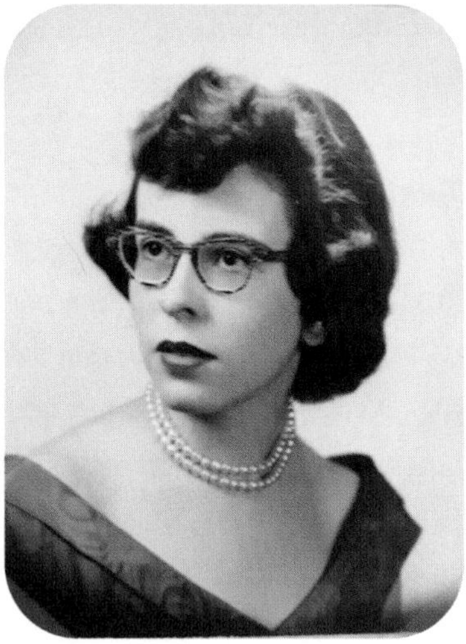

"My mother was a very economical cook. She often claimed that she could feed our family of four for under a dollar each night, which was a lot easier to do in the '60s! 'Bun Filling' was a regular entree at lunch time in our house, and I have returned to it from time to time, because it's surprisingly good. I've even modified the ingredients (sans buns) to make a hot dip. Just mix everything up, and place in a small prepared casserole dish, cover and bake at 350--375 degrees for 15 minutes or so. It's great with crackers, and you can make up your own name for it!"

½ pound ham, cubed
8 ounces sharp cheddar cheese, cubed
3 hard-boiled eggs, chopped
½ cup roughly chopped salad olives
½ cup chopped roasted red pepper strips
3 tablespoons mayonnaise (I prefer avocado mayo)
¾ cup chili sauce
Salt, to taste
1 dozen hot dog buns

Preheat oven to 400 degrees. Mix together ham, cheese, eggs, salad olives, and pepper strips. Mix together mayonnaise and chili sauce, then stir into the other ingredients. Stuff each bun with the filling, and wrap in foil. Place sandwiches on a cookie tray, and heat in the oven for 12 minutes. Note: Assembled in advance, these also freeze well for later use. Just add two or three more minutes in the oven.

Ode to Fried Chicken

Deborah Joy Corey • Castine, Hancock County

When frying chicken in my Maine kitchen, I never use poultry seasoning, buttermilk, eggs, garlic powder, onion powder, grape seed oil, sesame oil, a deep fryer, an electric frying pan, or a hair dryer.

Rather, I use a cast-iron skillet, milk, flour, paprika, salt and pepper, and Wesson Oil. The recipe I prefer is from Laurie Colwin's *Home Cooking* and it is the one that I adhere to most, with the exception of her love of a deep fryer. I much prefer a cast-iron skillet.

That being said, anyone who cooks should have Colwin's *Home Cooking* in their cookbook collection. Ms. Colwin was not only a brilliant writer but a sharp shooter in the kitchen, with her finger firmly placed on her cooking convictions, and her wit as reliable as a gun sight.

Chicken thighs are my favorite for frying with a drumette or two. Once and only once, I cut a boneless breast into several pieces, because I'd read that would help keep the meat moist. It did not, even with a complete flouring.

Still, I must admit that the best fried chicken that I ever had was a breast cut served room service at a hotel in Boston. A boneless breast with the small drumette attached. It was Valentine's Day and I was alone with my small daughters, both spiking high fevers, thus the splurging on a good hotel. The girls ate their mashed potatoes, but skipped their fried chicken, which left two extra servings for me. The Airline Chicken Breast cut or *frenched breast* was so perfectly cooked that I sometimes wished I'd never put my lips to another piece of fried chicken.

The flavor reminded me of partridge that my father fried in his trusted Lodge pan with sizzling butter. Sitting at our family table as the fall evening darkened, the taste of the crispy partridge skin released like a snappy prize in my mouth. The white interior was extra moist with warm rivulets as delicate as the thin rich gravy that Dad poured around the tiny breast.

Long ago, I knew that I would never achieve Dad's frying ability, but Laurie Colwin's fried chicken recipe has helped me get closer to his mastery.

Camp Kezar Baked Ducks

1923 • Favorite Recipes

Ladies' Circle, Church of the New Jerusalem • Fryeburg, Oxford County

A half hour to roast a duck? It seems impossible for those of us used to cooking domestic ducks. But wild ducks are smaller and much leaner, and can be cooked this quickly in a very hot oven (450-500 degrees). The recipe evokes a game hunting party at Camp Kezar, at the time owned by the New York City night club promoter Don Dickerman, whose Country Fair in the city's Greenwich Village imported "real Mainers" to entertain the Prohibition-era revelers. —DL

Rub ducks with salt and bake ½ hour in a very hot oven. Butter well when taken from oven. No dressing is used, and they come out brown and juicy, like broiled duck. —Mrs. E.E. Hastings

Brilliant Roast Chicken

Adrian du Plessis • Westport Island, Lincoln County

"In 2021, I married a man I've loved, and have corresponded with, for 50 years. It's a long story (obviously!), but we were born in wildly different circumstances, on different continents, met 50+ years ago at Stanford, and have kept in touch across oceans for all these years. That we've come together is a miracle...and so is his spectacular yet simple roast chicken. This is a simply delicious recipe for a family supper or a dinner party with friends. While Adrian prepares the chicken, I put together a mix of vegetables (page 104), which go into the oven halfway through the chicken's cooking time to create our favorite Sunday supper. There's nothing sacrosanct about this recipe, though it does provide a wonderful starting point if you are new to the joys of preparing a gorgeous roast chicken dinner." —Susie Stedman

1 free-range chicken, 3-5 pounds
Selection of fresh herbs, chopped
2 tablespoons olive oil
Salt, pepper, your choice of dried herbs and/or spices for a rub
1 lemon, cut into half-inch cubes
1 sprig rosemary
1 cup red wine
1 cup chicken stock

Preheat the oven to 425 degrees. Use a paper towel to pat dry your chicken. Select your favorite herbs–I use parsley, chives, basil, thyme, cilantro from our garden. Lift the skin off the breast of the chicken to insert the finely chopped herbs between the skin and the breast. Spread olive oil over the chicken and rub on your choice of seasoning: I use salt, pepper, sometimes dried herbs, cumin, harissa, curry powder–whatever you like. Put the cubed lemon and the rosemary into the cavity. There is no need to truss the chicken, slash the thighs or do anything else fancy!

Place the chicken on its back in an oiled roasting pan. Timing will vary with the size of the bird. After 40 minutes, take the chicken out of the oven, cut the skin on the inside of the thighs and open the legs wide to expose the part of the chicken that is hardest to get right. Stick a fork into the joint. If the flesh is still pink, give it another 10 to 15 minutes in the oven. The chicken will be fully cooked when a meat thermometer stuck into the thickest part reads 165 degrees.

When chicken is done, scrape the lemon and rosemary out of the cavity into the roasting pan; move the chicken to a warmed carving platter, and cover in foil for 10 to 15 minutes. Pour excess fat out of the roasting pan, then place pan on top of stove. Add the red wine and chicken stock, scrape the lovely dark bits off the bottom and stir occasionally while the liquid reduces until it has a nice light gooey texture. On lowish heat, this usually takes the 10-15 minutes the chicken needs to rest. Serve chicken with sauce.

Chicken and Wild Rice Casserole

Pamela Thompson • Caribou, Aroostook County

"This recipe came from my best friend of many years Judy Adler. She brought me this meal after I had surgery and whenever she knew I needed a pick-me-up. Then she gave me the recipe and I started making it for Christmas Eve dinner with my husband, our son and his wife, and our six grandchildren. The kids would always say 'This is Auntie Judy's.' Judy passed away two years ago and every time I make this I think of my best friend."

- 3 boneless chicken breasts
- 1 pound wild rice
- 2 tablespoons butter
- 1 medium yellow onion, chopped
- 3 tablespoons flour
- 1 cup milk
- 1 can cream of mushroom soup
- 1 teaspoon salt
- 1 teaspoon pepper
- ¾ pound sharp cheddar cheese, grated

Boil boneless chicken breasts, cool a little and shred. Set aside. In a separate saucepan, cook wild rice per package directions and drain.

In a skillet set over medium heat, melt butter, then add chopped onion and cook until soft.

Blend flour with the chopped onion and stir in the milk and the can of cream of mushroom soup. Mix together. You may add a little more flour if you want a thicker sauce. Add salt and pepper to taste.

Place a little sauce in the bottom of a 2-quart casserole dish. Layer cooked wild rice on top of this, then place a layer of chicken on top of the rice. Put shredded cheddar cheese on top of this, then repeat layers: sauce, rice, chicken, and cheese until you get to the top of the dish. End with cheese. Bake uncovered at 350 degrees for ½ hour, or until casserole is thoroughly warmed through and the cheese is hot and melted.

Memere and Ma's Cabbage Rolls

Jodie Mosher-Towle • Smithfield, Somerset County

"Memere, Dora Lessard Guertin, straight from Canada at age 11 or 12, learned quickly what it would take to live in Maine—hard work. She started working at the Hathaway, where she had to lie about her age to be hired. Speaking broken English and never learning to drive, she grew up, married my Pepere, Wilfred, and moved on to cleaning houses and scrubbing floors on her hands and knees to help support her family. All the while, she juggled her time to raise three children, including my mother, their only daughter, Nancy. My mother went on to have six kids, and Ma always went to her mother's recipes: filling, relatively inexpensive meals she made each afternoon in time for hungry mouths to devour at supper time. These cabbage rolls were one of our family favorites. We can fondly recall Memere, wearing her cat's eye-style glasses and with her thick French accent, making them at her small apartment in Waterville, and Ma making the at the counter at our house in Smithfield. It looked like a lot of work to us, but was a breeze for them! Memere remains in our hearts, and Ma just passed away in January of this year. Even when she suffered from dementia, and couldn't help us with the recipe in words, she smiled a huge smile after each bite when eating cabbage rolls prepared her way!"

- 1 medium to large head of cabbage
- 1 cup uncooked long grain rice
- 1½ pounds lean hamburg
- 1 large egg
- 1 large onion, peeled and rough chopped
- 1½ teaspoons salt
- 1½ teaspoons pepper
- 1 teaspoon onion powder
- 1 teaspoon garlic powder
- Two or three 15-ounce cans tomato sauce
- One 16-ounce can whole tomatoes or 1 quart canned stewed tomatoes
- ½ to 1 cup water, as needed
- Salt and pepper, to taste

Place a large pot of water on the stove, set the head of cabbage in the pot, and bring to a boil for 8-10 minutes. Halfway through boiling, turn the cabbage over, for even cooking.

In a large bowl, combine the uncooked rice, hamburg, egg, onion, salt, pepper, onion powder, and garlic powder, and stir until well mixed. (Memere and Ma did it with their bare hands, but today we use gloved hands or a wooden spoon.) Leave the mixture in the bowl and set aside.

Carefully remove cooked cabbage from the boiling water (Ma used 2 forks to stab each side of the hot cabbage). Keep the water at the boil, and set the cabbage on a cutting board. Let cabbage cool enough so that you can easily remove the outer leaves. These should be softened and easy to roll. Once all the cooked leaves are taken off, place the cabbage back into the boiling water for an additional 5-8 minutes, turning it over again about halfway through the boil.

While the cabbage is boiling, cut the stems out of the cooked leaves that are already on the cutting board. Place a scoop of the hamburg mixture onto the cabbage leave and roll it up (like a burrito, tucking the sides in then finishing the roll). Place a toothpick on the seam side to keep it closed and set aside. Repeat with the remaining filling and cabbage leaves.

Carefully take the cabbage out of the boiling water again, and repeat previous steps to remove the softened cabbage leaves. Replace the cabbage head in the boiling water if more leaves are needed and cook for an additional 5-8 minutes, turning halfway through and repeating the process if necessary.

Once all of the hamburg mixture is rolled up, and the final leaves are seam-side down, and secured with toothpicks, arrange the cabbage rolls in layers in a heavy-bottomed pot. (This can be the same pot you cooked the cabbage in, just pour out the water.)

When the cabbage rolls are arranged, pour 2 cans of the tomato sauce over them. Open the can of whole tomatoes and squeeze/squish them in your hands and scatter them over the top. (If you're using your own canned or stewed tomatoes, simply pour the entire jar over the cabbage rolls.) Add water to loosen the sauce, if necessary, to bring the liquid up to almost the top of the pot.

Cover the pot and let simmer for 2-3 hours, checking often to make sure there is enough liquid in the pot. If it needs more, add the remaining can of tomato sauce and/or water. After 2 hours, taste test a cabbage roll from the top layer to be sure the rice is cooked through. Once the rolls are done, turn off the burner and serve from the pot. Be sure to take out the toothpicks once they're on the plate!

Utilizing Odd Bits of Meat and Game

c. 1916 • St. Theresa's Parish Cook Book

St. Theresa's Catholic Church • South Brewer, Penobscot County

This slim cookbook contains more meat recipes than are usually found in community cookbooks, but the book's compilers were concerned with waste and frugality. Nearly a full page is dedicated to "How to Use Remnants" including leftovers, and this flexible recipe for a casserole of odd bits of meat is certainly watching the pennies. —DL

Line a casserole with slices of cooked veal, bacon, ham, or pork; fill with slices of cooked game, rabbit, quail or with pigeon; moisten with stock and cover the top with bacon; cook in the oven; this may be served cold. Hard boiled eggs make a pretty garnish. —Mrs. Carrie DeRusha

Poulet et Saucisse en Cocotte

Robyn Norton • Berwick, York County

"This is a classic French Canadian/Acadian recipe. Cassoulet has been passed down through the generations of my family because it's the ultimate comfort food and inexpensive to make, which was always important during the cold winter months."

- 2 tablespoons butter
- 2 tablespoons extra virgin olive oil
- 6 links Italian sausage
- 1 pound chicken legs
- 2 chicken breasts, cut into 4 pieces
- 1 large onion, coarsely chopped
- 2 stalks celery, chopped
- 2 cups halved carrots
- Two 15-ounce cans cannellini beans, rinsed well
- 2 cups chicken stock
- 1 cup tomato purée
- 28-ounce can diced tomatoes
- 3 garlic cloves, minced
- 2 thyme sprigs
- 2 tablespoons garlic powder
- 2 tablespoons onion powder
- 2 teaspoons smoked paprika
- 2 teaspoons Liquid Smoke
- Kosher salt and freshly ground black pepper, to taste
- 2 tablespoons cornstarch stirred into 2 tablespoons water, to thicken
- 1 cup toasted breadcrumbs mixed with Parmesan cheese, for serving
- Melted butter, for serving

Preheat oven to 325 degrees. In an oven-safe Dutch oven, melt the butter and oil, and brown the sausages. Remove sausages and set aside.

In the same Dutch oven, place the chicken legs and breast pieces skin side down, and brown. Remove browned chicken to a plate.

Add the onions and celery to the Dutch oven and sauté until translucent. Add carrots and beans, and stir to coat them in the butter and oil.

Stir in the remaining ingredients. Place the sausages and breast pieces in the pot and press into the bean mixture so that they are partially submerged. Add the chicken legs on top, skin side up, and season with salt and pepper. Bake for 4 to 5 five hours.

Remove from the oven, and scoop out the chicken and sausages. Place the meat on a plate. Place the Dutch oven on the stove top and bring everything to a boil. Add the cornstarch and water mixture, and stir to incorporate and thicken.

Place the chicken and sausages back on top of the vegetables. Sprinkle with the toasted Parmesan breadcrumbs. Pour a bit of melted butter over all and place under the broiler until golden. Serve in bowls.

Grum Damien's Stuffing (Kevin's Variation)

Kevin Flynn • Brunswick, Cumberland County

"My great-grandparents were immigrants from Quebec, Canada, who spoke a little English and a lot of French. My great-grandfather worked in the woolen mill in Orono, and at night built the house that my grandmother and I grew up in. This recipe has been in our family for as long as I can remember, and came from that tradition and that house. We had large family gatherings in Orono every Thanksgiving, and I was always tasked with helping Grum grind the ingredients when I got home. My career in the U.S. Secret Service moved my family to California and Maryland, but when my wife Wendy and I moved back to Maine we were fortunate enough to begin hosting our families at our home in Brunswick. It has been a tradition for over 23 years. The stuffing was continued in the new house with some tweaking, and it remains a family favorite."

1 pound meatloaf mix (beef, pork, veal)
½ pound bulk hot sausage
½ pound bulk sweet sausage
2 onions, minced
2 cups seasoned bread crumbs
2 teaspoons Bell's seasoning
1 teaspoon salt
2 teaspoons black pepper
2 teaspoons onion powder
2 teaspoons garlic powder
¼ cup parsley, chopped
Chicken stock, to moisten
1 cup turkey drippings, optional

In a hand grinder, grind all meat with onions. In a large pot, combine meat and onion mixture with bread crumbs. Add Bell's seasoning, salt, pepper, onion powder, garlic powder, and parsley to the pot and mix well. Cook about 1 hour over low heat, stirring often. Moisten with chicken stock, keeping the texture at stuffing consistency. Place in loaf pans and, if possible, pour turkey drippings over the top of each "loaf." Reheat stuffing in the oven when ready to use.

Kurací Paprikáš (Chicken Paprikash)

H. Lori Schnieders • East Machias, Washington County

"My mother was the 13th of 14 children and the first born in the United States. Her family came to the United States in 1912 from the Czech Republic. Chicken Paprikash was one of my favorite comfort food meals, and my mother prepared it using her mother's recipe. The name is derived from the ample use of paprika, a spice commonly used in Eastern European cuisine. It is traditionally served with spaetzle, a type of boiled egg noodles."

Whole chicken, cut in parts
(my mother used only wings and legs)
Salt and pepper, to taste
1 teaspoon ground caraway or cumin
Vegetable oil

For the paprika sauce:
3 tablespoons vegetable oil
1 onion, peeled and chopped
3 cloves garlic, peeled and crushed
2 tablespoons all-purpose flour
1½ cups water
1 teaspoon salt
½ teaspoon ground black pepper
1 cup sour cream
2 tablespoons paprika

Pat dry the chicken and season with salt, black pepper, and ground caraway or cumin. Distribute the chicken pieces around a large roasting dish and pour in a little oil, enough so that the pieces don't stick. Roast in the oven at 350 degrees for about 20 minutes, then turn chicken pieces over and continue cooking for another 20 minutes, basting with meat juices and water, if needed, to achieve a golden crust. Transfer the meat to a cast-iron skillet and pour the basting liquid over the chicken. Place skillet on the stovetop over low heat and keep at a simmer until you are ready to serve.

To make the paprika sauce, heat the oil in a deep-sided pan or medium saucepan over medium heat. Throw in the onion and sauté until translucent. Add the garlic and cook for a couple more minutes, stirring now and then to prevent it from burning. Sprinkle in the flour and continue cooking for another minute before removing from heat. Pour in ¾ cup of water and stir to combine well. Season with the salt and black pepper. Place over a medium heat again and bring to a simmer, stirring all the time until the mixture thickens.

In a mug or small bowl, mix together the sour cream, paprika, and remaining water. Add this mixture to the saucepan, return to heat, and stir until the sauce comes to the boil. Adjust the seasoning, take off the heat, and serve hot with the reserved chicken and a mound of boiled spaetzle.

Cow's Tongue

Savannah Sessions • Lovell, Oxford County

"My memere, Marie Francoise Theresa Caron Gagnon, better known as Teddy, was a spitfire with great legs and a great smile. Like so many Franco-Americans, she grew up pretty poor and ate accordingly. In spite of that, everything she made was delicious and somehow there was always enough to feed an army or two. One Christmas, we gathered in her home in Lisbon as was tradition. We all knew crabs, lobsters, and seafood stew would be the main course, but God forbid anybody go hungry, so there were tables full of appetizers, too. One nice looking charcuterie board with gherkin pickles and seedy mustards caught my sister Sarah's eye. Sarah, known for her weak stomach at the time, marched into the kitchen to enthusiastically announce that was the best tasting, most tender meat she had ever had. She then made the grave mistake of asking what it was. Mem simply replied 'cow's tongue' with a twinkle in her eye and the whole house erupted into laughter as Sarah sprinted to the bathroom, looking a little green. Mem left us in 1998, but Sarah went on to be an organic dairy farmer and mother of five; weak stomach no more! On one family visit to Sarah's farm, she served up a platter of absolutely delicious, tender meat. As she served it she beamed. What other cut would the farmer eat? We could almost hear Mem's laughter on the wind."

1 cow's tongue
(available from your local farmer)
1 cup vinegar
1 cup water
½ cup raisins
¼ teaspoon salt
Coarsely chopped or ground peppercorns

This works best in a pressure cooker, but a slow cooker will do as well. If using a slow cooker, place tongue in bottom of the pot and cover with water. Add remaining ingredients, close cover, and set cooking temperature to high. Cook for at least 6 hours, until the meat is tender and easily pierced with a fork. Score and peel the tough outer covering from tongue, slice and serve hot or cold with various breads and mustards. Enjoy!

Sunday Night Special

1955 • Lewiston Band Booster Club Cook Book

Lewiston Band Booster Club • Lewiston, Androscoggin County

Starting in the 1950s, many Maine community cookbooks were produced to support various school activities including sports teams and marching bands. To plan, produce, and market this fundraising book, the Lewiston Band Booster Club needed lots of volunteers, and we can see them in fold-out photos of the Grammar School and High School Marching Bands. Norman Phillips supplies a recipe for his Sunday Night Special, and is also listed as one of the "handprinters" in the credits. It took twelve "handprinters" to neatly write all the recipes and local advertisements we see. —DL

Bread
Cheese
Bacon

Toast bread, 3 or 4 slices per person. Fry bacon crisp. Butter toast, lay slice of cheese on toast, put on 4 slices bacon on cheese then top bacon with small strips of cheese. Place on broiler, heat until cheese melts and turns golden brown. Sprinkle with paprika on top (just for looks). Serve with piping hot coffee. Ham, chicken, deviled meats, sardines etc. can be used in place of bacon. It's easy to make and you don't use too many dishes. — Norman Phillips

High Concept Hamburger

John Hodgman • Hancock County

"Some summers ago I ate a hamburger sitting on a cannon at Fort Knox in Bucksport. I got the hamburger from Crosby's Drive-In, and it was not an ordinary hamburger: it was a Golden Buck.

I didn't ask what a Golden Buck was when I ordered it, because I enjoy mysteries. And I won't tell you what the two, truly inspired special ingredients are, not because it's some big secret (Crosby's will just tell you, as they did when I called them to refresh my memory to write this), but because I want you to go there and eat it. It is delicious. It is golden.

I've always been wary of high concept hamburgers. A burger's first appeal is simplicity. And while everyone's entitled to the condiments of their choice, it is perilously easy to go too far. Massive burgers, stuffed with cheese, flavored mayos, triple patties, multiple strata of bacon, custom grinds of wagyu beef, a sunnyside up duck egg, truffles—these burgers feel louche and desperate. They are dropped like grease bombs onto menus to tempt a visit from Guy Fieri, or are press-released as click bait for foodie websites. Almost none of these oddball improvizations balance with the burger to make it a new, good thing.

The Golden Buck is an exception. My burger, in my opinion, is another one.

It came about last summer in my kitchen in Maine. I happened to have a huge 6-pound tube of Taylor Pork Roll in my fridge (long story). If you don't know, Taylor Pork Roll is not a Maine product: it's a breakfast staple of New Jersey, a salty-savory ham-like processed meat that's shoved into a burlap sack. My aunts from Philadelphia gave this 6-pounder to me for my 50th birthday (OK, not so long a story after all). And while Pork Roll has a long shelf life, I was running out of ways to use it up before its August expiration date.

So I grilled up a slice and put it on a hamburger. And there I should have stopped, but I didn't. I also had some white American cheese, and a box of frozen hashbrowns. So I added those as well. Wait: I cooked the hashbrown first, of course. But I understand why you'd wonder, since what I was doing to this poor hamburger was already weird and criminal and was sure to taste like garbage.

But I am here to tell you it did NOT taste like garbage. It tasted good. A hamburger with a hashbrown, I'd later learn, is pretty well known in Japanese-based fast food places because it makes perfect sense. French fries and burgers go together already. But the pork roll added a vinegar tang that woke all the distinct flavors up and put them to work.

I realized what I had in my hand: an actual, functioning, non-bad concept burger. Maybe not a Golden Buck, but at least a bronze one. But what could I do with this burger? How could I share it with the world? I considered giving the recipe to Crosby's or The Brooklin General Store or any of the other Maine roadside places that I love, promising them that this recipe is a license to print money. But I knew they would look at it, and then at me, the same way you are looking at me now, and I would be asked to leave the premises.

So I share it with you here, now. Seriously: just try it. Here is the burger from the bottom up."

Bottom bun. Nothing fancy. Whatever you get at the Hannaford. Lightly toasted.

Put ketchup on that.

Griddle a frozen hash brown and put it on the ketchuped bottom bun.

I use Cavendish brand hash browns, which is from Quebec and (weirdly) is the official hash brown of Gillette Stadium in Massachusetts. But I get them at the Burnt Cove market on Deer Isle, so that feels pretty Maine to me.

At the same time, griddle 5 oz of ground beef, smash burger style, thin and crispy, as well as a quarter inch slice of Taylor Pork Roll in a cast-iron pan or whatever kind of pan you like.

For the beef, use whatever you like, but I'd be remiss if I didn't mention that Maine has lots of family farms who are raising cows and grinding beef locally: Caldwell Family Farm, Misty Brook Farms, Milkhouse Dairy Farm, A Wee Bit Farm—they're all great.

If it seems I'm really overplaying the Maine pedigree of this burger, you're correct. Because there is no denying that Taylor Pork Roll is absolutely From Away. That said, you can get it at Acadia Provisions in Ellsworth for some reason, and lots of folks on the Maine subreddit tell me they've seen it pop up elsewhere in the state. Maine already has Pennsylvania Dutch scrapple in the freezer case of many supermarkets and the people here like fried things, so I see no reason this pork should not continue its roll through the Pine Tree state. But if you absolutely can't find it, you can order it online. And if it just offends you, skip it. The burger is still good.

OK now that you've finished reading that lame defense, your burger and pork roll should now be cooked. Did you remember to cut little divots into the circumference of the pork roll at noon, three, six, and 10 o'clock to keep it flat? You'll remember next time.

Put the burger onto the hash brown.

Put a slice of white cheese onto the burger.

Put the slice of Taylor Pork Roll onto the cheese.

Remember when you put ketchup on that bottom bun? OK. Now put a little mayo on the lightly toasted top bun to top it all off.

CONSUME.

I still can't think of a name for this burger. "Bronze Medal Buck" is pretty good, but doesn't honor the Pork Rollishness of it. The "From Away Burger" leans too far toward New Jersey and no one will want to eat it. Porky Hashburger sounds like the name of a local creep. Call it whatever you want. It's finally out of my head and my greasy hands, and now it belongs to you, Maine. You're welcome.

MAINE COAST
LOBSTER
IN THE BASKET
BASKETS
Crosby's
CHICKEN
BASKET
HAMBURGERS
LOBSTER ROLLS

Giving Thanks

By Abdi Nor Iftin

Thanksgiving is one of my favorite holidays in the United States. I enjoy sharing the meal of turkey, mashed potatoes, stuffing, cranberry sauce and, my favorite dessert, sweet potato soufflé. None of this food is familiar where I originally come from.

Living in Maine, there is one thing I miss a lot: the chai and chats of Mogadishu's makeshift tea shops. This is a day of chatting about family affairs of men who gather for the joyful moment of sipping spicy tea cooked with cardamon, fresh ginger and dry cinnamon. I would sit in those shops surrounded by friends and the day would be filled with laughter. At nights there was this familiar sound that came from every house in my neighborhood. The sound of grinding corn using mortar and pestle to make white corn and beans boiled together for dinner.

Since I moved here seven years ago, I have learned that the dishes from Somalia can be even tastier here because there are many more ingredients to buy from the local groceries. Ingredients that come from anywhere on the planet. The Somalis have learned not only new skills and new languages to survive, they have learned to make their food ever more delicious. I still cook my meal as traditional as it used to be. For my beans and corn dinner, I follow the steps my family followed when I was a kid. Wash the beans and corn, soak them overnight with six cups of water, boil them for twenty minutes and eat them with camel milk. At the dinner table here in Maine, eating a Somali dish, I always have the strong feeling of being home—both homes.

There are more than 55,000 New Mainers in the state. Many of them are great cooks, and what makes neighbors love each other is sharing delicious food, and discussing culture and traditions. I work closely with Maine immigrant communities and I have the opportunity to meet and dine with people from different backgrounds, experiencing their food and culture. Despite the language difference, we get to know each other, sharing stories and meals. No two New Mainers are the same. I encourage Mainers who have lived here their whole lives to step out of their comfort zone and make the effort to integrate by inviting a New Mainer to dinner. Get to know the hopes of these New Mainers, what they find most surprising about living here and what can be done to live and thrive together.

How about sharing your food traditions with a newly arrived family? Know that some newly arrived Mainers won't eat meat unless it is halal meat, which they might buy from their preferred local grocery stores. But they could cook it at their house and bring the food to the host's home. All Mainers can show love and solidarity by sharing meals and giving thanks for one another. Sharing a meal will, for sure, bring so much joy.

I have lived here now for seven Thanksgivings. On my first Thanksgiving, I observed and learned. I did not do much except watch and exercise patience as I took notes. On my second Thanksgiving, I knew what to do. I picked one side dish to make, the Somali muufo, a popular Somali flatbread. White corn flour is used to prepare this side dish, which is best served with stews or sometimes eaten in pieces with shaah, a sweet and spiced Somali chai. On my third Thanksgiving, I learned to bake sweet potato soufflé. And someday when I return to my native country, it is one of the dishes I want to introduce. Mainers should be excited to integrate new foods and New Mainers into their meals, as well.

The recipe for Muufo Corn Bread can be found on page 24.

Abdi Nor Iftin is the author of the bestselling and award-winning memoir, Call Me American. *He has been featured on CNN, NPR, The New York Times, Washington Post, and The Boston Globe. Abdi is an advocate for refugee and immigrant rights and is dedicated to bringing people together through his stories of survival and resilience.*

COOKIES & BARS

Photo: Greta Wallace in her 1950s Westbrook kitchen. Greta's recipe for Crème de Menthe Bars can be found on page 210.

Auntie Azubah's Hermits

Sandy Garson • Bath, Sagadahoc County

"During the 1970s, Edith Berry Horne was the doyenne of Georgetown Island, the go-to source for its social histories, which she'd share with anyone willing to listen. Her memory was perfect. Edith was born in 1891 into the island center's most illustrious family and happily recalled that as a child, if the river wasn't frozen, she enjoyed a second Christmas: first at the Second church where the tree touched the ceiling and was decorated with popcorn and candy provided by its Ladies' Aid, then at her Aunt Azubah Berry Snowman's where the two plumpest chickens were killed to be served with homegrown squash, turnip, potatoes and onion. Edith's mother would bring molasses and sugar cookies as well as pies and cakes. 'Apple pies were too ordinary,' she said, 'because everybody had apples from their trees, but mince and pumpkin were special so that's what we had.' Into the 1970s and her '80s, Edith was still baking her Aunt Azubah's hermits for her adored grown grandson, and with great delight she passed on to the whole island her 19th-century recipe for New England's beloved cookie."

- ½ cup sugar
- 1 cup shortening
- 2 eggs, beaten
- ½ cup milk
- ½ cup molasses
- 2½ cups flour, less 2 tablespoons
- 1 teaspoon baking soda
- ¾ teaspoon cinnamon
- ¾ teaspoon ground ginger
- ½ teaspoon nutmeg
- ½ teaspoon cloves
- 1 cup chopped raisins

In a large bowl, cream together sugar and shortening. Add eggs, milk, and molasses. In a separate bowl, sift together flour, baking soda, and spices. Add sifted ingredients to sugar mixture, then stir in raisins. Mix well and pat dough into a 15x10-inch rimmed pan. Bake at 350 degrees for 25-30 minutes, or until done. Cool and cut into squares before serving.

Elizabeth's Famous Brownies

Colleen Crocker • Pittsfield, Somerset County

"This was my daughter Elizabeth's brownie recipe. She always said someday she would be famous for her brownies. Unfortunately she died as a teenager when she was struck by a drunk driver. Though Elizabeth only lived to be 15 years old, she made an impact on everyone who knew her. She was a loving girl who was known for getting along with everyone. She loved to bake and was so proud that she made the best brownies. She loved to make them for her dad and me, and her whole family. She and I baked together all the time and some of my best memories are the long mother-daughter talks we had as we baked, with love filling up our kitchen. We share her recipe whenever we can in the hopes that one of her dreams can come true."

- 2 cups sugar
- ⅔ cup cocoa
- 1 cup softened butter
- 2 teaspoons vanilla
- 4 eggs
- 1¼ cups flour
- ½ teaspoon salt
- ¼ teaspoon baking powder
- 1 cup nuts (optional)

Preheat oven to 350 degrees. In a large bowl, mix together sugar and cocoa, then cream in the butter and vanilla. Mix in the eggs. In a separate bowl, sift together dry ingredients, then add to the wet mixture and mix well. Stir in nuts, if using. Grease a 9x13-inch baking pan, and spread the batter evenly in the pan. Bake 25 to 30 minutes. Cool completely before cutting.

Baklava

Senator Olympia Snowe • Auburn, Androscoggin County

"Growing up in a large Greek family, every gathering was—and still is! —a grand affair filled with joyous conversation and an abundance of delicious Greek food. A particular favorite among the family was always my Aunt Mary's baklava. After her passing, my cousin Toni continued the tradition of making it for our family events. My husband, [former Governor] Jock [McKernan], and I always look forward to it when we all get together for holiday lunches and dinners—and Toni's sister, Georgia, introduced us to putting the leftover crumbs and syrup on ice cream to savor every last morsel. We highly recommend it!"

For syrup:
2 cups water
4 cups sugar
1 cinnamon stick
3 lemon slices
½ cup honey

For baklava:
1½ pounds walnuts, finely chopped
¼ cup sugar
1 teaspoon cinnamon
Zest of 1 orange
1 pound phyllo dough, thawed according to package directions (see Note)
1 pound butter, melted and cooled

Note: Packages usually come as 36-40 sheets measuring 9x14 inches or about 18-20 sheets measuring 14x18 inches. Either will work! If you get 14x18-inch sheets, just cut them in half for a total of 36-40 sheets measuring 9x14 inches."

To make the syrup: Combine water, sugar, cinnamon, and lemon slices in a saucepan. Stir over medium-high heat until all the sugar dissolves, then boil for 15 minutes. Remove mixture from heat and stir in the honey. Let cool completely.

To make baklava: In a bowl, combine walnuts, sugar, cinnamon, and orange zest and mix well.

Brush bottom and sides of a 9x13-inch pan with melted butter. Trim phyllo dough to fit pan. Keep in mind that phyllo dough dries out fast, so work quickly. To help, cover sheets with a damp towel while working.

Place 8 phyllo sheets in the pan, one at a time, brushing each layer with butter before adding the next.

After the 8th sheet, spread some of the nut mixture over phyllo into an even layer. Add three buttered phyllo sheets, then another layer of nuts. Repeat until you run out of nut mixture (about 4 times), reserving 8 phyllo sheets for the top. After the final nut layer, top with the remaining 8 phyllo sheets, buttering liberally between each.

Refrigerate the assembled baklava until cold, then score the top phyllo sheet in a diamond pattern. These are guide marks for cutting the baklava once finished. Bake at 350 degrees for 45 minutes, or until golden brown.

Remove from oven and pour cooled syrup evenly over baklava. Let sit at room temperature, uncovered, for 24 hours. Cut and serve. Store in airtight container at room temperature for up to 4 weeks.

Honey Treats

Jan Varnum • Bar Harbor, Hancock County

"My mother got this recipe from a friend about 75 years ago. She always made the cookies at Christmas; they kept well and softened up a bit when frosted and decorated. I've made them almost every Christmas since coming to Maine in 1962, and I'm 81 years old now! People love them."

- 1 egg
- ½ cup sugar
- ⅔ cup light-colored honey, strained
- ⅓ cup melted shortening
- 2¾ cups flour
- 1 teaspoon baking soda
- 1 teaspoon salt
- ½ teaspoon vanilla
- ¼ teaspoon almond extract

In a large bowl, beat egg thoroughly. Add sugar, strained honey, and melted shortening.

Sift flour, then measure and sift again with baking soda and salt. Add dry ingredients to the honey mixture. Add extracts and mix well. Chill thoroughly.

Preheat oven to 350 degrees. Roll dough thicker than usual on a flour-sprinkled surface, to about ¼ inch. Dough is quite sticky, so use plenty of flour in rolling. Cut out desired shapes and bake on a greased baking sheet (or parchment) about 10 minutes. Do not overbake. Frost and decorate, as desired.

Grammie's Molasses Cookies

Bessie Boulay • Bowdoinham, Sagadahoc County

"This recipe is great-great-grandmother Eunice Glidden Campbell's; handed down to great grandmother Caroline Campbell Douglass; handed down to my mother Minnie Douglass; handed down to me; handed down to my daughter Sherri St. Pierre and my daughter-in-law Lori Boulay; and handed down to Sherri's children and grandchildren."

- 1 cup molasses
- 1 cup sugar
- 1 cup shortening
- 3 teaspoons cream of tartar
- 3 teaspoons baking soda
- 1 teaspoon cinnamon
- 5 cups flour
- ¾ cup boiling water
- 1 teaspoon vanilla
- 1 teaspoon salt

In a large bowl, mix together molasses, sugar, shortening, cream of tartar, baking soda, cinnamon, and flour. Add the boiling water, then stir in the vanilla and salt and mix thoroughly. Roll out the dough. Use the rim of a glass to cut out the cookies and bake at 400 degrees for 8-10 minutes

Molasses, New England's Sweetener

Sandy Oliver • Islesboro, Waldo County

"Mainers' historic affection for molasses has endured even though molasses' flavor has been largely usurped by a modern preference for chocolate, with brownies favored now over gingerbread, and chocolate mousse taking the place of Indian pudding. Traditionally speaking, molasses-sweetened dishes rank high among New England comfort foods.

The syrup named molasses remains when cane sugar juice boils away and sugar crystals form. Today a centrifuge extracts sugar granules leaving molasses that may be further boiled to make more sugar. The darkest molasses, called blackstrap, has virtually all the sugar removed. Nutritionally speaking, molasses is high in calcium, iron, and carbohydrates. Brown sugar used to be sugar with some of the molasses left in it; nowadays, molasses is added back to granulated sugar to make brown sugars.

Bittersweet molasses created the characteristic flavor of many early New England dishes and was the main ingredient of rum, the beverage popular with Early American colonists and craved by sailors on sailing ships around the world. From the 1600s through the 1800s, sugar plantation development exploded to meet demand for sweetening. But inherent in the wealth created and the pleasures of eating and drinking was a great deal of brutality, misfortune and suffering. Molasses and rum were by-products of growing, harvesting, pressing and evaporating sugar cane, making for a brutally laborious production process that greatly expanded the growth of slavery in the West Indies and American South and perpetuated the trans-Atlantic slave trade.

During the 1800s, rum was demonized by Temperance workers and cane sugar was deplored by abolitionists, but molasses was cheap and popular and poured copiously into Indian pudding, brown bread, molasses cookies, gingerbread, and baked beans. Nicknamed 'long-tailed sugar,' molasses figured among the regular rations on American sailing vessels, used for sweetening coffee and tea, and as sauce for sailors' duff, a boiled pudding.

With time came change. At the turn of the 19th to 20th century, steamed gingerbread puddings gave way to chocolate steamed puddings. Marble cake was originally made by swirling together yellow cake and molasses-sweetened batter, but in the mid-20th century, marble cake was made with chocolate supplying the dark batter. Molasses cookies yielded to chocolate chip. Corn syrup has taken over taffy, popcorn balls, and nut brittles, all formerly made with molasses.

Hardly anyone alive today ever puts molasses-sweetened cream on apple dumplings or eaten molasses–sweetened apple pies. And pumpkin pie is more often than not sweetened with brown or white sugar instead of molasses.

Children growing up in the 1940s and '50s often enjoyed molasses spread on buttered bread for a snack. In some corners of Maine, relics of molasses sweetening continue, as in molasses doughnuts and molasses blueberry cake. Anadama, oatmeal, and brown bread all rely on molasses and enjoy continued popularity. And, of course, molasses and brown sugar sweeten Maine baked beans."

Zephyrettes

1907 • A Book of Selected Recipes

Pythian Sisters, Saco Valley Temple • Hiram, Oxford County

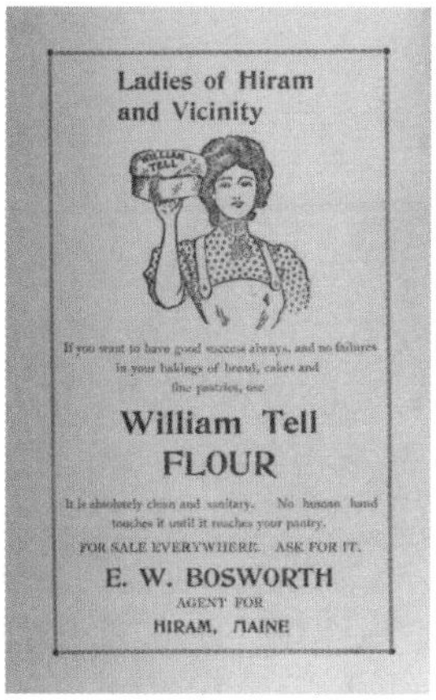

The contributor of the recipe, Mrs. E.W. Bosworth, likely had access to quality ingredients, as she was married to E.W. himself, agent for William Tell Flour, which we know from the full page advertisement in the front of the cookbook. —DL

Mix one-half cupful chopped nuts with one-half cupful cream; add sufficient confectioners' sugar to make a stiff frosting; flavor with vanilla. This mixture will spread about one pound and a half of saltines. Brown slightly in a quick oven. —Mrs. E.W. Bosworth

Memere's Filled Cookies

Lucky D'Ascanio • Falmouth, Cumberland County

"My Memere Roy used to have the best filled cookies when I was a little girl. Her kitchen always smelled so good and was so warm and comfortable. When I became a teenager, this was the first recipe that my mom taught me to bake. I made them for my children and they are still a favorite. I have since taught my daughter to make these yummy comfort food cookies and hope she too will share the recipe with her children one day."

1 cup shortening
2 cups sugar
4 eggs
2 teaspoons vanilla
5 cups flour
½ teaspoon baking soda
1 teaspoon salt
Jam for filling
(raspberry or strawberry tastes best)

Mix together shortening, sugar, and eggs in large bowl and beat until fluffy. Stir in vanilla. In a separate bowl, combine flour, baking soda, and salt. Add dry ingredients a little at a time to the shortening, mixture, stirring well after each addition. Chill overnight, or at least for a few hours.

When ready to bake, preheat oven to 400 degrees. Roll out dough on a floured surface to ¼-inch thickness and cut with a 2-inch juice glass or round cookie cutter. Place cookie bottoms on greased cookie sheet and drop scant teaspoon of jam on each round. Top with second cookie and pinch edges to seal. Prick tops with fork tines and bake for 8-10 minutes. Store in an air-tight container.

Pumpkin Chocolate Cookies

Andrea Hawkes • Portland, Cumberland County

"This was a favorite recipe of our Hawkes Family in Bangor. My beloved mother-in-law Dorothy 'Dolly' Averill Hawkes made these cookies for the 40 years that I knew her. These cookies were at every important family function and holiday, and everyone in the family loved them. She died in 2007, and to this day when we make them it is as if she is still with us, laughing in her kitchen as she presses more cookies on us."

- 2 eggs
- 1 can pumpkin purée
- 1 cup vegetable oil
- 2 tablespoons milk
- 2 cups sugar
- 2 teaspoons vanilla
- 4 teaspoons cinnamon
- 4 cups flour
- 2 teaspoons baking soda
- 1 teaspoon salt
- 12-ounce package chocolate chips

Preheat oven to 350 degrees. In a large bowl, mix together eggs, pumpkin purée, vegetable oil, milk, sugar, vanilla, and cinnamon. In a separate bowl, sift together flour, baking soda, and salt. Combine wet and dry ingredients and mix well. Add chocolate chips and mix until thoroughly incorporated. Drop cookies by spoonful onto a cookie sheet and bake for 10-15 minutes. Remove from trays and cool on a wire rack.

Lazy Man's Cookies

Jo Andrews • Brooksville, Hancock County

"I found this recipe in my Grammie Jessie's recipe box with MY name written across the top of the card, so I can only assume that Gram made these for me quite often. I think the filling was date jam, as I enjoy the taste of date-filled cookies. My parents, siblings, and I lived with my grandparents, Harris 'Babe' and Jessie (Clark) Vague in their Glenburn farmhouse from 1971-74. Grammie worked in Bangor shoe shops until her retirement in 1982, so for her to take the time to bake meant a lot. She was a good cook who made traditional baked beans and biscuits (sometimes cornbread to switch things up!) for Saturday dinner, homemade bread and butter pickles and many other time-honored Maine treats."

- 1 pound brown sugar
- 1 cup oleo
- 2 eggs
- 1½ teaspoons baking soda dissolved in ½ cup warm water
- ½ teaspoon salt
- 1 teaspoon vanilla
- 4 cups flour
- Jam, for filling

Mix together all ingredients and drop by spoonful onto a lightly greased cookie sheet. Make a hole in the dough and spoon filling into the hole. Drop a bit of dough on top of the filling. Bake 15-20 minutes at 350 degrees.

Koulourakia Greek Cookies

Donna Droggitis Thomson • Biddeford Pool, York County

"I have vivid memories of my Mum, Mary Droggitis, baking Greek pastries for church fairs and family gatherings, especially around the holidays. What I remember most is that she never followed a recipe. When baking with her, I would ask, 'How do you know how much flour to add?' And her answer would always be, 'You can feel it.' I was young back then and had no interest in baking or cooking and I certainly had no idea as to what she meant by 'you can feel it!' Luckily, my cousin's wife, JoAnn Droggitis, had the brilliant idea of actually watching my mother bake and she measured the ingredients as they went along. She generously shared all of my mother's pastry recipes with me after my mother passed away in 1980. Koulourakia are one of my family's favorites. I have, by the way, mastered the art of 'you can feel it' when adding flour. If you add too much, the dough is dry and crumbles, if you add too little, the dough is too sticky to handle. When I bake this particular cookie around the holidays, they disappear quickly as they come out of the oven and I often have to make another batch!"

1 cup unsalted butter, at room temperature
3 eggs
1½ teaspoons baking powder
1 cup sugar
1 teaspoon vanilla
3-4 cups flour
(start with 3—you can feel it!)
1 egg beaten with 1 tablespoon water, for egg glaze

In the bowl of a stand mixer, beat butter until creamy, then add eggs, baking powder, sugar, and vanilla. Gradually add flour, 1 cup at a time. Dough should be a soft consistency, moist but not sticky.

Roll pieces of dough in your hand and then twist the dough into a braid. Brush each cookie with a glaze of a little beaten egg mixed with a little water. Bake on ungreased cookie sheet at 350 degrees for approximately 20 minutes. Let cool and store in an air-tight container.

The Miller's Table Salted Rye Chocolate Cookies

Amber Lambke • Skowhegan, Somerset County

Sponsored by
Maine Grains

"This recipe comes from the personal collection of a former Maine Grains employee, the late Lisa Stern. The recipe has been adapted over time to use Maine Grains Organic rye flour and is frequently enjoyed by guests of The Miller's Table Café. They are soft, chewy, and fudgy, sprinkled with just the right amount of crunchy sea salt. Please note that precise measurements by metric weight appear in parenthesis for several ingredients."

- 2⅝ cups (450g) bittersweet chocolate chunks
- ½ cup (115g) unsalted butter
- 1 cup plus 2 rounded tablespoons (130g) Maine Grains rye flour
- 1 teaspoon baking powder
- ½ teaspoon salt
- 4 eggs, at room temperature
- 1½ cups (300g) granulated sugar
- 1 tablespoon vanilla extract
- Maldon's sea salt, for sprinkling

Melt chocolate and butter together in a double boiler, whisking to combine. Remove from heat and allow to cool slightly.

In a small bowl, combine Maine Grains rye flour, baking powder, and salt, and whisk together.

In the bowl of an electric stand mixer, whisk the eggs on high speed and slowly add the sugar, whipping for about 6 minutes. The mixture should triple in volume. Reduce speed to low, and add melted chocolate mixture and vanilla, scraping down the sides of the bowl if necessary. Slowly add the flour mixture, and using the paddle attachment, mix until combined. Refrigerate dough for 1 hour.

Preheat oven to 325 degrees. Using a 2-inch scoop or large spoon, scoop dough onto parchment-lined cookie sheet, leaving room for expansion. Flatten the top of each ball of dough slightly with your hand before sprinkling with a few grains of Maldon's sea salt. Bake for 18 minutes, rotating baking sheets halfway through. Cool thoroughly on a wire rack.

Annie's Christmas Cookies

Carmen Weatherbie • Cape Elizabeth, Cumberland County

"When I married my husband, Malcolm, in 1984, I was pleased that my mother-in-law, Annie Weatherbie, shared many of her recipes and Maine cookbooks with me. A long-standing family Christmas tradition was making rolled, cutout cookies. We know that Ethelyn Louise Tibbetts, Annie's mom, made these cookies. Where or when the recipe started is not known, but the tradition continues today with Annie's grand- and great-grandchildren. The recipe is easily doubled, and can be used for any rolled, cutout cookie."

Cookie dough:

⅓ cup shortening
⅓ cup sugar
1 egg
⅔ cup honey
2¾ cups flour
1 teaspoon baking soda
1 teaspoon salt
1 teaspoon vanilla

Icing:

Confectioners' sugar
Warm milk
Soft butter
Vanilla
Food coloring
Sanding sugar and sprinkles, for decorating

In the bowl of a stand mixer fitted with the paddle attachment, mix together all dough ingredients. The dough will be very stiff. Wrap and chill dough before shaping.

Grease cookie sheets and preheat oven to 375 degrees. On a floured surface roll dough to ¼-inch thick, or slightly thinner. Cut into desired shapes with cookie cutters and bake for 6-8 minutes. Cool completely before decorating.

To make the icing, combine confectioners' sugar with just a couple of teaspoons of milk and softened butter to desired consistency. Add a few drops of vanilla, and food coloring, if desired. Pipe or spread onto cooled cookies and decorate with sanding sugar and sprinkles, as desired

Mandelbrot

Nancy Schatz • Manchester, Kennebec County

"My mother came from a very close-knit Jewish family, she was the middle of five children, four of them girls. Her parents, Katie and Meyer came from Kyiv, and Meyer was a butcher and later in the soda business. All the sisters were great cooks, but this recipe came from my mother's sister-in-law, my Aunt Jeanette. She was a very cheerful woman, always smiling. She gave me the recipe years ago and I've been making it ever since. Now that I spend winters down in Florida, everyone down here knows my mandelbrot."

2 eggs, beaten
⅔ cup sugar
2 teaspoons lemon extract
½ cup vegetable oil
2 cups flour
1 teaspoon baking powder
½ teaspoon salt
¾ cup slivered almonds

Preheat oven to 350 degrees. In a large bowl, mix together the eggs, sugar, lemon extract, and vegetable oil. Stir in the flour, baking powder, and salt, and mix by hand with a rubber spatula. Add the slivered almonds, and thoroughly combine.

Separate dough into three pieces, and shape into logs 4 inches wide and about 2 inches tall. Place dough onto parchment-lined baking sheets, leaving room between them for the dough to spread. Bake for 20 minutes. Remove from oven and let cool for 10 minutes.

Using a serrated knife, cut baked dough into slices on a slight diagonal. Place the slices, cut side up, on the baking sheets, and return to oven for 20 minutes more, until mandel breads are crisp and slightly golden.

Honey's Heath Bar Cookies

Margaret Hathaway • Gray, Cumberland County

"My grandma Honey, Charlotte Lupien Buchholz, was famous for sending baked goods from her kitchen in Chicago to her children and grandkids all over the country—and the world. When I was living in France on my twenty-third birthday, I opened the mail to find a poundcake plastered in stamps. Well before every Christmas, she would send tins of cookies to all of us, and after Honey passed, I kept the tradition going. Now, with my daughters Charlotte, Beatrice, and Sadie, I pull out pages of recipes in Honey's handwriting, and get to work each December. We rarely get them in the mail as promptly as Honey did, but my aunts, uncle and cousins know to watch for a box from Maine."

1 cup butter, softened
1 cup brown sugar
1 egg yolk
1 teaspoon vanilla
2 cups flour
1 large Hershey bar
Lotsa (1 ½ cups)
ground pecans and/or walnuts

Preheat oven to 350 degrees. In a large bowl, beat together butter, brown sugar, egg yolk, and vanilla. Add in the flour and mix until thoroughly combined. Spread batter in a parchment-lined 9x13-inch baking dish, and pat smooth. Bake 15-20 minutes, until dough begins to shrink back from the sides. While cookie is still warm, place the chocolate bar on top, and once it's melted, use a spatula to smooth it over the top. Sprinkle with nuts and press them into the gloppy chocolate. Wait until the chocolate has hardened to cut into bars.

Coffee Bars

Barbie Sadler Humphrey • Bangor, Penobscot County

Sponsored by
Wicked Joe Organic Coffees

"I have been making this recipe for over forty years. It was given to me by my mother-in-law, and became one of my all-time standbys, especially for unexpected visitors. I kept all the ingredients on hand and could get it put together and in the oven in 10 minutes. It makes many servings depending on how you cut it. I've cut it into small 1-inch squares and put into mini-papercup holders to make fancy finger food at a party. This is delicious served with ice cream."

2 eggs
1 cup Wicked Joe's brewed black coffee, not boiling
1 pound (2¼ cups) brown sugar
3 cups flour
1 teaspoon salt
1 teaspoon baking soda
1 cup cooking oil
1 teaspoon vanilla
1 cup chocolate chips
½ cup chopped nuts (optional)

In a large bowl, beat eggs. Add coffee and mix. Stir in sugar, and mix. In a separate bowl, sift together flour, salt, and baking soda. Add sifted dry ingredients to the coffee mixture. Mix. Stir in oil and vanilla. Beat until completely mixed. Pour batter into a large ungreased jelly roll pan with sides. Dot the batter with chocolate chips and, if desired, nuts. Bake at 350 degrees for 20-30 minutes, until a toothpick comes out clean. Do not overbake. When fully cooled, cut into squares to serve.

Peanut Butter Fudge

1907 • Fairfield Cook Book Number One.
Favorite Recipes Club • Fairfield, Somerset County

This is not a recipe printed in the cookbook, but a handwritten recipe received by the book's owner, as part of a chain letter called the "Favorite Recipe Club." Mrs. F.S. Blodgett of Bucksport received this fudge recipe all the way from Jacksonville, Florida. This is a good example of how recipes travel, sometimes great distances, and then are taken in and made "local." —DL

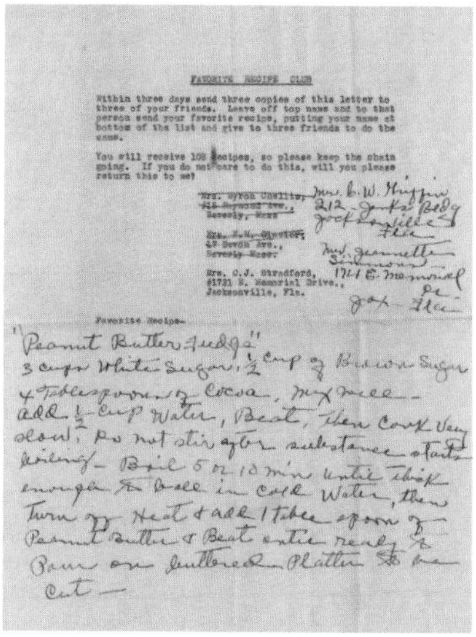

FAVORITE RECIPE CLUB

Within three days send three copies of this letter to three of your friends. Leave off top name and to that person send your favorite recipe, putting your name at bottom of the list and give to three friends to do the same.

You will receive 108 Recipes, so please keep the chain going. If you do not care to do this, will you please return this to me?

Mrs. C.J. Stradford,
#1721 E. Memorial Drive.,
Jacksonville, Fla.

Favorite Recipe-

"Peanut Butter Fudge"
3 cups White Sugar, ½ Cup of Brown Sugar
4 Tablespoons of Cocoa, mix well-
add ½ Cup Water, Beat, then Cook Very slow, Do not stir after substance starts boiling- Boil 5 or 10 min until thick enough to ball in cold Water, then Turn off Heat & add 1 Tablesp of Peanut Butter & Beat until ready to Pour on buttered Platter to be cut—

3 cups white sugar, ½ cup of brown sugar, 4 tablespoons of cocoa, mix well. Add 1 cup water, beat, then cook very slow. Do not stir after substance starts boiling. Boil 5 or 10 min until thick enough to ball in cold water, then turn off heat + add 1 tablespoon of peanut butter + beat until ready to pour on buttered plattered to be cut. — Mrs. C.J. Stradford of Jacksonville, Florida

Mom's Brownies

Marian Fowler • Norcross, Penobscot County

"My mother, Hope Herrick Hale, was born in 1902 and raised in Aroostook County. Until the early 1940s, she and my father, William W. Hale, lived with their four children in Easton, where he was a teacher-principal at Easton High School, and she ran a small store and raised the children. They then moved to Millinocket, where my younger sister and I were born. She hand wrote this recipe onto an index card when I was married in 1965. After many years, when the card had become smeared with chocolate and egg yolk and other baking detritus, I framed it and hung it in my baking area."

- Two 1-ounce squares unsweetened chocolate
- ½ cup butter (1 stick)
- 2 eggs, separated
- 1 cup sugar
- ¼ cup milk
- ½ cup flour
- Scant ½ teaspoon salt
- 1 teaspoon vanilla
- 1 cup chopped nuts (optional)

Preheat oven to 350 degrees. Grease an 8x8-inch pan.

In the top of a double boiler, melt the chocolate and the butter over hot water or very low heat. Remove from heat to slightly cool the mixture.

Separate the eggs. In a large bowl, stir the sugar and milk into the yolks. In a separate bowl, beat the whites into stiff peaks. Stir the chocolate-butter mixture into the egg mixture. Add the flour, salt, vanilla, and, nuts, if using. At the last, fold in the beaten whites and spread batter in the pan.

Bake for about 25 minutes. A light touch to the top should leave no imprint and the brownies should pull slightly away from the sides of the pan. Let cool and cut. Great with ice cream, whipped cream, or any favorite topping...or just plain!

Grammie Bibber's Raisin Oatmeal Cookies

Nancy Moore • Brunswick, Cumberland County

"I was lucky enough to grow up down the street from my grandparents' house in Falmouth. Some of my fondest memories are of the times I spent with Grammie Bibber in her kitchen, especially when she was baking her raisin oatmeal cookies. Once you taste these cookies, you'll understand why they are called raisin oatmeal cookies rather than the more common oatmeal raisin. Every time I pull out the recipe card she wrote out for me over 45 years ago I think of her. And when the smell of baking cookies starts wafting through my house, I'm immediately transported back to her kitchen."

- 1 cup raisins
- 1 cup water
- 1 cup soft shortening (butter works, if you prefer)
- 1 cup sugar
- 2 eggs
- 1 teaspoon vanilla extract
- 2 cups flour
- ¾ teaspoon baking soda
- 1 teaspoon salt
- 1½ cups rolled oats

Preheat oven to 350 degrees. Cook together raisins and water until about 5 tablespoons of liquid remains. Drain the raisins and save the cooking liquid.

In a large bowl, mix shortening, sugar, and eggs until they are thoroughly combined. Stir in the cooled raisin liquid and vanilla extract.

In a separate bowl, sift together the flour, baking soda, and salt. Stir dry ingredients into the shortening mixture, then add rolled oats and cooled raisins.

Drop by tablespoonfuls about 2 inches apart on a lightly greased cookie sheet. Bake 10-12 minutes. Makes 4-5 dozen cookies.

Crunchers

1961 • Copy Cat Cookies

Dorothea Dix Group of the Hampden Highland Methodist Church • Hampden, Penobscot County

This cookie recipe comes from a community cookbook of a church group named after social reformer Dorothea Dix (1802-1887), a native of Hampden and the daughter of an itinerant Methodist preacher. Dix identified the need for assistance to the indigent mentally ill and was an early advocate of the nursing profession. During the Civil War, those who worked under her included Louisa May Alcott. —DL

Sift together 1 cup sifted flour, ½ teaspoon soda, and ¼ teaspoon salt, set aside. Combine ½ cup shortening, ½ cup granulated sugar, and ½ cup brown sugar packed. Beat until light and creamy. Blend in 1 egg and ½ teaspoon vanilla. Stir in flour mixture, add 1 cup corn flakes (crushed), 1 cup quick cooking oat meal, and ½ cup coconut. Drop by teaspoonfuls on greased cookie sheet and flatten with bottom of glass dipped in flour. Bake at 350 for about 8 minutes. Cool.

Crème de Menthe Bars

Debra Wallace • Cumberland, Cumberland County

"My mother-in-law Greta Wallace called herself a kidda', never met a stranger and made everyone she met feel welcomed. Even the postman or repairman could not leave her doorstep without a homebaked treat to take along, or to share at her table. She and her husband Doug we gracious people who loved fellowship. Her specialty was baking and, in her delightful Maine accent, she would say 'Everybody loves my bahs!'"

Cake Layer:

1 cup granulated sugar
½ cup melted butter
4 large eggs, at room temperature
1 cup sifted flour
½ teaspoon salt
1 teaspoon pure vanilla extract
16-ounce can dark chocolate syrup

Mint Layer:

2 cups confectioners' sugar
2 tablespoons green crème de menthe extract
½ cup softened butter

Chocolate Glaze:

1 cup (6 ounces) chocolate chips
6 tablespoons butter

Preheat oven to 350 degrees. Grease and flour a 9x13-inch pan.

To make the cake layer: Mix all ingredients together and pour into the prepared pan. Bake for 30 minutes, until a cake tester comes out clean. Remove from oven and set aside to cool.

While the cake is baking, prepare the mint layer: Combine all ingredients and blend together until smooth. If the mixture is too firm to spread, add small amounts (just a drop or two at a time) of water or milk. Once the cake layer is cool to the touch, spread mint layer over the top.

To make the chocolate glaze: Melt together the chocolate chips and the butter over medium-low heat, stirring to incorporate. Cool the glaze slightly and spread over the mint layer.

Refrigerate bars until set up and firm, about 4 hours or overnight. To cut into squares, dip knife in hot water for a smooth cut. Enjoy!

STONEWALL KITCHEN
FAMILY of BRANDS
Make dessert the Maine event!
STONEWALL KITCHEN
Creators of Specialty Foods
Dark Chocolate Sea Salt Caramel Sauce
COMPANY CLASSIC
Net Weight 354g (12.5 oz.)
STONEWALL KITCHEN
Creators of Specialty Foods
Sea Salt Caramel Sauce
Net Weight 347g (12.25 oz.)
STONEWALLKITCHEN.COM

THE TAYLOR
WATERBORO

PIES & TARTS

Photo: Martha Speed, her cousin Joe Taylor and cousin-in-law Debbie Taylor, show off an array of pies baked for a reunion at the family camp in Waterboro. Martha's recipe for Anadama Bread can be found on page 26, and her sister Nancy Burnette's recipe for Apple Pie can be found on page 6.

Ada Frye's Perfectly Delicious Lemon Pie

Penelope Lord • Vinalhaven, Knox County

"This recipe is from the tattered and yellowed kitchen book of my grandmother and great grandmother, Ada and Sarah Frye. With her husband Frederick, Sarah built and lived at 58 Chestnut Street in Camden. It was a lovely, classic Maine townhouse with frosted panels in the front doors, an attached barn, and a full view of the harbor. I remember well running over the oil-soaked floors of the barn on my way to rummage for treasures in the attic, and the ceiling of the front porch painted a pale Penobscot Blue, holiday dinners around the oak table, the tin ceiling in the dining room, the old spinet in the living room. After Fred had moved in to town from North Haven—where his seafaring relatives from England had, long before, shown up—he married Sarah Smiley of Wiscasset; Ada was their daughter. In town, they called him 'Captain,' and among his many jobs and pursuits he worked at the Knox Mill and had a livery service moving people and things around town in a one-horse buggy. Sarah sounds so happy in her book, making notes about the progress of the house, such as the May day in 1883 when her curtains were hung and rugs were put down, as well as jotting down endless tips on household hints. Like most 19th-century cooks, she was proficient enough just to list the ingredients for most of her recipes—sometimes with just a hint, such as 'add all the flour it will take.' I bet most Mainers have what it takes. Ada would be proud."

1 cup sugar
2 heaping tablespoons flour
Piece of butter the size of an egg (about 2 tablespoons), melted
Pinch of salt
2 eggs, separated
Juice and rind of 1-2 lemons
1 cup milk
Pastry for single crust pie

In a medium-size bowl, beat together sugar, flour, melted butter, salt, and egg yolks until they are creaming. In a separate bowl, beat the egg whites until stiff.

Add to the sugar mixture the juice and rind of 1 or 2 lemons and the milk. Lightly fold in the beaten egg whites, to avoid leaving lumps. Line a 9-inch pie tin with pastry. Pour lemon filling into the crust and bake for 60 minutes in a "slow" oven (300-325 degrees).

My Nana's (Vegan) Pumpkin Pie

Lindsay Bileau • Portland, Cumberland County

"My Nana would make a non-vegan version of this pie for holidays, and I loved it so much that I'd often ask for it to be my birthday cake as well. She would clean out tuna fish cans and bake mini versions of this pie just for me. I went vegan in 2016 and I missed eating this delicious pie. After several failed attempts at figuring out a vegan replacement for sweetened condensed milk, I finally landed on the version you see here. My Nana passed away in 2017, and I've carried on her tradition of baking this pie every Thanksgiving."

Pastry for single crust pie
1½ cups soaked cashews (soak at least four hours OR boil for 20 minutes), drained
1 cup maple syrup
16-ounce can pure pumpkin purée
1 teaspoon cinnamon
½ teaspoon ginger
½ teaspoon nutmeg

Topping:
4 tablespoons all-purpose flour
½ cup coconut sugar (or other granular sugar)
3 tablespoons vegan butter (cold)

Preheat oven to 375 degrees. Line a 9-inch pie plate with pastry.

Blend soaked cashews and maple syrup in a food processor or high-speed blender until smooth and creamy. In a large bowl, mix together cashew mixture, pumpkin, and spices. Pour mixture into pie shell and bake for 15 minutes.

While the pie is baking, start making the topping. Mix the flour and sugar first, then start cutting the cold butter into it until you get a crumbly texture.

Remove from the pie from the oven, and sprinkle the topping all over the top. Return pie to the oven for another 40 minutes, checking after 35 minutes to make sure topping doesn't burn. Cool to room temperature before serving.

Lemon Cloud Pie

Georgia Hansen • Spruce Head, Knox County

"I made Lemon Cloud Pie at The Island Inn on Monhegan, where I was pasty cook for 10 years, the summers of 1969-1978. Our friends Larry and Lynda Goldsmith had purchased a cottage on the island (after years of renting Nigh Duck Cottage, where my husband Dennis and I were married in 1980). Houses are generally sold as is, so the cottage had a fully equipped kitchen, including cookbooks. One day Lynda found a newspaper clipping tucked in one of the cookbooks, and in a phone call, she told me that she found a recipe for a 'great sounding lemon pie,' but, she said 'it has an awful cutesy name.' I replied 'Is it Lemon Cloud Pie?' and it was! Wasn't she surprised. I hadn't made the pie in years, and started making it again. I later learned that it was the Pillsbury Bake-off winner from the first year of the competition in 1959. This had been an Island Inn favorite, and is now a Hansen family favorite. In 2012, I was asked by a neighbor on the cookbook committee for a Meals on Wheels fundraiser, to submit the recipe for the cookbook. Because mine was a late submission, I didn't know to write an anecdote to accompany the recipe. The cookbook, *The Community Table, Recipes and Stories from Midcoast Maine,* is no longer available from MCH (Making Communities Happen) in Rockland. So here is the recipe, now with the story behind it, and our wedding photo, on the porch of Nigh Duck Cottage."

Crust:

1 cup flour
½ teaspoon salt
⅓ cup butter or margarine
1 egg, slightly beaten
1 teaspoon grated lemon rind
1 tablespoon lemon juice

Filling:

1 cup sugar, divided
¼ cup cornstarch
1 cup water
⅓ cup lemon juice
3 egg yolks, slightly beaten
4 ounces (½ package) cream cheese
1 teaspoon grated lemon rind
2 egg whites
¼ cup sugar

To prepare the crust: Preheat oven to 400 degrees. In a large bowl, combine flour and salt; cut in butter. In a separate bowl, combine egg, lemon rind, and lemon juice, and stir into flour mixture, adding 1-2 tablespoons of cold water, if necessary, to form the dough. Roll dough to fit one 8- or 9-inch pie pan. Trim extra dough and make a fluted edge for the pie shell. Place extra pieces on a small baking sheet. Prick pie shell and extra pieces of dough with a fork. Bake for 12-15 minutes, till golden brown. Cool.

To prepare the filling: Combine ¾ cup sugar, cornstarch, water, lemon juice, and egg yolks in saucepan. Cook over medium heat, stirring constantly, until thick. Add cream cheese and stir until smooth. Remove from heat and stir in lemon rind. Cool.

In a medium-size bowl, beat the egg whites until soft mounds form. Gradually add remaining ¼ cup sugar and beat until stiff peaks form. Fold beaten egg white mixture into cooled lemon mixture. Pour into baked pie shell. Sprinkle crumbled pastry pieces over filling. Chill at least 2 hours before serving. Best to refrigerate uncovered so it doesn't get soggy.

Casco Bay (Pie) Crust

Alicia Menard and Jennell Carter • Scarborough, Cumberland County

Sponsored by Casco Bay Creamery

"We started Casco Bay Creamery 10 years ago to bring old-fashioned, good-for-you, real butter back to Maine dining tables. We were just a couple of crazy folks with a mixer in a rented church kitchen whipping up small batches of deliciously playful butter. We didn't realize how our butter journey would lead us to expand our product offerings and to grow from Casco Bay Butter to Casco Bay Creamery. Today, our story and mission remains the same: to support small, family dairy farms and to craft the best butter and cream cheese. We continue to be amazed by the support of our customers. It's an honor to be in your refrigerator, part of your recipes, and on your dinner tables."

- 1¼ cups all-purpose flour
- ¼ teaspoon salt
- ½ cup chilled and diced unsalted Casco Bay Butter
- 3 tablespoons ice water

In a large bowl, combine flour and salt. Cut in butter until mixture resembles coarse crumbs. Stir in water, a tablespoon at a time, until mixture forms a ball. Wrap in plastic and refrigerate for 4 hours or overnight. Roll dough out to fit a 9-inch pie plate. Place crust in pie plate. Press the dough evenly into the bottom and sides of the pie plate. Makes enough dough for a single crust pie.

Danish Puff

Marge Davis • Portland, Cumberland County

"My mother Edie McCormick, now 92, began making this recipe when I was growing up in Portland. Through her church, Trinity Episcopal in Portland, she was active for decades in Project Feed."

Pastry layer:
½ cup butter
1 cup all-purpose flour, sifted
2 tablespoons ice-cold water

Puff layer:
½ cup butter
1 teaspoon almond extract
1 cup all-purpose flour, sifted
3 eggs

Vanilla icing and toppings:
½ to ¾ cups confectioners' sugar, sifted
2 tablespoons butter
4 tablespoons milk or cream
½ teaspoon almond extract
Chopped walnuts, for decorating
Chopped maraschino cherries, for decorating

To make the pastry layer: Cut the butter into the flour until it's the consistency of fine crumbs. Add the ice water and beat by hand until mixture forms a ball and leaves the sides of the bowl. Divide the dough in half. Press each half onto an ungreased cookie sheet to form a rectangle 3 x 12 inches. Set the pastry bottoms 2 to 3 inches apart.

To make the puff layer: Preheat the oven to 350 degrees. Put the butter and 1 cup of water in a saucepan and bring to a boil over high heat. Add the almond extract. Remove from heat. Add the flour all at once. Beat until the mixture forms a ball in the saucepan. Let the mixture rest for 10 minutes, then add the eggs, 1 at a time, beating well between each. Divide the puff mixture in half and spread evenly over the pastry bottoms. Bring the puff layer over the edges of the pastry and seal well. Bake in preheated oven for 1 hour.

To make the icing and assemble the Danish puffs: Cream together the confectioners' sugar and butter. Add the milk and almond extract. Beat well to form a creamy icing. Ice the puffs while they are still warm. Decorate with chopped walnuts and cherries. Since this recipe makes 2 long puffs, you can freeze the second.

Custard Pie

Elizabeth Bailey-Mitchell • Union, Knox County

"My husband, Harbour, loves custard pie, and he loves my custard pie. However, Harbour often told me about a woman named Betty Bowley whom he met years ago at his church who was known for her 6-egg custard pie. Betty was a 'Holy Folder' (she, and other older women of the church, met each Saturday to fold the Sunday worship bulletins). Harbour and Betty became friends. He helped her out by snowblowing her driveway or helping with other chores around the house. She would always have a custard pie or cream puffs ready for him when he finished chores and a tall glass of milk to wash it down.

Betty passed away before I could meet her and get a copy of her custard pie recipe. I always wanted that recipe, because Harbour was so fond of both Betty and that pie. Well, God works in mysterious ways. I am a Methodist pastor, and the Bishop appointed me to serve a Methodist church where Betty's elderly niece, Faye, is a member! Making a home visit to Faye, I asked if she might have that custard pie recipe. She was delighted to give it to me!

It is the lightest, brightest custard I have ever had the pleasure of making. I find the virtual absence of directions charming. It indicates Betty assumed any baker worth their salt would surely know how to put together a custard pie, no instructions necessary except whipping eggs and the proper amount of heat and time to bake. I like to use whole milk, for the richest flavor, and while one can prebake the crust, I think that can be left to one's preference. You'll notice the quantity of milk and eggs. Therefore, a deep dish pie pan is necessary, which presents a lovely thick, yet light custard."

6 eggs
¾ cup sugar
1 teaspoon nutmeg
½ teaspoon salt
1 tablespoon flour
1 quart milk

Whip eggs with fork. 10 minutes 425 degrees; 35 minutes 350 degrees.

Bakewell Tart

Mike Fear • Bath, Sagadahoc County

"Going out for afternoon tea was a treat I loved as a child in England. We might have scones with clotted cream, lardy cake, eclairs, and more; however, my favorite was the moist almond-y Bakewell Tart. Its origin was a jam tart being made in Bakewell, Derbyshire, three centuries ago. The apprentice baker got confused about the order of the ingredients, and the resulting 'mistake' was adopted and adapted into today's Bakewell Tart. Although there are many versions of this lovely dessert, this one is a reliable crowd pleaser!"

Pastry:
1¼ cups all-purpose flour
½ teaspoon salt
½ teaspoon sugar
½ cup (1 stick) cold butter
½ tablespoon vinegar or fresh lemon juice
3 tablespoons cold water

Filling:
2-3 tablespoons raspberry jam
½ cup (1 stick) unsalted butter
½ cup caster sugar or granulated sugar
½ teaspoon vanilla extract
½ teaspoon almond extract
Juice and grated rind of ½ lemon
2 large eggs
Scant ¾ cup bread crumbs from fresh white bread
½ cup plus 2 tablespoons ground almonds
½ teaspoon baking powder
1 tablespoon milk

To make the pastry: Place flour, salt, and sugar in a bowl and toss lightly to mix. Cut your cold butter into ½-inch cubes and add to flour. Using your hands, a fork, or a pastry cutter, gently work the butter into the flour until it loosely resembles couscous. (If you "run warm" don't use your hands. You want to keep the butter cold.)

Add vinegar (or lemon juice) to the water and then pour into flour/butter mixture. Using your hands or a wooden spoon, mix together very gently until you form a ball. Avoid overmixing; as soon as all the flour and water are mixed, stop! Wrap dough in plastic wrap and place in the fridge for at least 1 hour.

Roll the pastry out to line a shallow pie dish. There will most likely be extra dough you can use for decoration.

To make the filling and assemble the tart: Preheat oven to 400 degrees. Spread the jam over the pastry.

Cream the butter and sugar together in a mixing bowl until light and fluffy. Add extracts, lemon juice, and grated rind, and then beat in the eggs until well blended.

In a separate small bowl, mix the bread crumbs and ground almonds together, then fold them into the mixture. Add the baking powder and milk. Pour this mixture over the jam.

Place tart in the oven and bake for 15 minutes. Reduce the temperature to 350 degrees, and bake for a further 20-25 minutes. You'll know it's done when the tart is a golden brown color and firm to the touch.

Pumpkin Chiffon Pie

Caitlin Hunter • Belfast, Waldo County

"This was my mother's recipe, and it was the most popular pie at every Thanksgiving. So light, you could go have another piece of pie! I still use her handwritten recipe—my mother had beautiful lettering. To make ginger whipped cream, simply add a little ground ginger to homemade whipped cream."

- 1 tablespoon gelatin
- ¼ cup cold water
- 3 eggs, separated
- ½ cup brown sugar
- 1¼ cups canned pumpkin or squash
- ½ cup milk
- ½ teaspoon salt
- ¼ teaspoon each cinnamon, nutmeg, ginger
- ½ cup granulated sugar
- Graham cracker crust

In a small bowl, soak gelatin in cold water. Set aside

Beat the egg yolks. Place beaten egg yolks, brown sugar, canned pumpkin, milk, salt, and spices together in the top of a double boiler. Cook and stir over hot water until thick. Stir in soaked gelatin until dissolved. Chill mixture until it just begins to set.

In a separate bowl, beat the egg whites until stiff but not dry. Gradually add granulated sugar, then fold into the pumpkin mixture. Fill pie shell and chill. Serve with ginger whipped cream.

Grandpa Gene's Onion Pie

Stacy (Lizotte) Cote • Sanford, York County

"My Grandpa Gene lived in Springvale all his life. He used to make onion pie every holiday! He and my Dad would enjoy every last bit because nobody else in the family has any interest in it. Grandpa passed away in 2002. I have tried to replicate his recipe since he never wrote anything down. My Dad is always thrilled when I bring one over, and that's all he asks for at Christmas and his birthday. Everyone I mention it to always has a look of confusion, but many end up loving it once they try it. Just don't set it down next to an apple pie or else one may be in for a surprise!"

Pastry for a single crust pie
(frozen pie crust is fine!)
5-6 of your favorite onions (we like Vidalia)
Butter
Flour
Salt and pepper
Pinch of sugar

Preheat oven to 400 degrees. Line a 9-inch pie plate with crust. Bake the pie shell for about 10 minutes, removing it from the oven before it starts to brown.

Reduce oven temperature to 350 degrees.

Slice your onions and cook them down in a pan with a little butter, flour, salt, pepper, and a pinch of sugar. Put the onion mixture in your pie crust. Bake the pie for about 25 minutes. Enjoy!

Tart Au Sucre (Sugar Pie)

Lisa Colburn • Orono, Penobscot County

"I grew up in Fort Kent during the baby boomer years. My mom, Rita, was French Canadian. She married my dad, Reynold Dubois, after he returned from the Korean Conflict in 1954. Food was an important part of our lives. My parents had a big vegetable garden in the back yard that provided lots of fresh fruit and vegetables for our family in the summer, and was canned and frozen for the rest of the year. We ate lots of beef—provided by my grandparent's dairy farm, Dubois Dairy—Joseph and Emily Dubois. And needless to say, we always had fresh milk. Holidays were marked by big family gatherings where great food (and lots of it!) was the focus. There were often so many aunts, uncles, cousins, and extended family in attendance that we ate in shifts. Kids would eat first, then were sent away to play. Adults ate next. Then we'd all gather again for desserts. This pie was a traditional French Canadian dessert served when you had special company. It is thick and rich and satisfied everyone's sweet tooth. My Québécois mom made sure company unfamiliar with Tart au Sucre had the opportunity to sample this special treat before they departed her home."

- Pastry for a double crust pie
- 3 cups packed brown sugar
- 1 cup flour
- 1 egg, slightly beaten
- 1 cup whipping cream
- ½ teaspoon salt

Preheat oven to 400 degrees. Roll out two circles of pastry and use one to line the bottom of a 9-inch pie pan.

Put all the filling ingredients into a heavy pot and bring to a boil on medium heat, stirring constantly, until thickened. Pour into the crust-lined pie pan. Add a top crust with slits cut into it. Bake for 45 minutes. Cool to room temperature. Serve with vanilla ice cream.

Pumpkin Pie

Rachel Tremblay • Moscow, Somerset County

"My mother enjoyed baking and her pies went quickly at bake sales. She liked her apple and berry pies extra juicy. In a family with five children, we sometimes would eat an entire pie for dessert, so one lucky child might get the last piece in the pie plate with lots of juice. Pumpkin pie was my Dad's favorite, and also my husband's. My mother liked the blend of spices in this recipe, and, of course, she grew her own pumpkins. She used a traditional pie crust, but I've found a graham cracker crust also goes well with the pumpkin."

Pastry for single pie crust
1½ cups cooked pumpkin
¾ cup sugar
½ teaspoon salt
1 teaspoon cinnamon
½ teaspoon ginger
¼ teaspoon nutmeg
3 eggs, slightly beaten
1¼ cups milk
⅔ cup light cream

Preheat oven to 400 degrees.

Line a 10-inch pie plate with crust.

In a large bowl, combine pumpkin, sugar, salt, and spices. Blend in eggs, milk, and cream. Pour into prepared pie shell. Bake for 15 minutes. Reduce heat to 325 degrees and bake for 30 minutes or until just set. Serve warm or cold with whipped cream.

Aunt Kathy's Cranberry Pie

Sylvia Smith • Seal Harbor, Hancock County

"An oldie but a goodie, and delicious with Maine cranberries."

2 cups cranberries
2 cups raisins
2 cups sugar
6 tablespoons flour
½ cup melted butter
1 cup hot water
1 teaspoon vanilla
Pastry for two double crust pies

Grind or process berries and raisins together. In a large bowl, mix in remaining ingredients. Fill two pie shells and top each with a lattice crust. Bake at 350 degrees until browned and bubbly, about 1 hour.

California Poppy

WILD MAINE BLUEBERRIES

Sponsored by Wyman's

Photo: Amy Wight Chapman's granddaughter Lila, picking blueberries at the family camp on North Pond in Woodstock. Amy's essay "How to Bake a Blueberry Cake Like Gramma Wight's" can be found on page 235.

Baked Blueberry Oatmeal

Jay Tall • Swanville, Waldo County

"Nearly 20 years ago, my wife and I fell in love with Maine. Each year for our annual family vacation, we would head to Acadia National Park where we would hike and pick wild blueberries. We are now fortunate enough to have a home in Swanville and make the 7-hour drive once a month. We leave our house at 5 a.m. I am up that time anyway and my wife and kids fall back asleep in the car to nap for the next 3 hours. When they wake, I have breakfast ready to sustain them for the long ride ahead and, well, to bring back the taste of Maine. What's more hardy than oatmeal and what is more Maine than wild blueberries? I started making this for them and it quickly become their favorite. If there are leftovers, I cut them into sticks and fry them in butter with a little brown sugar."

⅔ cup roughly chopped pecans (omit if you are not a nutty person)
3 cups old-fashioned oats
2 teaspoons cinnamon
2 teaspoons baking powder
¾ teaspoon salt
½ cup sugar
¼ teaspoon nutmeg
1¼ cups milk or half-and-half
⅓ cup maple syrup or honey
2 large eggs
4 tablespoons (½ stick) melted butter
2 teaspoons vanilla extract
1 pint wild Maine blueberries, fresh or Wyman's frozen
1 tablespoon brown sugar, for topping (optional)

Preheat oven to 375 degrees. Grease a 9-inch square baking dish. If using, toast the pecans on a rimmed baking sheet for 4 to 5 minutes, until fragrant.

In a bowl, combine the dry stuff: oats, toasted nuts, cinnamon, baking powder, salt, sugar, and nutmeg. In another bowl, the wet stuff: milk, maple syrup or honey, eggs, butter, and vanilla together; everything except the blueberries, as they will break. Then combine it all in whichever is the larger bowl. After everything is mixed and happy, gentle as you can, mix in the berries.

Gently place the oatmeal in the greased pan. Some of the liquid may still be in the bowl; pour it around the pan and sprinkle the brown sugar on top if you'd like some extra sweetness and crunch. Cover with foil and bake for 20 minutes. Uncover and bake another 25 minutes, until the top is nice and golden. Remove your baked oatmeal from the oven and let it cool for a few minutes before serving. Optional toppings for serving include: vanilla yogurt, heavy cream, additional maple syrup or honey for drizzling, additional blueberries, or brown sugar.

Easy Blueberry Cobbler

Barbara Lovely • Topsham, Sagadahoc County

"I never really knew how wonderful blueberry cobbler could taste until we moved to Maine eight years ago and I began making this cobbler with those special Maine-grown blueberries. *Quelle difference!* Now I freeze Maine blueberries in the summer and make this through the winter months. It's always a great treat for all who share it. Although this recipe can be made with any fruit, I can't imagine making a cobbler without those delicious blueberries grown right here in The Great State of Maine!

3 cups wild Maine blueberries, fresh or Wyman's frozen
1 tablespoon lemon juice
1 cup all-purpose flour
1 cup sugar
1 egg, beaten
¼ cup plus 2 tablespoons butter or margarine, melted
Mix of cinnamon and sugar

Preheat oven to 375 degrees. Place blueberries in an 8-inch baking dish. Sprinkle with lemon juice.

In a large bowl, combine flour, sugar, and egg; stir until mixture resembles coarse meal. Spread over blueberries. Drizzle butter over the top and sprinkle heavily with cinnamon sugar. Bake for 30 minutes. Serve warm, either plain or with ice cream.

Blueberry Buckle

Ellen Moore • Ellsworth, Hancock County

"The following account wasn't *my* worst nightmare but it certainly was for good friend, Cina! One summer our two families went camping for the weekend. My friend knew that my favorite dessert was her blueberry buckle, so she brought all of the ingredients. That afternoon, her husband made a fire and prepared the coals for the reflector oven. My friend prepared the buckle and her husband baked it to PERFECTION! Just before dinner, she asked if I would like to try a little bite—naturally I said 'yes.' I put the beautiful morsel in my mouth and proclaimed 'Oh Cina!' She had mistakenly measured out salt for the sugar in the topping! That was the end of that blueberry buckle!"

Batter:
¼ cup shortening
½ cup sugar
1 egg
1 cup flour, sifted
1½ teaspoons baking powder
¼ teaspoon salt
⅓ cup milk

Topping:
½ cup sugar
⅓ cup flour
½ teaspoon cinnamon
¼ cup butter

2 cups wild Maine blueberries, fresh or Wyman's frozen

To make the batter: In a large bowl, cream shortening and sugar. Add egg and beat well. In a separate bowl, mix dry ingredients together. Add dry ingredients to shortening mixture in two parts, alternating with the milk. Mix just enough to incorporate.

To make the topping: In a small bowl, mix together all ingredients.

To assemble the buckle: Preheat oven to 350 degrees. Grease an 8-inch square baking pan. Spoon batter into the prepared pan. Spread blueberries evenly over the batter. Sprinkle topping over the berries and bake for 30-40 minutes.

Blueberry Cream Cheese Bundt Cake

Nancy Marshall • Carrabassett Valley, Franklin County

"In 2011, the Carrabassett Valley Academy Parent Support Organization put together the *Big Dog Cookbook* as a fundraiser. My mother, Martha Briggs, contributed this cake to the book, with the note that it's 'excellent for breakfast or dessert.' Later, when my sons were older, my mom, who was known to all as 'Oma,' often brought her cake to the college ski races. All the racers from other teams would come to the Colby table because they knew we had the best food for lunch!"

- 18.25-ounce regular yellow cake mix
- 4 large eggs
- ½ cup milk
- ¼ cup vegetable oil
- ½ cup sugar
- 1 teaspoon almond extract
- 8-ounce package cream cheese, softened and cut into 1-inch pieces
- 2 cups wild Maine blueberries, fresh or Wyman's frozen, rinsed and drained
- 1 tablespoon flour
- Sprinkling of confectioners' sugar, for garnish

Preheat oven to 350 degrees. In a large bowl, combine the cake mix with eggs, milk, oil, sugar, and almond extract. Beat on low speed until just blended. Add cream cheese and beat on medium speed for 2 minutes, scraping sides once or twice. In a small bowl, combined blueberries with the flour and shake to coat. This helps to keep them from sinking to the bottom fo the cake. Gently fold the berries into the batter and pour into a greased and floured bundt pan. Bake for 50 to 55 minutes. Place pan on a wire rack and let it cool for 10 minutes. Invert onto a serving platter. Sprinkle with powdered sugar.

Maine Charoset

Judy Stein • Belfast, Waldo County

"My husband, Mike, and I were first-generation American children of Eastern European Jews. We both grew up in suburban New York Ashkenazi communities. We were young adults before we realized that there were communities of Jews for whom 'Jewish' food was very different from the food our parents and grandparents considered Jewish. Jews cooked the food grown and raised in the areas in which they lived and used the spices of the region to create their Jewish food. That realization began a lifelong interest in Jewish food around the world.

Passover provided a great opportunity. Charoset, which in the Passover Seder represents the mortar Jews used when they were slaves in Egypt building the Pyramids, is eaten at every Seder. Mike made the charoset each year until his death, adding new varieties as he discovered them. Some years there were seven kinds of charoset on the table–charoset from Venice with chestnuts and charoset from Surinam with coconut competed with charoset from Eastern Europe with apples and walnuts.

When we moved to Maine in the early 1990s we invited new friends, Jewish and not Jewish, to Seder. As always, charoset became a major topic of conversation when we got to eating it in multiple variations. What would charoset created in Maine include? Obviously you start with blueberries; cranberries were a quick second. Cooked and mashed it is a whole lot more like mortar than chopped apples. Somewhere we read it should have something in it that resembles hay—thinly cut threads of ginger. For several years we played with ingredients and quantities. This Maine Charoset is always on the table—not just for Seder but through the Passover holiday and sometimes as a condiment with grilled meat at other seasons. This recipe also appeared in Joan Nathan's book, *King Solomon's Table*."

- ¾ cup Wyman's whole dried wild blueberries
- ¾ cup dried cranberries
- ¾ to 1 cup sweet kosher wine
- 1 tart apple, diced and peeled
- ⅓ cup ginger, peeled and sliced into toothpick-size strips
- ⅓ cup golden raisins
- ¼ cup wine vinegar
- ½ teaspoon ground cinnamon
- 2 tablespoons maple syrup or local honey

In a medium-size bowl, soak the dried blueberries and cranberries in ¾ cup of the wine until soft, several hours or overnight.

Put the berry and wine mixture into a medium saucepan and add the apple, ginger, raisins, wine vinegar, and cinnamon. Cook over medium heat for 10-12 minutes, until the apples have softened. Place the mixture in the bowl of a food processor and pulse until combined, but not puréed. Add maple syrup or honey, and, if needed, up to ¼ cup more wine. Makes about 2 cups.

Gram's Blueberry Cake

Heather Cox Richardson • Bristol, Lincoln County

"When I was a girl, I got this recipe from Elizabeth Prior on Loud's Island. She got it from a friend when she was a girl. She didn't write it down and never measured when she cooked, so she estimated the proportions for me. This is good, but it's not quite like hers.

Over the years, I have found this recipe in local community cookbooks reaching back to the 1880s, attributed to a different person every generation. So what I knew it as—Gram's Blueberry Cake, because I knew her through her grandsons—is the very definition of a community recipe."

- ¾ cup molasses
- ¾ cup oil
- ¾ cup hot water with 1 teaspoon baking soda stirred in
- 2 cups flour
- ¾ cup sugar
- 1 teaspoon nutmeg
- 1 teaspoon cinnamon
- ½ teaspoon salt
- Wild Maine blueberries, fresh or Wyman's frozen (at least two cups of them)

Combine molasses, oil, and hot water mixture in a large bowl. Sift the dry ingredients into the wet mixture. Mix well. Stir in at least 2 cups blueberries. (Note: To keep blueberries from sinking to bottom during baking, coat them with flour before mixing them into the rest of the cake.) Pour batter into a lightly greased 9x13-inch pan, and bake at 350 degrees for about 30 minutes or until done.

Blueberry Grunt

Jane Cleaves McKenna • Bowdoinham, Sagadahoc County

"A grunt is a really traditional New England, Maritime Canadian recipe. As kids we just loved the name 'Grunt!' A grunt is part cake, part pudding, baked over a fruit base...the result is a gooey, sweet mass of fruit, dripping over a really really moist cake pudding. I usually make this with wild blueberries—August rolls around, and blueberry picking or raking berries is the order of the day. Summer hiking and camping trips late summer always involved seeking out berries, and picking into caps, or coffee cups, whatever was available. Usually a small cast-iron fry pan (8- or 9-inch) and a bowl were in the camping kit, and the dry ingredients. This dessert can be baked in a reflector oven, like a Sproul oven. And it was! In Baxter State park, Downeast on Grand Lake Stream, and now at our camp near Bigelow Mountain. No need to get too hung up on perfectly creaming sugar and butter, and tinned milk works just fine. Try it first at home to test the waters, enjoy."

2 cups wild Maine blueberries, fresh or Wyman's frozen
Juice of ½ lemon
3 tablespoons butter
1¾ cups sugar, divided
1 cup flour
1 teaspoon baking powder
½ teaspoon salt, divided
½ cup milk
1 tablespoon cornstarch
1 cup boiling water

Preheat oven to 375 degrees.

Line a greased 8-inch pan or small cast-iron fry pan with berries and sprinkle them with lemon juice.

In a large bowl, cream together butter and ¾ cup sugar. In a separate small bowl, blend together flour, baking powder, and ¼ teaspoon salt. To the creamed butter and sugar, add milk alternately with flour mixture. Spread batter evenly over berries.

In a small bowl, combine remaining 1 cup sugar, cornstarch, and ¼ teaspoon salt, and sprinkle this mixture over the batter in the pan. Pour boiling water over the top and bake for 1 hour. The grunt will brown and bubble when done. Makes 6 servings but can be doubled.

Blueberry Gingerbread

Jennifer Pinkham • Hollis Center, York County

"This has always been such a homey, and delicious recipe. Several years ago, my daughter and I submitted the recipe and a beautiful baking pan full of blueberry gingerbread to the parent/child baking contest at the Fryeburg Fair. We won 3rd place. You will be amazed by how delicious this simple recipe is! It's a go-to recipe because it's quick and easy. Such a great way to use such a staple Maine crop!"

- 1 cup sugar, plus 3 tablespoons for sprinkling
- ½ cup vegetable oil
- ½ teaspoon salt
- 1 egg
- 2 cups flour
- ½ teaspoon ginger
- 1 teaspoon cinnamon
- 1 teaspoon baking soda
- 3 tablespoons molasses
- 1 cup milk to which 2 tablespoons vinegar has been added
- 1 cup wild Maine blueberries, fresh or Wyman's frozen

Preheat oven to 325 degrees. Grease a 9x13-inch baking pan. Set aside 3 tablespoons of sugar.

In a large bowl, mix together all ingredients (except reserved sugar), adding blueberries last. Pour batter into prepared baking pan, and sprinkle the top of the batter with reserved sugar. Bake until a toothpick inserted into the center comes out clean, about 30-40 minutes. Serve with whipped cream or vanilla ice cream. Great for breakfast too!

How to Bake a Blueberry Cake Like Gramma Wight's

Amy Wight Chapman • Greenwood, Oxford County

"'Gramma Wight' was my mother, who, if she were still with us, would've turned 100 in 2020. She and my father were both native Mainers, but were 'living in exile' in Connecticut when they purchased a lot on North Pond in Woodstock in 1954 and began to build our family camp. There was a clump of wild high-bush blueberries at the edge of the pond, and my family has been picking them for more than 60 years. What follows is instruction for how to bake a blueberry cake like Gramma Wight.

Start with the berries. Go out the front door. (At camp, that's the door on the lake side; the door toward the road is the back door.) Go down to the edge of the lake and pick two cups of berries from the clump of wild high-bush blueberries that has (without fuss or fertilizer, attention or interference) been producing berries for pancakes, muffins, and cakes for more than half a century.

If you tie a cut-down plastic milk jug around your waist with a piece of clothesline rope, you'll be able to use both hands to pick; this is helpful.

Go barefoot, and wear shorts, because to pick the ones on the lake side of the bush you have to stand in the water. (Gramma Wight did not wear shorts. She wore skirts. I do not wear skirts at camp, or anywhere else, for that matter, if I can help it.)

The best time to go is early in the morning, because if you get there before the sun burns off the dew, there will be fairy dresses to admire, stretched between the branches of the bushes and spread out on the little patch of grass behind them.

Use Marjorie Standish's Melt-In-Your-Mouth Blueberry Cake recipe, from her first cookbook, *Cooking Down East*. Marjorie says this is 'undoubtedly the most popular recipe ever used in my column.' Marjorie was a great cook, a true professional. There's no real reason to make any changes to her recipe at all, but I modify it with the addition of a crumb topping, because who doesn't like a nice crumb topping?

You'll need: two eggs, separated; a half-cup of shortening (next time I might experiment with using butter instead, but today I went with Marjorie's recommendation and used Crisco); a cup of sugar; a teaspoon of real vanilla; a cup and a half of flour; a teaspoon of baking powder (I like Rumford brand because it's aluminum-free and doesn't give your baked goods a weird, metallic aftertaste); a quarter of a teaspoon of salt; a third of a cup of milk; and two cups of blueberries. (Marjorie's recipe actually only calls for a cup and a half, but I like to use two cups if I have them. The cake will come out just fine, not too heavy or soggy, and it will have a lovely amount of blueberry taste in every bite.)

Separate the eggs and beat the whites until stiff. It's best to use Gramma Wight's old Pyrex mixing bowl for this; the red one should be the right size.

If you're a purist, you can use the ancient hand egg-beater that is hanging on the pegboard to the left of the sink. Be sure to clean the cobwebs off it first; it probably hasn't been used in a while. But it's okay to use the electric mixer if you're not feeling energetic. It's a lot of work to beat egg whites stiff with a rotary egg-beater.

Add some of the sugar from the recipe to the beaten egg whites to keep them stiff, about a quarter of a cup.

Cream the shortening in a bigger bowl; the yellow Pyrex one is perfect. Before you put the shortening in it, turn it over. That 'R. Wight' on the bottom, in faded Magic Marker, was put there several decades ago, so that the big yellow bowl would always be sure to come home from potlucks and picnics, after the coleslaw or potato salad or brownie pudding was gone.

Add the sugar, vanilla, and egg yolks and beat until nice and fluffy. It's best if you're able to use free-range local eggs, because they have the loveliest dark yellow yolks. My farmer friend tells me it has to do with the higher protein content of their diet, from eating bugs and grubs along with the usual grain. Whatever the reason, using local eggs will give your blueberry cake a nice, rich color.

Sift together your dry ingredients, but first, measure out your blueberries in a two-cup glass measuring cup—the chipped spout won't matter—and mix just a little of the flour from the recipe with the berries so they won't settle to the bottom of your cake; a couple of teaspoons should be enough.

If you still have the green Pyrex bowl that originally came with the set, it's about the right size to sift the dry ingredients into, but if it has disappeared or gotten broken over the years, the stainless steel bowl that fits into the copper-bottomed Revereware saucepan (for use as a double boiler) will work just fine.

Add your dry ingredients alternately with the milk, mixing with the old wooden spoon—just dig around, and you'll find it in the drawer with the sharp knives (don't worry; none of them are actually sharp enough to cut you), the broken vegetable peeler, and that heavy little glass thing nobody wants to throw out because one day someone might figure out what it is.

Gently fold in the beaten egg whites and then, even more gently, the blueberries. You don't want to crush the berries—Marjorie used a rubber scraper for this step, but you may find that the rubber scraper from the knife drawer has gotten all cracked and crumbly over the winter. If so, don't worry; just use the wooden spoon. But be gentle!

Spread the batter in a greased 8x8-inch pan. Marjorie says to sprinkle the top lightly with granulated sugar, but I do love a nice crumb topping. So mix half a stick of softened butter with a quarter cup of brown sugar, a half cup of flour, and a half teaspoon of cinnamon. Use a pastry blender—that ancient one with the crazily bent wires that was brought to camp fifty years ago because it 'wasn't good enough for home' will work just fine.

Sprinkle the topping onto the batter and bake it at 350 degrees for 50-60 minutes, or until it springs back when you press the center.

Put it on a wire rack on the table to cool while you go to a meeting, or out for a walk, or to the dump and the post office. If you're lucky, there will be a piece left for you when you get back."

Ma's Blueberry Pie - Fresh, Cold

Sarah Dillinger • Winter Harbor, Hancock County

Sponsored by **Wyman's**

"Every summer my mother would make not just the traditional baked blueberry pie, but using Wyman's fresh wild blueberries, she made this amazing fresh blueberry pie. Generally it was made for when friends from out of town were visiting, but I always made sure I was around for a piece! Now I make it myself, and while she made her own crust, I actually like to use the pre-made graham cracker crust. I think it goes well with the cream cheese on the base of the pie. Delicious!!"

- Single pie crust, fully baked and cooled, or graham cracker crust
- 8-ounce package cream cheese, softened
- ¾ cup sugar, divided
- ¼ cup sour cream
- ½ teaspoon vanilla
- 1 cup wild Maine blueberries, fresh or Wyman's frozen
- ½ cup water
- 1 tablespoon cornstarch
- 1 tablespoon lemon juice
- 2 cups fresh wild Maine blueberries

In a large bowl, mix the softened cream cheese with ¼ cup sugar, sour cream, and vanilla until smooth. Spread over the baked pie shell. Refrigerate to chill until firm.

Meanwhile, in a small saucepan mash 1 cup of the blueberries. Add water to the mashed berries; bring to a boil.

In a small bowl, combine the remaining sugar and cornstarch. Pour in a little juice from the saucepan to dissolve the sugar. Add the sugar and cornstarch mixture back to the saucepan and cook until it thickens. Remove from heat and add lemon juice. Set aside to cool.

Place the remaining 2 cups of blueberries over the chilled cream cheese layer. Spoon the sauce evenly over the top. Chill for 3 hours.

Fighting Hunger in Maine

By Kristen Miale

Over the past ten years leading Good Shepherd Food Bank, Maine's largest hunger-relief organization, there is no greater lesson I have learned than that food is so much more than food. We know this somewhat intuitively, even if we take it for granted some days. Food is warmth, safety, and comfort. Food is family, friends, and belonging. Food is health, fuel, and strength. Food is nourishment for the body, mind, and soul.

I came into hunger-relief work through my passion for food and cooking. After a decade working in the private equity and business consulting fields, I developed a heightened awareness of the growing wealth gap during the Great Recession. Wanting to give back to the community, I started volunteering one day a week at food pantries—and what I saw opened my eyes to the realities of hunger in Maine. Seniors on fixed incomes were cutting back on their prescriptions to buy food. Parents were facing grocery budgets that would run out before the end of the month and foregoing meals so that their children could eat. Individuals were working multiple jobs and still not making ends meet. My neighbors were coming to community food pantries run by dedicated volunteers to get enough food to meet their basic needs.

I was shocked by the need, but also by the solution. Much of the food provided at that time was less healthy, and the healthier food that was distributed through food pantries was often left on shelves because not everyone knew how—or had the time—to prepare it. I saw an opportunity to help and started offering cooking classes for low-income families to teach people how to cook healthy, delicious meals from scratch and on a budget. This led to the formation of Cooking Matters, a cooking and nutrition education program of Good Shepherd Food Bank that continues today. I fell in love with the work and saw how a home-cooked meal shared around the dinner table provided much more than nourishment. That meal reduced the stress of families and provided an opportunity for connection, conversation, and joy.

Eventually I had the opportunity to take on the role of president at Good Shepherd Food Bank and over the past ten years, we have worked to transform our work to focus on providing nourishing, healthy meals to more Mainers. Today, more than 30,000 families have participated in our Cooking Matters program. We created a network of school-based food pantries to make fresh, healthy food more available to families with children. We launched Mainers Feeding Mainers, a local buying program that brings farm-fresh vegetables, fruit, and protein to community food pantries while supporting local farms and food producers. We began to understand that food is medicine and started partnering with physicians and health-care centers to help identify food insecurity and refer food resources among patient populations. And we greatly improved the nutritional quality of the food our network distributes; of the food provided by the 31.6 million meals the Food Bank distributed last year, 82 percent was classified as healthy and nourishing. Over the past decade we've transformed from an organization that distributes surplus food to nonprofit organizations to living our mission of eliminating hunger in Maine by improving access to nutritious food for people in need, building strong community partnerships, and mobilizing the public in the fight to end hunger.

As our mission indicates, we do not do this work alone. Good Shepherd Food Bank partners with more than 500 organizations across the state to distribute food and implement programming. We also rely on tens of thousands individuals, businesses, and foundations who support our work through food and financial contributions, volunteering, and advocacy.

Today Maine is grappling with continued high rates of hunger as we recover from the COVID-19 pandemic. Despite the progress we have made, we are acutely aware that there is more work to be done. While the increase in healthy food distribution has helped many, there are populations that are disproportionately impacted by hunger whom we are not adequately reaching, especially in communities of color. While 13.6 percent of Maine households suffered from food insecurity before the pandemic, the rate for households headed by people of color was more than twice that, at 28 percent.

While the impacts of hunger in our state are devastating, there is reason to have hope. Hunger in our state was once a hidden epidemic, but the pandemic has shined a light on the problem and Mainers have rallied in response with community support. Our local, state, and federal legislative leaders have implemented unprecedented policies to help stabilize low-income families. Working together, we can truly end hunger in Maine.

Today, as you flip through this cookbook and select a wonderful recipe to prepare for your family and loved ones think about how food is a connecting, nourishing, joyous force in your life and please consider how you can help your neighbors experience the same. By ending hunger, together, we can help Maine children reach their highest potential, assist our senior citizens to age in place with the dignity they deserve, and build hope and resiliency for future generations.

Kristen Miale is the President of the Good Shepherd Food Bank of Maine. She and her team of more than 80 employees, plus numerous volunteers, work with a network of more than 500 nonprofit organizations to distribute 25 million meals a year, making Good Shepherd Food Bank Maine's largest hunger-relief organization.

CAKES

Photo: Ellen Moore, her son John, and Francine Thurlow at Moore's camp on Green Lake in Ellsworth in 1984. Francine's recipe for Blueberry Buckle (submitted by Ellen) can be found on page 230.

Isabel's Cranberry Cake

Sylvia Trueworthy Pease • Hiram, Oxford County

"My mother, Isabel, was a wonderful cook and an awesome mother. She took great care of her five children in addition to working outside the home. In the early years she worked for the school lunch program and also found time to help tend the family gardens. It was not unusual to see her drive a tractor or the hay truck. In summer months she sold vegetables door to door in the Kezar Falls Village. Mother never graduated from high school, however she made certain that all five of her children graduated. My three brothers joined three different branches of the service: Army, Marines, and Navy. My older sister and I both attended college and became teachers. Mother was always so proud of her 'kids.' Yes, we were still her kids even when she was in her 80s. When we sat around the dinner table, we enjoyed her homemade biscuits with freshly made butter. On Saturday morning she would make and fry donuts for the glass jar that was kept on the counter. We did not own an electric stove so all her cooking was done on the black kitchen cook stove. It was amazing how she was able to bake perfect pies and cakes in that stove. I don't remember her using a recipe. Her pies, cookies, and cakes often used what was available to her from our farm. The Trueworthy Family owned a cranberry bog and every year she kept the shelves stocked with her homemade cranberry sauce. The bog was located across the road from our farm house and in the winter months the five of us would skate around the edge of it. The cranberry bog is still owned by my brother Arlyn and this year it was abundant with berries. My brothers and I were able to pick and freeze plenty of cranberries for the winter months before the turkeys arrived. What a wonderful feeling to be able to pick berries in the very same bog that my grandfather wrote about harvesting in his 1930 journal."

- 2 eggs
- 1 cup sugar
- ½ cup butter, melted and cooled to room temperature
- ½ teaspoon vanilla
- ¾ cup flour
- ½ teaspoon baking powder
- 1 cup cranberries, mixed with 1 tablespoon flour (see Note)

Note: Cranberries can be frozen or fresh. If frozen let them set a few minutes in a bowl before adding to the batter.

Preheat oven to 350 degrees. Grease and flour an 8x8-inch pan. In large bowl beat eggs and sugar together until light yellow. Add cooled butter and vanilla and mix until smooth. Mix in flour and baking powder. Stir in cranberries. Pour batter into the pan and bake 30-35 minutes, or until a toothpick comes out clean.

Chocolate Zucchini Cake

Joan Benoit Samuelson • Freeport, Cumberland County

"A few years ago, I did a cookbook of my grandmother's recipes. She was a very good baker. She had a famous poundcake and a famous spongecake that she always filled with raspberry jam and sprinkled powdered sugar on the top. I can still smell and taste the cake. She had an old cutting board that I remember her cutting everything on. It was a round well-worn cutting board that said, 'give us our daily bread,' and she gave us our daily treats whenever we visited....I became a master gardener years ago, and I grow as much as I possibly can. I incorporate all those things into my cooking. In my family, one of my most famous recipes was originally out of the Portland symphony cookbook, the chocolate zucchini cake. That's what everybody wants. When they come to the house for dessert, they all want the chocolate zucchini cake."

- 2½ cups flour
- 1½ cups sugar
- 1 medium-size zucchini, grated (about two cups)
- ½ cup milk
- 2 eggs
- 1 teaspoon vanilla extract
- 4 tablespoons cocoa powder
- 1 teaspoon cinnamon
- 1 teaspoon baking soda
- ½ teaspoon baking powder
- 1 cup chocolate chips (I use dark chocolate)

Like everything I bake, I mix all the ingredients together and have no set order in what I put into the mixing bowl. Pour the mixture into a greased 9x13-inch baking pan and bake at 325 degrees for 45-50 minutes. May be served slightly under that time for a molten quality.

Celebration Carrot Cake with Cream Cheese Frosting

Nancy Wanderer & Susan Sanders • Falmouth, Cumberland County

"If a recipe can be the tie that binds two people together for life, this recipe for carrot cake is the one. On September 30, 1979, while sitting at my Waterville kitchen table, I discovered an article by Maine Sunday Telegram staff writer Millie Stewart called 'These Vegetables Take the Cake.' As a vegetable lover, I was intrigued by the idea of including pumpkin, potatoes, tomatoes, zucchini, and carrots in cakes. Meanwhile, my future life partner, Susan Sanders, was in her own Belgrade kitchen, cutting out the same article. Little did we know that, seven years later, we were destined to meet and join our lives with that recipe for carrot cake as a centerpiece of our life together. Since then, we have baked and served this delicious carrot cake at virtually every special family event, including milestone birthdays and our commitment ceremony in 1990. Susan's outstanding ability to decorate carrot cakes by squeezing colored frosting from tiny holes in the corners of zip-lock bags made each cake an artistic and culinary treasure."

Carrot Cake:

2 cups sugar
1½ cups vegetable oil
4 eggs
2 cups plus 2 tablespoons flour
2 teaspoons baking soda
1 teaspoon salt
2 teaspoons cinnamon
3½ cups grated raw carrots
½ cup chopped walnuts

Cream Cheese Frosting:

1 stick butter
8-ounce package cream cheese
2 teaspoons vanilla
3½ cups (one 16-ounce bag) confectioners' sugar

To make the cake: In a large bowl, mix together sugar, oil, and eggs. Add dry ingredients and mix well. Stir in grated carrots and nuts. Pour batter into a greased 9x13-inch baking pan and bake 35-40 minutes at 350 degrees. Cake is fully baked when a toothpick inserted into the center comes out clean. Remove from oven, and cool on a wire rack.

To make the frosting: In a large bowl, beat butter with cream cheese and vanilla. Gradually beat in the confectioners' sugar. If the mixture becomes too thick, add a little milk. Spread on cooled cake, and decorate as desired.

Refrigerator Fruit Cake

Millie Stewart • Brunswick, Cumberland County

"My mother, Lucy Ward Simpson, grew up in North Bath and lived all of her married life on a farm in East Brunswick. In her day, there were no cookbooks as we know them today. Cooks relied on publications for recipes, like the Farm Journal, advertisements on packaging, friends and neighbors, and Parade Magazine, which published this recipe in December 1950. I found this in my mother's recipe book, mostly filled with clippings she had saved."

- 1½ cups raisins
- 1 cup sliced prunes
- 1 cup pitted and sliced dates
- 1½ cups mixed and diced other fruits and peels (fruitcake mix)
- ½ cup butter
- ½ cup powdered sugar
- ¼ cup light corn syrup
- ½ cup orange marmalade
- 1 teaspoon cinnamon
- ¼ teaspoon ground cloves
- ½ teaspoon salt
- ½ cup chopped walnuts
- 5 cups fine graham cracker crumbs

Rinse and drain raisins and prunes. Combine with dates and all other fruits and peels. Set aside.

In a large bowl, cream together butter and powdered sugar. Blend in corn syrup, marmalade, spices, and salt. Fold in fruits, and mix "lightly." Let stand 2 hours or more.

Blend in walnuts and graham cracker crumbs. Line a large loaf pan or several smaller pans with wax paper or parchment. Fill pans with fruit cake mixture. Refrigerate for at least 48 hours to firm. Serve in small slices.

Raspberry Riches

Jayne Farrin • Presque Isle, Aroostook County

"My dad and his brother were in business together, and that business was the building of roads. Farrin Brothers & Smith, Inc. roads can be found from Jackman, Livermore Falls, to Palermo. Several times when I was growing up, my dad, mom, and I lived on a 'road job' that was too far away for my dad to easily travel to every day. The summer I turned 9 we were living in a trailer on a road job site. mom explained that she wouldn't be able to bake me a birthday cake, but instead would get me a quart of raspberries. I love raspberries! I call them the 'jewels of summer.' I am 66 and have had raspberries on my birthday ever since that year I turned 9. Before I married my husband, Mom made him promise that he would see that I had raspberries on my birthday. My husband Steve put in a raspberry patch the first summer we were married and has faithfully provided them since."

Sugar Crumb Topping:

½ cup firmly packed light brown sugar
2 tablespoons flour
1 tablespoon unsalted butter, cut in small pieces
1½ teaspoons finely grated semi-sweet chocolate

Cake:

1 cup sifted all-purpose flour
¾ cup sugar
½ teaspoon baking powder
½ teaspoon baking soda
¼ teaspoon salt
1 egg
⅓ cup buttermilk
½ teaspoon vanilla extract
⅓ cup unsalted butter, melted and cooled
1¼ cups fresh red raspberries

To make the topping: In a small bowl, mix together all ingredients with a fork or pastry blender. Alternatively, pulse ingredients in the bowl of a food processor until they are the consistency of corn meal.

To make the cake: Preheat oven to 375 degrees. Butter a 9-inch round or an 8-inch square baking pan. Sift together the dry ingredients into a large mixing bowl. In another bowl, beat together the egg, buttermilk and vanilla until smooth. Stir in butter. Pour the liquid mixture into the flour mixture. Beat with a wooden spoon until nearly smooth. Spread batter evenly in prepared pan. Sprinkle with raspberries. Finish with a layer of sugar crumb topping.

After sprinkling the crumb topping over the berries, bake until richly browned, 40-45 minutes. Remove from oven and let cake cool on rack, but serve warm. This will make 10 servings.

Orange Raisin Grind-Up Cake

Deborah Hayden • Brunswick, Cumberland County

"My mother, Olive Fielding, made this cake pretty often because it's easy and popular. She used an old-fashioned, hand-cranked meat grinder to grind the oranges, but I chop them in the Cuisinart. There were no instructions about pans or time, but I've figured it out over the years. I thought of sharing this with you today because I baked it yesterday for my brother's birthday. He asks for it every year. I use a cream cheese frosting."

- 1 cup raisins
- 1 whole orange
- 1 cup sugar
- 1 tablespoon butter
- ¾ cup sour milk
- 2 cups flour
- 1 teaspoon baking soda
- ½ teaspoon salt

Grind together the raisins and the WHOLE orange (rind and all). If you do it all at once it gets gooey, so it's best to do this in two batches, including both raisins and chunks of orange in each one. Set aside ground mixture.

This next direction sounds impossible: "cream the butter and sugar." Obviously, the proportions are off, but it works! I use my hands to just rub the two ingredients together.

When sugar and butter are thoroughly incorporated, add the milk, then stir in dry ingredients. Finally, add the ground fruit and stir to combine.

Pour batter into a greased 8x8-inch pan and bake at 350 degrees until a toothpick comes out clean, about 35 minutes.

Strawberry Shortcake

Suzanne Trussell • Stetson, Penobscot County

"My mother, Dorothy May, was born in 1910. She married my father, Fred Trussell, in 1938 and began a family of my two brothers and me. Every June, our family would visit a local farm and pick strawberries. My mother would make this strawberry shortcake for dessert on Sundays. She would also bring it to the Woman's Club and the Garden Club, where it was admired for its appearance, and especially for its taste. My mother's recipe was handed down to me in 1972 when I married my husband, Joe Stupak. Joe and I adopted our own tradition of visiting local farms to pick strawberries in season to make this special dessert. Eventually, our daughter Emily joined us in those strawberry picking outings. Since 1999, this strawberry shortcake has become the centerpiece of a new tradition. Joe and I have met at our home every year in late May or early June with four of our close friends and neighbors to review the applications for a scholarship in Emily's memory, the Emily Trussell Stupak scholarship. Every year, without fail, once our committee of six has reached a consensus on one or more graduating seniors to recommend to receive the current year's award, we all dig in to a piece of this delicious shortcake!"

Shortcake:
2¼ cups flour
4 teaspoons baking powder
2 tablespoons granulated sugar
½ teaspoon salt
A few grains of nutmeg
⅓ cup butter
1 extra large egg
⅔ cup milk

Strawberry Filling:
1 quart fresh strawberries
Granulated sugar to taste, if desired

Whipped Cream Topping:
1 pint whipping cream
1 teaspoon vanilla extract
1-2 tablespoons confectioners' sugar

To make the shortcake: Preheat oven to 425 degrees. Lightly butter and flour a 7x11-inch baking pan. In a large bowl, mix all dry shortcake ingredients together. Add butter to dry ingredients, and use a pastry blender to cut in butter until well mixed.

In a separate bowl, combine egg with milk, and mix together well. Pour the egg mixture into the other ingredients, and combine quickly until well mixed. Spread with clean hands into the prepared pan. Bake for 15 minutes, until golden. Remove from oven and cool on a rack. When cake is at room temperature, cut the shortcake into 8 pieces, then slice each piece in half horizontally to create a top and bottom.

To make the strawberry filling: Pick out the 8 prettiest strawberries to decorate the top, and set them aside. Hull the remaining berries. With a potato masher or other utensil, mash strawberries to the point where they are juicy and chunky. Add a little granulated sugar, if desired, to sweeten the berries.

To make the whipped cream topping: Pour whipping cream in a large bowl, and add 1 teaspoon of vanilla extract and 1 or 2 tablespoons confectioners' sugar, to taste. Using an electric mixer, whip cream until soft peaks are formed. Be very careful not to overbeat.

To assemble the strawberry shortcakes: Arrange the bottom pieces of shortcake on a serving platter or large plate. Spoon all the mashed strawberries onto the bottom pieces. Spread half of the whipped cream on top of the mashed strawberries. Be sure to save enough cream for the top. Put the top pieces of shortcake on the finished bottoms. Spread the rest of the whipped cream on the top, covering each piece. Place a whole strawberry on each piece of shortcake. Serves 8.

Pork Cake

1908 • Tried and Tested Recipes, Ninth Grade Cook Book

Ninth Grade Pupils, Emerson Grammar School • Bar Harbor, Hancock County

The Emerson Grammar School in Bar Harbor had a four-year home economics program. The "Ninth Grade Pupils" (probably about ten of them) offer us Pork Cake, a recipe which in recent years has been claimed by some as a Southern recipe. However, there are decades of recorded recipes for Pork Cake from Connecticut and the Hudson Valley that precede any from the South. This simple version of the recipe by the students of Bar Harbor further anchors this dish's American roots in New England. —DL

One cup molasses, 1 cup sugar, 1 cup chopped pork, 1 cup raisins, 1 cup sweet milk, 2 eggs, 1 heaping teaspoon soda, flour enough to make stiff batter. — E.M.

Frieda Berry's Chocolate Snacking Cake

Taylor Bickford • Portland, Cumberland County

"I grew up in a family with a long history of women who baked, and baked well. But it wasn't just a product of the times—they weren't baking because that's what women did, their baking was the most direct representation of their love. The Kendrick women weren't outspoken about their love, nor were they very physical, showering you with hugs and kisses. Now they would say that these women possessed the love language of giving gifts. Holidays, birthdays, happy times, sad times, or just because they were thinking of you—a Kendrick woman would bring you a fresh baked good. You knew if you were on the receiving end of my mum's Christmas baking, you were someone near and dear to her. Growing up, this chocolate cake, passed down through generations of Kendrick women, was baked for me more times than I can count. When I was young, I considered it just my mum making food. As I grew up and began baking myself, learning first hand the joyous labor that went into baking, I understood this chocolate cake was my mum's love in bite-sized, easily digestible form. As an adult, I look back fondly at all the desserts my mum baked and recreate them for those I love, knowing the generations of love baked into every recipe card. This cake is just chocolatey enough to satisfy your sweet tooth, not rich enough to not be able to have more than one piece, the perfect balance of moist but airy, makes enough to be shared, and shares the love of the person who baked it."

Cake:

1 stick margarine
½ cup cooking oil
4 tablespoons cocoa powder
1 cup water
2 cups flour
2 cups sugar
½ cup milk mixed with ½ teaspoon vinegar
1 teaspoon baking soda
2 eggs
1 teaspoon vanilla

Frosting:

1 stick margarine
3 tablespoons cocoa
⅓ cup milk mixed with ⅓ teaspoon vinegar (soured milk)
¼ teaspoon salt
1 teaspoon vanilla
1 cup chopped nuts
3½ cups (one 16-ounce bag) confectioners' sugar

Preheat oven to 400 degrees. In a sauce pan, bring to a boil the margarine, cooking oil, cocoa powder and water. In a large bowl, sift together flour and sugar. Pour the chocolate mixture over the dry ingredients and mix well. Add to that mixture the soured milk, baking soda, eggs, and vanilla, and mix well. Pour into a greased broiler pan or large jelly roll pan at least 1-inch deep. Bake 15-20 minutes.

While the cake bakes, make the frosting. In a large saucepan, mix together margarine, cocoa powder, and soured milk, and bring to a boil. Remove from heat and add salt, vanilla, chopped nuts, and confectioners' sugar. Mix well. Frost cake while hot, and serve warm.

Park House Gingerbread

Karole Clark • Sweden, Oxford County

"Our mother, Beverly Forbus, was manager and head cook at the Park House Restaurant in Hartland in the 1980s and 1990s. The restaurant served home-cooked diner-style meals and catered to workers from Irving Tanning in town, and church-goers after Sunday services. One of Beverly's most popular desserts was the Park House Gingerbread, served warm with a generous dollop of homemade whipped cream. One patron was dubbed the 'Gingerbread Man' because he often ordered three helpings for breakfast. What a great way to start the day!"

- ½ cup sugar
- ½ cup shortening
- 2 eggs
- 1 cup molasses
- 2½ cups all-purpose flour
- 1 teaspoon cinnamon
- 1 teaspoon ginger
- ½ teaspoon salt
- 2 teaspoons baking soda dissolved in 1 cup boiling water

Preheat oven to 325 degrees. Grease and flour a 9x13-inch baking dish. In a stand mixer, beat together sugar and shortening until fluffy. Add eggs and molasses and mix until well combined. In a separate bowl, sift together flour, cinnamon, ginger, and salt. Add dry ingredients gradually to the mixer, and mix well. On low speed, gradually stir in baking soda mixture. Pour batter into prepared pan. Bake for 55-60 minutes. Serve warm.

Patriot Subaru Legacy Peach Crumb Cake

Jackie Parker • Saco, York County

Sponsored by
Patriot
Subaru

"Our mission statement at Patriot Subaru is 'to serve,' and one of the ways we do this in our local community is our team involvement with the Bon Appetit Community Meal Program in Biddeford. We applaud all efforts that help to ensure that no Mainer goes hungry. We're lucky that we have multiple associates who have peach trees growing in their yards, and every late summer we look forward to sharing in their bounty! You are bound to 'Impreza' your friends and family and we're sure they'll 'Ascent' the highest peaks to sing your praises if you serve this dessert or tea-time favorite! Legacy Peach Crumb Cake has huge crumbs, bold peach flavor, and a delectable soft cake base. It tastes even better on day two, after everything has settled a bit and the crumbs adhere better, though it is infrequent that it lasts that long to find out!"

Peaches:
1½ pounds peaches (see Note)
Juice of half a lemon
1 teaspoon ground cinnamon
1 tablespoon granulated sugar

Crumb topping:
½ cup salted butter, melted
⅓ cup brown sugar (light or dark)
⅓ cup granulated sugar
1 teaspoon ground cinnamon
1⅓ cups all-purpose flour

Cake:
6 tablespoons salted butter, softened
½ cup granulated sugar
1 large egg
⅓ cup sour cream
1 teaspoon vanilla extract
1¼ teaspoons baking powder
Pinch of kosher salt
1 cup all-purpose flour

Note: 5 small or 4 medium peaches should do it. Blanch and peel if you wish, and cut in to ½-inch wedges. Frozen peaches work well in this recipe, but make sure they are thoroughly thawed and room temperature before using.

Preheat oven to 325 degrees. Lightly coat an 8-inch square cake pan with butter. You can also line the bottom with a sheet of parchment paper to ensure easy removal and no sticking.

In a large bowl, toss sliced peaches first with lemon juice, then with cinnamon and sugar and set aside.

To make the crumb topping: Whisk the butter, sugars, and cinnamon together until evenly mixed. Add flour and mix until it disappears–the mixture will be thick. Set aside.

To make the cake: In the bowl of a stand mixer fitted with with paddle attachment, beat butter with sugar until light and fluffy, 2-3 minutes. Add egg, sour cream, and vanilla and beat until combined. Sprinkle surface of batter with baking powder and salt, and beat well to combine. Add the flour and mix only until it is no longer visible.

Assemble the cake by scraping cake batter into the prepared pan and smoothing the surface. Arrange peaches on the cake with slices overlapping. Pour any of the juices left in the bowl over the peaches. Sprinkle the crumbs all over the cake. If you find you have bigger crumbs, squeeze them in to smaller pieces and break these up for a couple of larger chunks over the cake.

Bake for 1 hour 10 minutes, or until you see juices bubbling around the peaches. Cool to room temperature before cutting in to squares. You can dust with powdered sugar for a sweeter bite, but we often aren't patient enough to remember to add the extra sweetness. This cake will keep for 3 days at room temperature, if kept in an airtight container.

Chocolate Pudding Cake

Pam Libby-Lussier • Durham, Androscoggin County

"When my mom, Arlene Brown Libby, made this for our family of 14, she had to triple it and bake it in a very large pan so there was plenty for all of us. This recipe is so good with whipped cream on top."

- 2 tablespoons shortening
- ¾ cup sugar
- 1 cup flour
- 2 teaspoons baking powder
- ¼ teaspoon salt
- ¼ cup plus 2 tablespoons cocoa, separated
- ½ cup milk
- 1 cup brown sugar
- 1¾ cups water

Preheat oven to 350 degrees. In a large bowl, mix shortening and sugar well. In a separate bowl, combine flour, baking powder, salt, and 2 tablespoons of cocoa. Add dry ingredients to the shortening mixture, alternating with the milk. Pour batter into a greased 9x13-inch cake pan.

In a small bowl, mix together brown sugar and remaining ¼ cup of cocoa. Sprinkle this mixture onto the batter. Pour water on top. Bake for 20 minutes. Serve with whipped cream, if desired.

The Wassookeag Special

Randy Hatch • Bangor, Penobscot County

"Wassookeag School Camp, located on Lake Wassookeag, was founded in Dexter in 1926 by my grandfather Lloyd Harvey Hatch, Sr. My great aunt, Elsie Mae Sharpe, Lloyd's sister-in-law, was legendary for the home-cooked meals she served the students. The story goes that one day there were some unexpected, exclusive guests for a luncheon, and 'Auntie' did not have an appropriate dessert. With the supplies on hand, she developed a dessert that was beloved for years. When asked for the name of the dessert, she replied 'The Wassookeag Special.'"

Cupcakes:
1½ cups flour
1 cup sugar
½ teaspoon baking soda
1 teaspoon cream of tarter
Dash salt
Scant ¼ cup butter, melted
1 egg
Roughly ½ cup milk
½ teaspoon vanilla

Chocolate Sauce:
2 tablespoons butter
3 squares unsweetened chocolate
2 cups sugar
Dash salt
⅔ cup hot water
1 teaspoon vanilla

Whipped cream, for serving

To make the cupcakes: Preheat oven to 350 degrees. Grease and lightly flour a muffin tin.

Into a large bowl, sift together the flour, sugar, baking soda, cream of tartar, and salt. Pour melted butter into a glass measuring cup. Crack egg into the butter, then fill with milk until you have 1 cup. Add vanilla. Stir liquid ingredients into the dry. Scoop batter into the muffin tins and bake until a toothpick inserted into the center comes out clean, about 18 minutes.

To make the sauce: Place butter in a medium saucepan over low heat. When butter has melted, add chocolate squares and stir until melted. Then add sugar, salt, and hot water. Boil 12-15 minutes, until consistency is a thick syrup. Flavor with vanilla.

To serve: Have cupcakes warm. When ready to serve, pour on warm sauce and whipped cream.

The Dreaded Fruitcake

Sydnia (Welch) Czarnecki • Gouldsboro, Hancock County

"Although most people (like me!) don't care for fruitcake, many people love this recipe! My mother, Glennice Welch, always made this around Thanksgiving since it needs to sit for several weeks before serving. People always raved about it at the holidays, though I never did develop a taste for it!"

- 2 cups candied red and green cherries
- 1 pound candied orange and pineapple
- 1 cup seedless raisins
- 1 cup whole pitted dates
- Brandy or pineapple juice
- ½ pound butter or margarine
- 1 cup sugar
- ½ teaspoon each of nutmeg, mace, cloves, and cinnamon
- 6 eggs
- 2½ cups flour, separated
- 1 teaspoon baking powder
- ½ teaspoon salt
- 5 cups whole unsalted mixed nuts (pecans, walnuts, filberts, Brazil nuts, almonds)

In a large bowl, mix the candied fruit, raisins, and dates together and cover with brandy or unsweetened pineapple juice (my mother only used brandy). Let soak for several hours or overnight.

In a separate large bowl, cream together the butter and sugar, then add the spices and mix until fluffy. Add the eggs, one at a time, beating well after each addition. Stir in 2 cups of flour, and the baking powder and salt.

Add the nuts to the fruit mixture, sprinkle with the remaining ½ cup of flour, and mix to coat. Pour the batter over fruit and nut mixture, and mix well.

Preheat oven to 300 degrees. Pour batter into four well greased and floured 1½ pound loaf pans. Pans should be about ⅓ full as this doesn't raise much. Bake for 2½ hours.

After baking, cool cakes completely, then wrap with several layers of brandy-soaked cheesecloth. Place in an airtight container for at least 2 weeks, dampening with more brandy as needed. The cheesecloth should remain damp but not wet. After 2-3 weeks, discard cheesecloth and wrap tightly in plastic wrap or aluminum foil.

My Christmas Cake, aka Gram's Fruit Cake

Marjorie Pfeiffer • Clinton, Kennebec County

"My grandmother was married in 1916. This fruitcake was only made at Christmas time and she gave this cake to every family member. I always looked forward to it, and after she died in 1981, I started making it myself. This cake was so good that even people who said they didn't like fruitcake would eat it and like it, especially if I called it 'my Christmas Cake.' My husband said once, 'Can't we have 4th of July fruitcake?' I told him that this cake was made only once a year. This is a family tradition that I hope will go on for years to come."

- 1 pint mincemeat
- 1 cup chopped walnuts
- 1 cup raisins, cut up
- 1 teaspoon vanilla
- ½ cup melted oleo or shortening
- 1 cup sugar
- 2 cups flour
- 1 teaspoon baking soda mixed with 3 tablespoons cold water
- 2 egg yolks
- 2 stiffly beaten egg whites
- Walnut halves, for garnish

Preheat oven to 350 degrees. In a large bowl, mix together all ingredients in the order given, gently folding in the beaten egg whites last. Pour batter into a greased and floured tube pan. Place walnut halves decoratively on top of the batter. Bake for about 1 hour, until a toothpick comes out clean. Cool completely before removing from pan.

DUMPLINGS, PUDDINGS, & ICE CREAMS

Photo: Marsha Merryman and her brother Leslie at their home in Oakland for Leslie's 12th birthday in 1970. Their mom Luella's recipe for Pumpkin Ice Cream Pie can be found on page 262.

Pumpkin Ice Cream Pie

Marsha Merryman • Oakland, Kennebec County

"This recipe was my brother Leslie's favorite, and is now loved by my great nephew Seth. We always had it at Thanksgiving and Christmas, and on Leslie's birthday. He was six years older and we were close because Mom had him watch out for me, especially back in the day, when we walked to and from school. Leslie served our country as a Marine embassy guard, serving in Ankara, Turkey during the Iranian hostages, and in Paris, France. Unfortunately we lost him in 2015. Every time I make this, I think of him."

Graham Cracker Crust:

36 graham crackers, crushed and rolled fine
½ cup sugar
1 cup butter, melted

Pumpkin Ice Cream Filling:

15-ounce can pumpkin
½ cup brown sugar
½ teaspoon salt
½ teaspoon cinnamon
¼ teaspoon ginger
¼ teaspoon nutmeg
1 quart vanilla ice cream, softened

To make the crust: In a large bowl, combine graham cracker crumbs, sugar, and melted butter. Press mixture into two 9-inch pie plates. Refrigerate for 45 minutes.

To make the ice cream filling: While crusts chill, combine all ingredients in a large bowl. Beat with a wooden spoon or rubber spatula to thoroughly combine. Divide between chilled crusts and freeze until ready to serve, at least 2 hours. Makes 2 pies.

Coffee Marshmallow Dessert

Martha Turner • Yarmouth, Cumberland County

"My mother, Ruth Turner, graduated from Colby College in Waterville, as did her aunt, Winnibel Gower. (Her aunt must've influenced her to go to Colby, as she'd gone there before going to Columbia to study library science; Winnibel was a librarian at Deering High School in Portland for many years.) My mother paid her college tuition by modeling shoes at Stearns, the Waterville department store, when Boston shoe salesmen came up to Maine. When we were growing up in the 1960s, my brother Warren and I loved this dessert. My mother used Sanka coffee, and had a mug of hot water that she dunked her scissors in while cutting up marshmallows. This was before mini-marshmallows were on the market!"

- ½ pound large marshmallows, cut into pieces, or mini-marshmallows
- 1 cup hot coffee
- ½ pint whipping cream

Put the cut-up marshmallows in a bowl and pour the hot coffee over them. Stir so the marshmallows look foamy and softened. In a separate bowl, whip the cream.

Mix whipped cream into the coffee mixture and put dessert in the freezer. After 30 minutes, go back to the freezer and stir, as the coffee settles to the bottom. Check again in 30 more minutes, and stir if the coffee has settled again. The mixture will look choppy, but the coffee usually needs mixing into the whipped cream as it starts to freeze. Once the mixture is totally frozen, serve and enjoy!

Spirited Moxie Shake

Toby Conroy • Lisbon, Androscoggin County

Sponsored by
Three of Strong

"Back in the dark ages of 1997, I found myself volunteering for the Moxie Festival. As a young'un I felt that the festival offered very little for teenagers and focused solely on the older and younger generations. What was billed as a weekend event was more of a Saturday event with the street sweepers running cleanup around 4 p.m. The sidewalks were rolled up and the festival was over for the year. My goal was to increase the events to be more inclusive to all ages and spice up the festival to fill more of the weekend it was advertised as. My mother, Sue, and I found ourselves organizing the festival after a year of volunteering. Together with the help of a small crew we increased the attendance from an estimated 8,000 people to roughly 40,000! At one point, we hosted the largest parade in the state, lasting for 2 hours. Sunday provided the perfect day for what was the longest flat water river race. While the crew has changed many times since, and the overall festival has evolved, some of our additions still stand today: The Friday Night Fireworks and The Moxie Chuggin' Challenge, to point out a few. We hope to see you at the Moxie Festival, always scheduled around the second Saturday in July."

- 1 cup ice
- 2 ounces Three of Strong Merrymeeting spiced rum
- 2 ounces Georgia corn whiskey, or other bourbon
- 1 teaspoon vanilla
- 1 can Moxie, room temperature
- 4-5 cups vanilla ice cream
- Chocolate syrup

Place ice, liquor, and vanilla in a blender. Add 4 cups of ice cream. Pour Moxie over mixture slowly, to avoid fizz. Mix in blender until you reach the consistency of a shake. Serve in tall glasses with chocolate drizzled down inside the rim.

Poutine au Chômeur (Poor Man's Pudding Cake)

Lisa Colburn • Orono, Penobscot County

"My mom was known as a fabulous dessert cook. She'd spend most Saturdays baking sweets—mostly pies and cookies—enough to last the entire week. We had dessert after every meal! In later years, we dubbed her the 'Dessert Queen.' This Acadian recipe was supposedly the cake that was made when you couldn't afford more expensive fancy ingredients. Make no mistake about it, this dessert is special! Serve warm with vanilla ice cream."

Sauce:
1½ cups brown sugar
¾ cup water
2 teaspoons margarine or butter

Cake:
1 cup flour
1½ teaspoons baking powder
½ teaspoon salt
1 teaspoon sugar
1 egg, beaten
½ cup milk

To make the sauce: Mix the sauce ingredients together in a saucepan and bring to a boil. Cool slightly while making the cake mixture.

To make the cake: Preheat oven to 350 degrees. Mix all cake ingredients together and pour into a greased 8x8-inch baking pan. Pour the hot sauce mixture over the cake mixture. Do NOT mix together. Bake 30 minutes, or until cake springs back when touched.

Chocolate Bread Pudding

Marjo (Sawyer) Meade • Milbridge, Washington County

"This recipe has been handed down from my great-grandmother, Winifred Wallace Sawyer. She was from Milbridge and moved to Camden in the early 1900s with her husband and children."

Bread Pudding:
3 cups soft bread crumbs
3 tablespoons sugar
3 tablespoons cocoa powder
1 quart milk, scalded
1 egg

Sauce:
1 egg
1 cup sugar
1 tablespoon butter, melted
1 teaspoon vanilla

To make the bread pudding: Mix together bread crumbs, sugar, and cocoa powder in a large bowl. Add scalded milk, then stir in the egg. Pour into a greased baking dish and bake 1 hour in a 400-degree oven.

To make the sauce: Combine all ingredients in a bowl and beat until creamy. Place mixture in a saucepan over medium heat, and whisk until thickened.

Serve bread pudding warm, topped with sauce.

Beignets

Colleen Baker • Sanford, York County

"My mother, Leona Hebert Paradis, grew up on a potato farm in far Northern Maine, near Fort Kent. Her heritage was French Acadian. She was a ball of energy, a petite woman who spoke Franglaise (a combination of French and English) a good part of the time. We loved most of her cooking, but her beignets were special, and full of family history. She remembered: 'When we were small and lived on the farm, eggs were very scarce in the winter. Our hens stopped laying eggs when the days shortened and increased their laying in the spring when the daylight lengthened. Come Easter, we would always have beignets because the eggs had become more plentiful by then. These were so special to us and such a delicacy!' My mother, following her family's tradition, always made these for us at Easter dinner. They can be boiled in pure maple syrup, but she made the syrup in this recipe."

Syrup:
2 cups brown sugar
½ cup dark Karo syrup
1 teaspoon butter
Dash of maple essence or Maplene, for flavor
Water, to make a thinner syrup

Beignet Dough:
1½ cups flour
1½ teaspoons baking powder
½ cup sugar
Pinch of salt
3 eggs
½ cup milk
1 teaspoon butter, melted

In a skillet, add syrup ingredients and blend. Bring to a slow boil.

While syrup is boiling, prepare the dough. Sift the dry ingredients into a medium-size bowl. Set aside. In a separate small bowl, beat the eggs, then add the milk and the melted butter. Add the egg mixture to the dry ingredients, and stir to mix. The dough should be quite stiff.

Drop the dough by teaspoonfuls into the hot syrup. Cover the skillet and adjust burner heat to keep it at a slow boil. Cook for about 10 minutes. Serve in small bowls with the syrup. Makes 10-15 beignets.

Maple Mousse

1925 • Rebekah Cook Book

Members of the Mizpah Rebekah Lodge no. 62 • Winterport, Waldo County

This is such a simple recipe for one of Maine's signature ingredients! When I first read it, I stopped everything to give it a try. Instead of the freezer, I put the mold of mousse outdoors on a bitterly cold night which helped to freeze it extra quickly. An easy and delicious treat. —DL

Boil one-half cup of maple syrup and pour gradually over the beaten yolks of four eggs. Beat well and when cool add one pint of whipped cream. Pack in mold and freeze. —Mrs. L.K. York

Blackberry Dumplings

Marianne Pinkham • Nobleboro, Lincoln County

"Growing up on Borland Hill Farm in Damariscotta Mills, blackberry dumplings were a Sunday supper favorite during the summer months, when fresh blackberries ripened in my father's gentleman's garden. Rich, sweet, filling, warm, and luscious berry dumplings were a simple, easy-to-make, one-pot meal that could be viewed as a stew, a dessert, or a combination of both."

Blackberry Mixture:

2 quarts fresh Maine blackberries
1 cup sugar
½ cup water

Dumplings:

1 cup unbleached flour
1 teaspoon baking powder
½ teaspoon baking soda
¼ teaspoon salt
½ cup milk
¼ cup vegetable oil

To make the blackberry mixture: Place fresh blackberries, sugar, and water into a heavy-bottomed 3-quart saucepan. Using a potato masher, gently crush blackberries. Place saucepan containing the mixture on the stove. Using a low to medium level of heat bring to a boil, stirring occasionally. Turn heat down and let the mixture simmer on very low heat while you make the dumplings.

To make the dumplings: Sift together the flour, baking powder, baking soda, and salt in a medium-sized mixing bowl. In a separate small bowl, combine the milk and the vegetable oil. Add the wet mixture to the dry ingredients, stirring together until just moistened.

To assemble the blackberry dumplings: Bring the blackberry mixture to a boil. Drop the dumpling mixture by heaping tablespoons into the boiling blackberry mixture. Cover tightly with a close-fitting lid and return to a boil. Immediately reduce the heat, but DO NOT lift the cover. Simmer, covered, for 15 minutes, but NO longer.

Serve immediately in large bowls. Depending upon your preferences, the dumplings can be topped with a bit of butter, a dollop of sour cream or yogurt, or even ice cream. Makes 5-6 dumplings.

Lemon Curd Dessert

Frances Bosman • Brunswick, Cumberland County

"I grew up in Johannesburg, South Africa, and as far back as I can remember, Sunday lunch has been the time when the whole family gathers to eat together. Grandparents, parents, and children. Now that my siblings are all adults with families of their own, the party is up to 25 people or more. We all bring and share a part of the meal from salads to meat to bread to dessert. My grandmother's lemon dessert recipe is easy to double or triple for a large party, or switch out lemons for limes or grapefruit. Now that we are in Maine, we have been pleasantly surprised to be welcomed by new friends to join in their family gatherings such as Thanksgiving, Christmas, and Easter celebrations. Sharing my lemon dessert with them lets me embrace the new American traditions while still keeping my own family traditions near to mind."

2 tablespoons butter
¾ cup sugar
2 eggs, separated
2 tablespoons flour
Grated rind and juice of one lemon
1 cup milk

Preheat oven to 350 degrees.

In a large bowl, cream the butter and sugar. Mix in the egg yolks, flour, lemon zest and juice. Stir in the milk. Whip the egg whites stiff and fold into the mixture.

Pour into a greased baking dish and stand in a slightly larger baking dish. Pour hot water into the larger dish, until it comes about halfway up the sides of the pudding. Bake until set and golden, around 45 minutes. While it bakes, the pudding will separate out into a lemon custard with a light sponge on top. Serve warm with a dollop of whipped cream.

ACKNOWLEDGMENTS

It takes a community to create a community cookbook. It has been our honor and privilege to gather and share recipes from families all over this great state. Now, more than ever, we are thankful for the multitude of people who have helped create goodwill and community around these books.

There are many we would like to thank by name, but there are countless others, whose identities are lost to the centuries, without whom this book would not have been possible. The tireless work of all those who put together previous community cookbooks, whose traditions and recipes are the foundation of our continued project, deserve our biggest thanks. Gathering and testing recipes, typesetting them, and working outside the traditional publishing channels to bring a book to fruition is hard work, and we applaud all those who took it on before us and offer them our deepest thanks.

This book is the second volume in a series, and without the early boosters who encouraged and supported the *Maine Bicentennial Community Cookbook*, we would never have had the tenacity to attempt it again. Thanks to everyone who helped us shape the first book, and whose unflagging enthusiasm made that book such a pleasure.

Many of those who were instrumental to the creation of the first book were part of this second volume. As in the first volume, we are grateful to the Jewish Farmer Network and Maryland's Pearlstone Center for their inspiration and example for the creation of our Land and Food Acknowledgment.

This book would not have been possible without our lead sponsor, the Department of Agriculture, Conservation and Forestry. Thanks particularly to Commissioner Amanda Beal, Nancy McBrady, and Leigh Hallet.

At Islandport Press, thanks to Dean Lunt, Shannon Butler, Piper Wilber, and Holly Eddy. For her infinite patience and flexibility while designing a gorgeous book, abundant thanks to Ashley Halsey. Thank you to proofreader Amy Paradysz for her keen eye, attention to detail, and delicious recipe contribution!

Thanks always to Leslie Oster, Director of the Blaine House, for her unconditional support (in all our endeavors!), thoughtful suggestions, and enthusiasm for connecting people. Thanks to Nancy Harmon Jenkins for her unwavering support and passion for Maine's culinary history. Special thanks to Nancy Marshall for making so many introductions on our behalf. Thanks also to Christine Burns Rudalevige, Ben Coniff, Jessica Donahue, Beth McEvoy, David Freidenreich, Wayne Gray, Zach Heiden, Muhadin Libah, Gary W. Libby, Clare Morin, and Carolyne Obery for connecting us to so many fascinating Mainers.

For their enthusiasm and help gathering additional recipes, thanks to Savy Kuch, Meaghan Dillon, and members of the University of Maine Cooperative Extension: Hannah Carter, Dana Rickman, and Lynne Holland. Special thanks to Holli Francis at Passamaquoddy Wild Blueberries for putting out the call for recipes, and also to Cara O'Donnell and Ayana Green at Micmac Farms.

Discussions of food touch on many facets of our state's history. For providing a rich context to the culinary history and contemporary challenges of our state, thank you to those who contributed essays and narrative pieces to the book: Myron Beasley, Amy Wight Chapman, Matthew Dunlap, Senator Craig Hickman, John Hodgman, Avery Yale Kamila, Nancy Harmon Jenkins, Kristen Miale, Sandy Oliver, and Pamela Sweetser Snowe. Thank you to Senator

Olympia Snowe and Heather Cox Richardson for their thoughtful additions to the text, and to Tom Easton and the Foss Family, especially Jayne Farrin, for their generosity in sharing family reminiscences.

It's quite an endeavor to illustrate a cookbook without images of food. Many thanks to the contributors who rummaged through their attics and albums to find the perfect photos to share. For historical images, we are grateful to the Maine Historical Society, especially Sofia Yalouris and Kathleen Neumann; the New Sweden Historical Society, especially Carolyn Hildebrand; Mike Valenoti and Jennifer Pappas of Crosby's Drive-In; Gene Wright, publisher of the original Ma Dudley cookbook; and The Good Life Center.

Thanks to so many who spread the word about this project, and its predecessor: Gillian Britt, Rob Caldwell, Anestes Fotiades, Mindy Fox, Meredith Goad, Peggy Grodinsky, Lousia Kasdon, Erin Ovalle, Vanessa Santarelli, and Karen Waterson.

Enthusiasm for the first book helped us consider compiling a second. Thanks to Kathy Gunst, Cynthia Finnemore Olin, and to Paula and Bob Smithson for their relentless cheerleading; to Elizabeth Bailey-Mitchell for cooking her way through the first book, and documenting it on her blog; to Cat Morrow at Legacy Acres; and to Millie Stewart for hunting through her files to share some delicious slices of Maine's food history.

Various and sundry thanks to Larry and Sophie Westler, Lucian Berg, Jan Nowinski, Monika Eichler, and Forest Lytle.

Don would particularly like to thank the private collectors of cookbooks like Dorothy Ross, formerly of Belfast, food historians like Sandy Oliver of Islesboro, and booksellers like Scott DeWolfe and Frank Wood, of DeWolfe & Wood Booksellers in Alfred, all of whom have helped source books, lend advice and direction, and express delight and enthusiasm with their interest in the community cookbooks of Maine.

Margaret and Karl would particularly like to thank Don for joining us on this journey through Maine's community cookbooks. His scholarship and contagious enthusiasm has been an inspiration.

Fertile soil, clean water, and fresh air keep our state's agricultural life strong. For their passionate activism on behalf of Maine agriculture, thanks to the staff and volunteers at Maine Organic Farmers and Gardeners Association and the Maine Farmland Trust, particularly Sarah Alexander, Katy Green, and Ellen Sabina.

Thank you to our families! This book would not have been possible without the ongoing support of Bruce and Nancy Schatz, Jeanine Hathaway, and Charlotte, Beatrice, and Sadie Schatz.

We are grateful to the many organizations working to fight hunger in our state, and to their staff and volunteers, who work every day to feed hungry Mainers and solve the problem of food insecurity.

Finally, thank you to everyone who cooks from this book, makes the recipes their own, and adds their family to the next chapter of Maine's food story.

Great thanks to all the amazing Mainers who opened their homes, family cookbooks, recipe boxes, and family photo albums to us:

Denise Alexander, Linda Alperin, Jo Andrews, Cindi Annis, Mary Bagley, Roberta Bailey, Elizabeth Bailey-Mitchell, Colleen Baker, Jessica Battalana, Amanda Beal, Myron Beasley, Joan Benoit Samuelson, Robert Bernheim, Taylor Bickford, Lindsay Bileau, Cathy Billings, Jim Birkett, Pamela Fesq Bonney, Frances Bosman, Bessie Boulay, Lori Boulay, Margaret Brandes, Carol Brown, Nancy Burnette, Karen Bustillo, Patricia L. Campbell, Joyce Carson, Jennell Carter, Chenda Chamreoun, Karole Clark, Jane Cleaves McKenna, Lisa Colburn, Paula Collier, Toby Conroy, Karen Conroy, Deborah Joy Corey, Patricia Cote, Judith Couture, Heather Cox Richardson, Colleen Crocker, Lindsay Crooker-Mazariego, Vickie Croteau, Marnie Reed Crowell, Gail D'Agostino, Lucky D'Ascanio, Anne Dailey, Betsy Daus, Marge Davis, Rebecca DeLisle, Cynthia DiBiase, Sarah Dillinger, William Doukas, Tom Doyle, Donna Droggitis Thomson, Adrian du Plessis, Matt Dunlap, Mary Durost, Jodie Dyer, Thomas W. Easton, Elyse Eichler, Lennie Eichman, Janet Erickson, Cindy Eves-Thomas, Jayne Farrin, Mike Fear, Heather Fear, Kevin Flynn, Ada Foss Cobb, Marian Hale Fowler, Mindy Fox, Rachel Freedman, Sandy Garson, Geri Gay, Alex Gayton, Meg Gerritsen, Edythe Gervais, Victory Glenar, The Good Life Center, Jamie Gordon, Mona Grandbois, Charlotte Grass Shaw, Ayana Green, Joan Gregoire, Peggy Grodinsky, Susan Hall, Georgia Hansen, Betsy Harding, Randy Hatch, Margaret Hathaway, Andrea Hawkes, Deborah Hayden, Kelsie Hayes, Sam Hayward, Craig Hickman, Karen Soderberg Hinchliffe, John Hodgman, Luke Holden, Lynne Holland, Caitlin Hunter, Kate Huntress, Jasen Hutchinson, Heidi Inman, Nina Interlandi Bell, Angel Jamison, Nancy Harmon Jenkins, Karen Jennings, Avery Yale Kamila, Jennifer Kreckel, Amber Lambke, Kris Lape, Jane Legard, Pamela Leone, David Lewis, Susan Lewis Baines, Pam Libby-Lussier, Craig Littlefield, Stacy (Lizotte) Cote, Penelope Lord, Barbara Lovely, Diane Lukac, Sue Mackey Andrews, Faye Macomber, Diane Mann, Allison Marcoux, Ellie Markovitch, Nancy Marshall, Silvia B. Mathewson, Jack McAdam, Lauren McKenna, Faye McNall, Alicia Menard, Marsha Merryman, Ellen Moore, Nancy Moore, Heidi Morin, Cat Morrow, Jodie Mosher-Towle, Nokomis Regional High School Cooking Club, Sheila Norman, Robyn Norton, Shana Nowinski, Virginia Oliver, Leslie Oster, Amy Paradysz, Jackie Parker, Dean Paterson, LouAnna Perkins, Marjorie Pfeiffer, Sherry Pike, Jennifer Pinkham, Marianne Pinkham, Joan Prentice, Karen Prouty, Rachel Quinlan, Eric Rector, Marnie Reed Crowell, Barb Rehmeyer, Laurie Reynolds, Cindy Rogers, Margo Rowen, Barbie Sadler Humphrey, Shawn Saindon, Habiba Salat, Marjo (Sawyer) Meade, Nancy Schatz, Phoebe Schilla, H. Lori Schnieders, Barbara Seaver, Dave Seddon, Savannah Sessions, Caitlin Shetterly, Zhenya & Schelene Shevchenko, Craig Sipe, Sylvia Smith, Paula Smithson, Pamela Snow Sweetser, Senator Olympia Snowe, Susan Spector, Martha Speed, Brian Stanley, Susie Stedman, Judy Stein, Millie Stewart, Gerri Stiles, Kathleen Sturtevant, Jay Tall, Carol Tanner, Alisha Targonski, Pamela Thompson, Jackie (Mrs. Paul E.) Tower, Chris Toy, Rachel Tremblay, Victor Trodella, Sylvia Trueworthy Pease, Suzanne Trussell, Martha Turner, Jan Varnum, Karen Walker, Debra Wallace, Kate Wallace, Daria Walton, Nancy Wanderer, Carmen Weatherbie, Kathleen Webster, Richard Webster, Sydnia (Welch) Czarnecki, Amy Wight Chapman, Katherine McGee Wilson, Doris Wong, Patricia Worth, Chhom Yay, Lynn Young, Evan and George Zarkadas.

**Huge thanks to all of our business sponsors —
we could not have done this without your support:**

Lobster Bake: Real Maine (Maine Department of Agriculture, Conservation, and Forestry)

Clam Bake: Maine Homes by Down East; Stonewall Kitchen; Wyman's

Grange Hall Dinner: Atlantic Sea Farms; Casco Bay Creamery; Maine Harvest Credit Union; Native Maine; Sherman's Books

Bean Pot Supper: Austin Street Brewery; Camden National Bank; Eat, Drink, Lucky; Hannaford; Home Remedies; Law Offices of Joe Bornstein; Maine Coast Waldorf School; Now You're Cooking; Oakhurst Dairy; Rabelais Inc; Rosemont Market; Southern Maine Community College; Wicked Joes Organic Coffees, Wilbur's of Maine

Seafood Platter: Bar Harbor Foods; Lee Auto Mall; Maine Farm and Sea Cooperative; Maine Organic Farmers and Gardeners Association; Rose Foods; The Sausage Kitchen; Sebago Lake Trading Company; Three of Strong

Blueberry Pie: Luke's Lobster; Maine Farmland Trust; Maine Grains; Patriot Subaru; UMaine Cooperative Extension

Special thanks to: Rachel Ambrose, Jake Austin, Jesse Bains, John Bennett, Kayla Bess, Brandon Boey, Ben Bornstein, Scott Budde, Jennell Carter, Ben Coniff, Chad Conley, Toby Conroy, Colleen Craig, Jeff Curtis, Jimmy Davolio, Amy Denuzzio, Meaghan Dillon, Heather Fear, Peter Fitch, Bob and Carmen Garver, Keri Guddeck, Luke Holden, Lawrence Hollins, Jess Joyce, Christopher Kasprak, Sue Konkel, Amber Lambke, Adam Lee, Holly Martzial, Sam May, Dave McConnell, Alicia Menard, Melissa Motejunas, Amy Mullen, John Naylor, Jackie Parker, Jennifer Pride Collins, Matthew Robertson, Mike Sansing, Dave Seddon, Renée Smyth, Tom Talbott, Deb Taylor, Theanna Twitchell, Briana Warner, Andy Wilbur.

You will find the advertisements and sponsored recipes on the following pages:

COPYRIGHTS & CREDITS

All photographs appearing with a recipe are courtesy of, or reprinted with permission of the submitter or submitter's family, unless otherwise noted below. All additional photographs are courtesy of, or credited as follows: p. xi: A full list of credits for the Faces of the *Maine Bicentennial Community Cookbook* can be found at maine200cookbook.com; pp. xii, xvi-xvii: Cookbook collection of Don Lindgren; p. xvii: David Lewis; p. 2: Kathleen Webster; p. 9: Collection of Don Lindgren; p. 10: Collection of Don Lindgren; p. 15: Collection of Don Lindgren; p. 17: Apples by John Bunker, reprinted with permission of MOFGA; pp. 18-19: Cookbook cover and photographs reprinted with permission of Gene Wight; p. 20: Margaret Hathaway; p. 22: Courtesy of Passamaquoddy Wild Blueberry Company; p. 24: Muhadin Libah; p. 37: Collection of Don Lindgren; p.38: Reprinted with permission of Gene Wight; p. 40: Faye McNall; p. 43: Collection of Don Lindgren; p. 46: Collection of Don Lindgren; p. 48: Michael Hurley, with permission of Marika Kuzma; p. 52: Brianna Soukup / Portland Press Herald; p. 54: Collection of Don Lindgren; p. 61: Anne Dailey; p. 68: Collection of Don Lindgren; p. 70: Collections of Maine Historical Society, item #23859; pp. 70-71: Re.Past photos by Jop Blom, with permission of Myron Beasley; p. 72: Faye McNall; p. 76-77: Courtesy Micmac Farms; p. 84: Jop Blom; p. 85: Collection of Don Lindgren; p. 88: Collections of New Sweden Historical Society, courtesy of MaineMemory.net, item #22293; p. 92: Karen Soderberg Hinchliffe; p. 101: Collection of Don Lindgren; p. 107: Potatoes by Katherine McGee Wilson; p. 109: Potato farm by Katherine McGee Wilson; p. 110: Collections of Maine Historical Society, item #3124; p. 111: Courtesy of Toni Fiore; p. 112: Greta Rybus; p. 119: The Good Life Center; p. 132: Collection of Don Lindgren; p. 133: Nowinski family; p. 134: Nancy Harmon Jenkins; p. 141: Geri Gay; p. 143: Collection of Don Lindgren; p. 144 (Thomas Reed): Benjamin Brady/Levin Handy/Library of Congress; p. 148: Michael D. Wilson; p. 154: Collection of Don Lindgren; p. 162-163: Courtesy of Craig Hickman; p. 164: William Doukas; p. 166: Collections of Maine Historical Society, item #17361; p. 177: Collection of Don Lindgren; p. 181: Collection of Don Lindgren; p. 186: Collection of Don Lindgren; p. 189: Courtesy of Mike Valenoti; p. 190: Courtesy Abdi Nor Iftin; p. 194: Collections of the Georgetown Historical Society; p. 199: Collection of Don Lindgren; p. 207: Collection of Don Lindgren; p. 209: Collection of Don Lindgren; p. 212: Martha Speed; p. 226: Amy Wight Chapman; p. 233: Peter Stevens (https://flickr.com/photos/28435100@N00/50855723308); pp. 240-241: Good Shepherd Food Bank; p. 242: Ellen Moore; p. 245: City of Boston Archives (https://www.flickr.com/people/48039697@N05); p. 251: Collection of Don Lindgren; p. 260: Marsha Merryman; p. 264: Steve Yenco; p. 267: Collection of Don Lindgren; p. 285: Author photo taken by Forest Lytle (top), Greta Rybus (bottom).

INDEX

N

O

P

Q

R

S

T

COUNTY INDEX

Knox

Lincoln

Oxford

Penobscot

Piscataquis

Sagadahoc

Somerset

Waldo

Washington

York

Sipayik

ABOUT THE AUTHORS

Margaret Hathaway and Karl Schatz are the wife and husband team behind seven books on food and farming, including the memoir *The Year of the Goat*, the guide *Living With Goats*, two volumes of the *Portland, Maine Chef's Table* cookbook, and the *Maine Bicentennial Community Cookbook*. Margaret is a writer and goat farmer who has worked in cookbook publishing and as manager of New York's landmark Magnolia Bakery. Karl is a photographer, journalist, and goat farmer who has worked as a Photo Editor at Time Magazine and as Director of Aurora Photos. Since 2005, the couple has lived with their three daughters on Ten Apple Farm, their homestead and agritourism business in southern Maine, where they raise dairy goats, tend a large garden and small orchard, lead goat hikes, teach workshops, and operate a guest house. You can visit them at tenapplefarm.com

Don Lindgren is an antiquarian bookseller specialized in printed and manuscript books about food and drink. His bookselling business, Rabelais Inc., acquires, researches, and sells rare books, manuscripts, ephemera, and other materials related to culinary history. He has served as a Governor of the Antiquarian Booksellers' Association of America and is a member of the International League of Antiquarian Booksellers. He has lectured or presented at the Oxford Symposium on Food & Cookery, the Colorado Antiquarian Book Seminar, and the Rare Book School's Boston Seminar. In 2019 he published the first part of a multi-volume exploration of the American community cookbook, titled *UnXld: American Cookbooks of Community & Place*. Visit him at rabelaisbooks.com.

To learn more about community cookbooks, you can listen to Margaret, Karl, and Don on their podcast, Cooking is Community. Find it at communitycookbook.com or wherever you get your podcasts.